RASIKA

RASIKA

FLAVORS OF INDIA

STORIES BY **ASHOK BAJAJ**

RECIPES BY **VIKRAM SUNDERAM**

COAUTHORED BY **DAVID HAGEDORN**

ecco

An Imprint of HarperCollins*Publishers*

HarperCollins
PUBLISHERS
Since 1817

HarperCollins books may be purchased for educational,
business, or sales promotional use. For information please
e-mail the Special Markets Department at
SPsales@harpercollins.com.

FIRST EDITION

Designed by Renata De Oliveira
Photographs by Shimon and Tammar Photography

Library of Congress Cataloging-in-Publication Data has
been applied for.

ISBN 978-0-06-243555-2

17 18 19 20 21   ID/LSC   10 9 8 7 6 5 4 3 2

TO MY LATE PARENTS
—Ashok Bajaj

CONTENTS

INTRODUCTION
THE HISTORY OF RASIKA AND THE RISE OF FOUR-STAR INDIAN COOKING

When I moved to Washington, D.C., in the late 1980s, it was a world capital with a small-town feel. Nancy Reagan, one of the most prominent members of the "in crowd," would often have lunch with friends at the Jockey Club in The Fairfax Hotel, then known as the Ritz-Carlton, near Embassy Row. I was working to open my first restaurant in the city at the time and would read about these visits in the local papers, imagining what it would be like to have the first lady or the president in my dining room.

Now, ten restaurants later, I remember that early ambition and think about how frequently Michelle Obama has dined at some of them, whether enjoying a tasting meal and wine pairings with friends at Rasika or celebrating her husband's birthday at its sister restaurant, Rasika West End. I can't help but smile at the thought of how Washington and its dining scene have evolved over the years.

Rasika restaurant opened in December 2005 and Rasika West End six years later. *Washington Post* restaurant critic Tom Sietsema named Rasika the best restaurant in Washington, declaring it "the most fabulous Indian cooking in the country."

He asked rhetorically, "Remember when Indian food meant samosas and curries washed back with a Kingfisher?" The game, he pointed out, had changed.

Indian cooking had long been dismissed in America as mere "ethnic" food that was too greasy and fiery hot. The accolades for Rasika and for its executive chef, Vikram Sunderam, are proof that

Indian food today has broken free of the stereotypes to take its place among the world's most refined cuisines.

But recognition as one of America's finest restaurants, and of its chef as one of the best in the country, did not happen overnight or easily. Rasika could not have happened without my first restaurant, The Bombay Club, which opened a stone's throw from the White House in 1988. And the entire journey started in India.

IN THE BEGINNING: THE BOMBAY CLUB

My mother, Kamla, was an excellent cook, and she delighted in preparing special local dishes for friends and family. Growing up in New Delhi, I remember eating this fresh, natural food every day, and how our home became a place where cousins, aunts, and uncles would gather to eat. She would walk to the market daily and buy whatever vegetables and fruits were freshest. Hawkers would pass by on the street calling out that they had zucchini, eggplant, potatoes, or peas for sale from baskets and carts. She would use these ingredients to prepare simple, delicious meals.

When I was in school, I would sometimes come home for lunch and find that my friends were already there eating. My mother would be bustling about the kitchen, serving up *aloo tikki,* vegetable jalfrezi, *baingan bharta,* or kormas and dropping hot bread fresh from the *tawa* onto their plates while they all laughed and gossiped. She loved to welcome people into her kitchen and dining room and often meals would extend to midnight and beyond.

Perhaps that's why I was drawn to the hospitality business, and especially to the food side of things. When I was twelve or thirteen years old, my uncle Prem Arora would take me to lunch at the hotels where he was an executive. These were elegant restaurants, and the experience made a lasting impression. I remember always being in awe of the glamorous setting. The formality of how the waiters would present the elaborate creations of the chefs was so different from the casual way we ate at home, yet the flavors and ingredients were familiar.

It was my uncle who first thought that this might be a career that would suit me. He encouraged me to enter the food and beverage training program at the Ashok Group of Hotels while I was getting my degree from the University of Delhi.

After earning a postgraduate diploma in tourism and hotel management from the University of Rajasthan, I was fortunate to get a position with the Taj Hotel Group, which operated some of the best restaurants and hotels in India. I learned a great deal about the business and about which parts of it I most enjoyed. The front of the house, the kitchen, room service, lounges, and other areas were each like separate worlds with their own cultures. In all of them, I learned that hospitality is about more than just serving food correctly.

In 1983, the company asked me to go to London to help manage its first restaurant there. Bombay Brasserie, in the Bailey's Hotel in South Kensington, was one of the most sophisticated Indian restaurants in London. Every night was like a Who's Who of London society, where Mick Jagger might be dining a few tables away from members of the royal family. The expectations were high, and making all of the pieces fit together smoothly was an adrenaline rush.

By 1987, I was ready to move on from Bombay Brasserie. Since India is a former British colony, Indian food is common in London, but there were surprisingly few high-end Indian restaurants in major American cities. I saw that as a great opportunity for innovation, but it was also a great risk.

While searching for the right place to open my own restaurant, my business partner at the time thought Washington stood out as the best location for what I wanted to create. As a major world capital, it had many people who had traveled extensively. All of the embassies were there, as were global organizations like the International Monetary Fund and the World Bank. They employed large numbers of people who had lived abroad and understood other cuisines of the world.

Washington was also large enough to support something new, but not so large that one more place to eat would simply get lost in the crowd. I wanted my restaurant to have influence—to be noticed. The Bombay Club would be a place where Indians would be proud to bring their American friends and where Americans would be proud to bring their Indian friends.

I wanted to build a first-class restaurant, so it needed to be in a first-class building. But I couldn't find anyone who wanted to rent me space. I spoke to landlords and brokers, but when they heard "Indian restaurant," they worried that it would make their lobbies smell.

Finally a landlord was willing to listen. He had space in a building right across Lafayette Square from the White House. The location was perfect, and I knew that it could become exactly what I was dreaming of. It took months of persuasion, including convincing him to go to London so he could see for himself the high-end restaurants I was trying to emulate. Once he went there, he got it, and we struck a deal. The process was long and difficult, but it was a useful reminder that this would be a great opportunity to open people's eyes to a cuisine that was still largely unknown to them.

When The Bombay Club opened, there was nothing else like it in Washington. The restaurant had a style reminiscent of the old Raj clubs of colonial India. The menu featured authentic, regional Indian cooking that combined flavors and spices quite unfamiliar to many people. It was so far outside many diners' experience that I began handing out small, 2 x 4-inch cards

telling people how to order in an Indian restaurant. It would say, "If you like spicy food, you may enjoy the lamb vindaloo or green chili chicken," or "If you have never tried Indian food before, you might start with something from the tandoor."

I was nervous about our chances of succeeding, and it was sometimes exhausting trying to always appear positive. But I had a passion to create this restaurant and introduce the public to this cuisine. Anyone who has ever struggled to create something must understand this feeling.

In Indian restaurants, there is a tradition. The staff gathers in the warmth of the kitchen before every service and drinks chai—spiced tea with milk. At these meetings, I would give a pep talk to the staff, explaining that our goal was to have the best Indian restaurant we could and that the rest would follow.

It did follow, and very quickly. *Esquire* magazine named The Bombay Club as one of the top 10 new restaurants of the year in 1989. The *Washington Post* gave us a smashing review, and the restaurant started getting busy. People would come in and ask for exactly what had been mentioned in the reviews. They were taking a chance by trying something new, and we were determined to make sure they loved the food and the experience. As the restaurant became an accepted part of the city's dining scene, so did the food.

Perhaps the biggest moment came in October 1993, when we got a call from the White House. President Clinton would be coming for dinner that night

with his family and a half-dozen guests. The president had a reputation as an adventurous eater, and he was familiar with Indian food from his university days in England. But it was actually his daughter, Chelsea, who visited us first. She had come in with some friends a few weeks prior, and I think she must have been the one who recommended us to her parents.

When people would tell me that they didn't think they'd like Indian food because it was too spicy, I responded that it wasn't spicy, it was flavorful. As more people dined with us, they understood this distinction for themselves. They also learned that an Indian restaurant could be refined and elegant, not the image they might have in their mind.

The growth of Indian cuisine in Washington and other American cities was dramatic in the early 1990s, but that was nothing compared to how the cuisine changed in the years to follow.

CREATING RASIKA

Throughout the nineties, Indian cuisine continued gaining popularity in cosmopolitan cities like New York, Brussels, San Francisco, and Sydney. People's tastes were becoming more sophisticated, and ingredients that we had previously imported from India were more easily available for home cooks. We were well past the days of handing out cards telling people what to order. Now, guests were starting

to tell us what they wanted us to cook, perhaps something they had sampled on their travels to India.

Still, I worried that the demand was not yet there for another high-end Indian restaurant. I focused instead on opening restaurants that took different approaches to modern American cuisine.

But around 2002, I started to notice a very interesting shift. People were going out to eat in a more casual way. Celebrated chefs and restaurateurs were opening less formal versions of their fine-dining restaurants. In New York, Daniel Boulud built on the success of his Daniel by opening the casual db bistro

moderne. Thomas Keller balanced The French Laundry in Napa with Bouchon. This allowed them to experiment with new techniques and combinations. Their main restaurant might be quiet and staid, and their casual place would be noisy and animated. Both would be comfortable, but in different ways.

At the same time, Washington's population was growing. Young people were moving back into the city, and more neighborhoods were being revitalized. People were looking for new experiences. They didn't necessarily want to go out to the same restaurants as their parents. This was a worldwide trend, really. In India, restaurateurs were opening new places, expanding on traditional cuisine with more modern presentations and new ingredients not local to Indian cuisine. For example, Dover sole was suddenly appearing on menus, flown in from Europe. By 2003, I decided the time was right for me to embark on a project that would build on this expansion.

I kept coming back to the idea of modern Indian cuisine that was firmly rooted in tradition but approached the dishes and the hospitality in a contemporary way. The idea was that you would feel comfortable having a full meal, or just two or three small plates and a glass of wine. Modern Indian food, modern design, and a world-class wine list.

Unlike at The Bombay Club, there would be no tablecloths. There would also be an open kitchen. Part of the hospitality of fine-dining restaurants is that the work is hidden from the guests. The food is presented like a theatrical production—you don't show what is going on backstage. But now people were watching television programs about what happens in restaurant kitchens. They wanted to see the action as part of the show. That wall had to come down.

I knew exactly who the chef should be to help me bring this vision to life: Vikram Sunderam, who at the time was the executive chef of Bombay Brasserie in London and whose skill and creativity I greatly admired. He was enthusiastic about coming to work for me on the project.

Eating in restaurants is emotional. There are many great home cooks who still want to eat out a lot. They look for a place that suits their mood at that moment. My new restaurant would be aimed at those times when people were looking for something very different from The Bombay Club.

Take the music, which is so important to ambience. At The Bombay Club, the music was quiet and in the background, with a piano player helping to create a refined and relaxed atmosphere. I wanted this new restaurant to have more vibrancy. My girlfriend, Andrea Reid, and I spent a lot of time shopping for music that would set the right tone. I was also inspired by the music at Buddha Bar in Paris, so eclectic and interesting that it launched a series of compilation CDs. The beats combined elements from European, Indian, and Asian music, forming a new sound that helped define the restaurant's atmosphere.

Naturally, the whole time I was thinking about this new project I was pondering what to name it. My restaurants had always had what could be considered very conventional names, such as The Bombay Club and The Oval Room. Now I was looking for a name that was softer and more captivating, something that would evoke the sensuality of the colors and flavors of the various herbs and spices so strongly associated with Indian cuisine.

My longtime controller, Pat Minter, showed me a Sanskrit website during one of her many late nights at work. There I came across the word *rasika,* which roughly translates as "flavor."

Sanskrit is not widely spoken in India, but it is the liturgical language of Hinduism. So there is an ancient connection to the language, a bridge to the past and the heritage. Rasika is also a girl's name referring to someone who is passionate and discerning. That seemed perfect. It combined all of the themes that I was looking for. And if you roll the R, it sounds beautiful when you say it—RAH-see-kuh.

For the design, I wanted to create a place that would look modern, with an Indian feel and Indian tones. I hired an architect named Harry Gregory from London, with whom I had worked on other

projects in the past. He had been to India many times and understood what I was trying to accomplish.

Together Harry and I walked around the neighborhood I had chosen: the Penn Quarter area of Washington. This was a very young and vibrant neighborhood. A few years earlier it had been a pretty run-down part of town, but now there were theaters, the city's sports and entertainment arena, bars, new condo buildings, and many restaurants—including another one of mine, 701 Restaurant. We wanted to make

Rasika a place where people could walk in wearing smart, casual clothes and feel as comfortable as someone wearing a suit.

We split the space into a lounge, the chef's table with a view of the kitchen, and the main dining room. The flow among the three would help to create the energy that we wanted. It would be loud. It would have buzz. The laughter from one table would spread to another. Your attention would naturally be drawn outward, to the action and the people around you, as much as inward toward your own table. The sights and sounds of the restaurant would build on one another to help define the way people experienced the food.

While Harry worked on the physical space, Vikram and I worked on the menu together—over many glasses of single malt Scotch. He spent time in the kitchens of some of my other restaurants—The Oval Room and 701—to gain exposure to contemporary American tastes.

As we got closer to opening, I traveled to India, searching for inspiration and shopping for artwork and furnishings for the new restaurant. I visited places like the famous Chor Bazaar in Mumbai, which has been around for well over a century, looking for antiques to add authenticity to the modern design. At one gallery in the Colaba neighborhood of Mumbai, I found some large paintings by an artist named Arunabha Karmakar. He is an Eastern artist who was not well known in the United States. I was captivated by the colors in these paintings as well as by the sensuality. Here again, the art caught the softness that I was looking for. It also drew from the colors of the spices that would infuse the cooking: turmeric, cloves, cumin, cinnamon, coriander, mace.

BUILDING A TEAM

In the restaurant business, service is as important a part of the hospitality as the food is, so I started assembling the team that would make everything work. There needed to be a mix of people with different strengths to help execute my vision.

Indian restaurants are not known for wine, but we had always had a very good wine list at The Bombay Club. I wanted it to be a focus at Rasika as well. I brought in Sebastian Zutant, who had been sommelier at one of the best and most adventurous restaurants in Washington, the Greek-inspired Komi. Sebastian worked up a wine and cocktail program that paired beautifully with the spicy and sweet flavors that were features of many of the dishes on our menu.

Atul Narain moved from being manager at The Bombay Club to head up the front of the house at Rasika. As the core of the team took shape, we built on it by picking some of the best staff from my other restaurants and assigning them to open Rasika. With five other restaurants by this time, I had some of the most talented cooks and professional waitstaff in Washington. This would allow us to provide excellent service right from the very beginning.

At this point in my career, I knew how to open restaurants. In my heart and soul I believed that Washington was ready for a modern take on Indian cuisine. Although I should have been as confident as anyone could be in a new venture, opening a new restaurant is always difficult and risky. Aside from the financial commitment of signing a ten-year lease, I also felt a moral responsibility toward Vikram, whose wife and two children were being uprooted from London along with him.

This was the same kind of nervousness and anxiety that I experienced when I was first going out on my own. Am I doing the right thing? Are people really ready for this? Will I just be taking customers away from The Bombay Club and competing with myself?

OPENING DAY

Setting aside all of these doubts, we opened Rasika on December 9, 2005. It was popular from day one with a noticeably younger crowd than we had at The Bombay Club.

Sometimes we didn't even understand how people had discovered us so quickly. On the first day, we had a visit from Erin Hartigan, who wrote for a blog called *Daily Candy*. The site was very popular in New York, but was just starting in D.C. Frankly, I had never heard of it before. She wrote about the restaurant, and the next day we had a lot of young people coming in. I asked how they had heard about us, and they said from *Daily Candy*. Our new customers immediately seized on items like the Palak Chaat (page 53), Black Cod with Honey and Dill (page 169), and Tandoori-Style Mango Shrimp (page 140), and these became our signature dishes.

The kind of endorsement people used to seek from professional restaurant critics at large newspapers had expanded to include the new social media. Blogs, online review sites, knowledgeable amateurs who shared their enthusiasm—they were now important tastemakers just like the established reviewers. I had understood something about this shift before, but I had never seen it play out so dramatically in person, and I was delighted by it.

Rasika grew in its cuisine, its standards, and in its reputation every day. Vikram, Atul, and the entire team were constantly building, evolving, updating. The young professionals of Washington really embraced the concept of pairing food with wine and cocktails, and they reveled in the noise and excitement.

Esquire named us one of the best new restaurants of 2006 and we got very positive reviews locally, too. The *Washington Post* started off by giving us two and a half stars out of four, a very good showing for a new restaurant. Over time, they recognized that we just kept getting better, and bumped up our rating.

The staff was doing excellent work, and we continued to bring in talented people to help us grow. We were very fortunate to add a great master chef, Mohamed Issak Qureshi, soon after Rasika opened. He is from Lucknow, the capital of Uttar Pradesh in Northern India and a city known for its gastronomy. He has many years of experience dating back to his days in his

family's restaurant there. Mohamed not only executes Vikram's vision with aplomb, he enhances it and maintains its quality.

Another great chef, Neraj Govil, would come several years later from Taj Mahal Palace hotel in Mumbai to work under Vikram. Adding to a restaurant family like this injects new ideas and new vitality into a kitchen. It is the best kind of change.

In the fall of 2009, I got a call from a newspaper reporter saying that the *Washington Post* had awarded us four stars, its highest rating. Word had gotten out on the Internet, but this was the first I had heard of it. The reporter asked how it felt.

How did it feel? There were only a handful of restaurants in the region to have received four stars. Among them was the Inn at Little Washington—one of the top dining and hotel destinations in the entire country. I felt proud, validated, and very nervous. I really couldn't sleep for a few nights.

This would be a big change. The staff would be elated, but now there was even more pressure not to let anyone down—pressure on the whole staff, not just on Vikram to be a great chef. We had to keep doing exactly what we had been doing, but to a greater degree. We added more hosts, chefs, servers, and dishwashers. I didn't want to leave any room for error.

Now we started getting customers from all over the world. People were booking reservations months in advance. At the staff briefing every day, we would stress that we simply could not let anybody down. People were going to have the highest expectations, and from now on we would be judged by a new standard.

Also in 2009, Vikram was nominated for a prestigious James Beard Foundation Award for Best Chef, Mid-Atlantic. Having come from India and England, he didn't grasp just what that honor meant. I explained that the James Beard Awards, named after the dean of American cuisine, were like the Oscars of the food world. After that, he really wanted to win and tried harder and harder to improve so he could win. He was nominated for the award every year for the next five years, finally winning it in May 2014. I was delighted for him. He had grown incredibly as a chef and now had won the recognition we all knew he deserved.

CONTINUING TO GROW: RASIKA WEST END

As Rasika was building its reputation, we were in the unexpected and uncomfortable position of having to turn people away. To anyone who had followed our journey from the first days of The Bombay Club, it seemed incredible, and we tried everything we could to accommodate people.

I was truly disappointed whenever we couldn't find a space for someone. That's not what we want to do in the hospitality business. We want to serve people and to make them happy. If we absolutely didn't have a table, we would often pack up food for guests to take home. It wasn't ideal, but at least it was a way to share the cooking that we were so proud of.

Because of Rasika's popularity, I started to get questions about opening a second location. Vikram and Atul were eager to do another Rasika. I was very hesitant. I didn't want us to lose our focus and was worried about maintaining our standards at a second location. These were some of the same concerns that I'd had about opening Rasika in the first place, when there was a danger that it would damage The Bombay Club. In retrospect, I realized that The Bombay Club's business grew faster once Rasika opened. The two were such counterpoints to each other that they weren't really in competition. The younger crowd from Rasika viewed The Bombay Club as a quieter and more grown-up

alternative for when they wanted that option.

Once it became clear that one restaurant wasn't taking business away from the other, I gradually began building a team within Rasika to plot what an expansion might look like. I started scouting locations and saw that the West End of D.C. was very attractive. There were new hotels and condos nearby, including a Ritz-Carlton, and a lot of new residents. It was also a part of town without a lot of fine dining options.

In many ways, it reminded me of the potential I had seen in Washington many years earlier, except that now our food was widely understood and accepted, and our audience was already familiar with Rasika.

In order to make sure that we were continuing to push the cuisine forward, I wanted our second location to be a very different restaurant. It would share a name—Rasika West End—and it would have the same basic idea of progressive Indian food. In fact, because Vikram would be designing the menu at this new restaurant as well, some of the same dishes would inevitably appear at both places. We had to include our signature dishes— the *palak chaat* and the black cod—on

the menu, for instance. Our customers expected it. But we wanted everything else to be as dissimilar and new as possible. I wanted the menu to have new dishes, along with new cocktails and a more advanced wine list.

(By the way, over the years we have never revealed the recipes for palak chaat—which is crispy fried spinach with yogurt and tamarind—or the black cod, although countless guests and publications have asked us for them. We always intended to share them if we were to ever write the Rasika cookbook, so now, here they are, on pages 53 and 169 respectively.)

For Rasika West End, we also went for a totally different look, centered around a sculptural banyan tree, with its branches spreading across the ceiling. Booths took

the shape of *palaki,* carriages in which the Indian nobility used to be carried. We used bright jewel tones like turquoise, pink, and purple to remind people that they had come into a very new place, not a copy, and, god forbid, not part of a chain.

Rasika West End has garnered its own reputation as a great restaurant, and the staff has worked hard to make sure that they are not thought of as just the younger sibling of Rasika Penn Quarter. It is a sort of rivalry that brings out the best in both restaurants. Whether it is the Clintons celebrating their wedding anniversary, President Barack Obama coming for his birthday, or out-of-town guests like Bill Gates and Jeff Bezos stopping in for working dinners with their staffs, every notable visit reinforces the staff's success and pride. It also reminds us how important it is that we treat every diner with the highest level of hospitality and respect.

Today, both Rasikas continue to evolve. No great chef wants to keep repeating himself or rest on his laurels, and Vikram is undeniably a great chef. He is always drawing inspiration from new trends and looking to push his own ideas. We continue to visit different restaurants together, including progressive Indian restaurants in other cities.

Remaining current is vital. As people's tastes change, restaurants must take on different personalities but preserve their character and their commitment to superlative food and gracious hospitality.

We have come a long way since I first brought my vision of fine Indian dining to America almost thirty years ago. There is no way of knowing how things will progress over the next twenty-five years, but every day is a new opportunity to try new things, to find new ways to expand our style, and to introduce new guests to our dream.

I am proud of the part we've played in the evolution of Indian cuisine in America and am delighted for this opportunity to help readers be part of that evolution in their own kitchens.

—Ashok Bajaj

1

THE FOUNDATION OF
RASIKA'S COOKING

THE ORIGIN OF RASIKA'S RECIPES: TRADITION WITH A MODERN TWIST

FROM CHEF VIKRAM SUNDERAM

When Ashok brought up the idea of writing a cookbook, he had a clear idea in his mind. Through stories and anecdotes, he wanted to explain what Rasika is all about—how it came to be, what role it plays in Washington's dining scene, and who the dedicated people are who help us do what we do every day. Above all, he and I wanted to present the recipes in a way that would inspire all cooks, including connoisseurs and those unfamiliar with, or perhaps daunted by, Indian cooking, to give it a go.

All of the recipes in this book are for dishes that we serve or have served at Rasika, with scant compromising on methods of preparation and no cutting back on the ingredients we use. All of the offerings are rooted in tradition, but with modern twists. They reflect a balanced representation of India's diverse regions and distinctive flavor profiles.

An idea for a dish usually starts with an ingredient I want to feature, so I will begin the process by researching, poring through cookbooks looking at various preparations, say, for a southern-style coconut curry I may want to pair with lobster, such as the Lobster Moilee (page 161).

There really is no set way to make any Indian dish, be it a curry, a biryani, or a chutney. Recipes are often handed down within families over generations, with each cook putting his or her own twist on them. You'll not find a *Larousse Gastronomique* for Indian food that lays out exactly what the ingredients, preparations, and accompaniments of a dish should be, like that encyclopedia does for French cuisine. If you were to ask twenty cooks how to prepare the basic, home-style chicken curry *tariwala murgh,* like the one on page 184, you would likely receive twenty different recipes.

I may decide to stay fairly faithful to a particular style of preparation, or I may deconstruct it, switch it up with American ingredients or riffs on American dishes. Ashok, always on top of trends, gives his input. "You should do something with artichokes. People love them!" he suggested one day, and soon Cremini Mushroom and Artichoke Korma (page 120) was on the menu. Avocado Chaat with Banana (page 59) came to be in a similar way.

But what I rely on the most is the exposure I had to culinary excellence, starting with my childhood and extending through a thirty-two-year career. I was born and raised in Bombay, now Mumbai, the capital of the state of Maharashtra in Western India. The major food influence in my life was my mother, Vimal, a Maharashtrian who loved to cook and enjoyed a reputation for being good at it.

Bringing people together at the table to share company and conversation over a multidish meal was a passion for her.

As many Indians do, she fasted on certain days of the week, serving only vegetarian dishes then. (Fasting doesn't necessarily mean not eating.) On other days, seafood or fresh fish that fishmongers would bring right to the door from the harbor's boats first thing in the morning would be the centerpiece of the meal. Silver pomfret, a butterfish as delicate as Dover sole, was a particular favorite. Sunday lunches were elaborate meals, always including a lamb, mutton, or chicken curry that required long, diligent preparation.

My father, Trikoor, is a Tamil Brahmin from Kerala, in Southern India, so my mother would often serve foods from that region, such as sambar (a vegetable and dal stew cooked with tamarind and spices), carrot and bean *poriyal* (a stir-fry seasoned with mustard seeds, split black gram, curry leaves, and coconut) and *avial* (a vegetable stew made with squash, yams, plantains, and drumsticks, which are long, thin, okra-like pods that resemble green sticks).

But frankly, I can't say that I had a tremendous interest in food when I was young. I just wanted to play sports with

from Sophia Polytechnic in Bombay. There I was exposed to all aspects of the food industry—cooking, baking, housekeeping, and restaurant service. Cooking appealed to me more than anything else.

I joined the prestigious Taj Group of hotels in Bombay in 1985, starting as a chef trainee and producing mostly European-style dishes. It wasn't until I was sent to a three-month cross-training program at the New Delhi Taj that I had my first real exposure to preparing Indian cuisine.

Working in Haveli, one of the premier restaurants in the hotel, I learned all about tandoori foods and their marinades and the various curries and gravies, particularly for typical northern dishes like *paneer lababdar,* chicken tikka masala, and chicken *makhani,* the beloved Punjabi dish known as butter chicken. I even tried my hand at *rumali roti,* a thin bread made from stretched dough thrown into the air like pizza dough.

After Haveli, I was transferred to Tanjore, the Indian restaurant in the Taj Mumbai, and then to various other outlets throughout India, which gave me the opportunity to work with accomplished cooks and chefs from all over the country.

Into my culinary repertoire went dishes and styles from India's diverse regions, each distinctive in its own way, among them the luxuriant Moghul and Persian kormas of Northern India, rich from nut pastes, saffron, butter, cream, dried fruits, and warming spices; the Portuguese-influenced vindaloos and *balchãos* of Goa, adobe red,

my friends. My decision to pursue cooking as a career was serendipitous. After high school, I applied to colleges for engineering and catering. As fate would have it, I was accepted at the latter first, so that was that—catering it would be! I obtained a bachelor of arts degree from Osmania University (Hyderabad) and a diploma in hotel administration and food technology

tangy, and fiery from vinegar and red chili peppers; the Malvani masalas charged with cinnamon, clove, cardamom, black pepper, and coconut.

In 1991, I had the opportunity to move to London, where the Taj Group opened Bombay Brasserie in the Bailey's Hotel in Kensington. Under Chef Udit Sarkhel, I further refined my skills in cooking traditional Indian curries, tandoori dishes, breads, and vegetables. In 1997, I was promoted to executive chef and began to develop my own signature dishes, some of which I brought to Rasika with me, such as Palak Chaat (page 53)—a wispy, wafery pile of delicately fried spinach topped with yogurt, tamarind, and bits of tomato— and Black Cod with Honey and Dill (page 169).

In 2004, Ashok reached out to me to discuss the possibility of my becoming the chef at Rasika. He spoke with great enthusiasm about creating a vibrant, buzzy environment with a lively cocktail lounge, a great wine list, and an open kitchen that would make diners feel like they were part of the action. The food, he said, would be a modern take on Indian cooking, with lots of appetizers and small plates, bursts of flavors, and tie-ins to what was going on in the American food scene.

That was an opportunity that could not be passed up, and I came to Washington with my wife, Anjali, and our two children, Viraj and Nidhi, in 2004. And the rest, as they say . . .

THE RASIKA SPICE PANTRY—THE ESSENCE OF INDIAN COOKING

HOW SPICES FUNCTION

Spices are dried plant materials, other than leaves, whose first use as food additives dates back six millennia. Ever since then they have been a fundamental part of human life, whether for their medicinal qualities, their trade value, or their appeal as food flavorings and preservatives.

India is the greatest producer and exporter of spices and provides the majority of the world's supply. Spice is, rightly so, the first association people make with Indian food. It is quite simply fundamental to our health and cuisine.

Ayurvedic medicine, the cornerstone of Hindu culture for thousands of years, identifies six tastes, or *rasas,* necessary to achieve gustatory pleasure, promote good digestion, and provide the body's vital nutrients. (*Ayur* means "life," *veda* means "knowledge.") The tastes are: sweet, sour, salty, pungent (hot), bitter, and astringent. Striking a balance of rasas with all of the ingredients, including spices, that go into dishes and meals contributes to physical and mental well-being as well as pleasure.

That all of these factors go into the creation of our food, based on knowledge and traditions that have been passed down through generations over centuries, is what makes Indian cooking so rich, refined, and complex.

That complexity is rooted in how we use spices to create aroma (cardamom, fenugreek seeds, fennel seeds, star anise, mace, nutmeg, cumin seeds, asafetida, dried roses), sourness (mango powder, tamarind), pungency (black peppercorns, red chili peppers, mustard seeds, cloves), bitterness (fenugreek seeds), and astringency (turmeric). Spices also provide color (deggi mirch, Kashmiri chilies, saffron, turmeric) and thicken sauces (white poppy seeds). But the most important function of spice is to add flavor.

ADDING SPICES TO THE POT

The combination of spices and how and when they are added to a dish is not arbitrary.

Some spices take longer to release their flavors than others. Some burn more easily than others. Whereas it might be tempting and easy to add spices and flavorings all at once, it is a bad idea; the complexity, and therefore the quality and balance, of the dish will suffer.

Overall, whole spices should be cooked before being integrated into a dish in order to release their essential oils and aromas and to make them more digestible. There are two ways to do this:

1. **TOAST THEM (SOMETIMES REFERRED TO AS DRY-ROASTING):** Simply place whole spices in a dry pan over medium heat until their aromas are released. Cooking them over too high a flame will burn and ruin them. Once cooled, grind the toasted spices and incorporate them into the recipe as directed.

2. **QUICK-FRY THEM:** Add whole spices to oil or ghee that has been heated almost to the smoking point. (Or, in the case of mustard oil, until heated to the smoking point and cooled slightly. This removes its bitterness and blooms its pungency.) Related to this is tempering, known as *tadka,* which is quick-frying spices with flavorings such as curry leaves, chopped ginger, chopped garlic, asafetida, and dried chili peppers, then adding them to a dish either at the beginning or end of its preparation. This creates an extra burst of flavor, richness, and complexity.

GLOSSARY OF SPICES, DRIED HERBS, MINERALS, FLAVORINGS, AND ELEMENTS

AMCHOOR POWDER: See **mango powder.**

ASAFETIDA POWDER (HING): A resin extracted from the taproot or rhizome of *ferula,* an herb in the parsley and fennel family, and sold in chunks or powder form. It has a strong sulfuric odor, but when cooked releases an onion-flavored umami bomb, which makes it an important spice for religious sects, such as the Jains, who don't eat onions. Asafetida is also thought to be an antiflatulent, which is why it is commonly used in legume dishes.

BLACK CUMIN SEEDS (SHAHI ZEERA): See **cumin seeds.**

BLACK PEPPERCORNS, WHOLE (KALI MIRCH): Berries from the *Piper nigrum* plant that have been dried just before maturity. They are used to add pungency, which diminishes quickly after being ground, so it is best to grind only the amount you need for a recipe.

BLACK SALT (KALA NAMAK): A rock salt that contains sodium sulfate, which gives it a distinct sulfuric profile and a faint violet hue. It adds tartness to foods and is often used in chaat masalas (see **chaat masala**).

CARDAMOM GROUND AND WHOLE PODS (ELAICHI): Highly aromatic, dried, seed-filled pods from the ginger family. **Green cardamom** (*choti elaichi*) seeds (and sometimes the pods, too) are used for ground cardamom. Whole pods are used often in Indian cooking to perfume sauces and *pulaos*. The profile is lemon, menthol, and camphor—a little goes a long way. **Black cardamom pods** (*kali elaichi*) are not interchangeable with green ones, which are brighter and more citrus noted. Black cardamom is smoky and earthier than green cardamom.

CHAAT MASALA: A spice blend of salty, pungent, and sour notes, often consisting of mango powder (*amchoor*), cumin, coriander, black salt, red chili powder, black pepper, and asafetida. Used in chaats and snacks to add a burst of flavor.

CHAI MASALA: A ground spice mix used for flavored tea or in desserts, the latter similar to how Americans might use pumpkin pie spice mix. It's made with fennel seeds, cardamom pods, cloves, cinnamon stick, ground ginger, star anise, and black pepper.

CHANA DAL: See page 15.

CHAROLI SEEDS: Small seeds, resembling brown lentils, from the *Buchanania lanzan* bush. They taste like a cross between pine nuts and almonds.

CINNAMON STICK (DALCHINI): The aromatic bark of the cinnamon tree or the cassia tree. Cinnamon bark is much thinner, and slightly sweeter, than cassia, which is slightly more bitter. They can be used interchangeably.

CITRIC ACID POWDER: Used to add a sour note and acid at the same time.

CLOVES (LAVANG): Shaped like nails, whole cloves are dried unopened flower buds of the evergreen clove tree.

CORIANDER SEEDS (DHANIA): The dried seeds of the coriander plant, whose leaves, also known as cilantro (*hara dhania*), are widely used in Asian cooking. Coriander often goes hand in hand with cumin in curries and ground spice mixtures. It's aromatic with citrus tones when whole and produces nutty, earthy tones when toasted and ground.

CULINARY ROSEBUDS AND PETALS, DRIED: Edible roses used as garnish or ground to lend sweet, floral, and perfumed notes to spice blends.

CUMIN SEEDS (JEERA): White cumin seed is one of the most predominant spices in Indian, North African, Middle Eastern, and Latin American cooking. It imparts aroma and smokiness with a mild licorice note and is considered a digestive aid. Cumin appears throughout the Indian repertoire in masalas, kormas, curries, and spice blends. **Black cumin seeds** (*shahi zeera*) are a relative of the white cumin family, but are more deeply aromatic and bitter with a slight menthol note. They're used in Northern Indian dishes, such as biryanis and shammi kebab.

CURRY LEAVES, FRESH (KADI PATTA): See page 14.

DEGGI MIRCH: A bright red chili powder made from a ground mix of Kashmiri and other dried red chili peppers. See page 12.

EDIBLE SILVER OR GOLD FOIL: See **vark.**

FENNEL SEEDS (SAUNF): Dried seeds from a variety of fennel related to that eaten as a vegetable. The flavor profile is anise and licorice.

FENUGREEK, SEEDS (METHI) AND DRIED LEAVES (KASOORI METHI): Dense, bitter, aromatic seeds of a plant in the Fabaceae family (legumes, peas, and beans) that resemble small yellow pebbles. They are generally toasted to mellow their bitterness and bring out their maple-like profile before being added to masalas, especially for pickles. **Dried fenugreek leaves,** used whole or ground, are much less bitter than the seeds and have a fennel, celery, and herbal profile.

GARAM MASALA: A spice blend, differing from region to region, household to household, that contains warming spices, such as cinnamon stick, cloves, mace, cardamom, black peppercorns, cumin seeds, and coriander seeds. Commercial garam masalas are available. The word *garam* means "to heat the body."

INDIAN BAY LEAVES (TEJ PATTA): Dried Indian bay leaves come from the cassia tree and are not related in appearance, flavor, or species to bay laurel leaves used in America. *Tej patta* are larger, paler, thinner, and more brittle than laurel leaves and have more of a cinnamon profile, whereas bay laurel has a more lemony profile.

KASHMIRI CHILI, DRIED: A long, dark red chili with mild heat and a fruity flavor profile. When ground, these peppers imbue sauces with a pleasing reddish orange hue. See page 12.

KEWRA WATER: An aromatic water made from a distilled extract of flowers from the screw pine (pandanus) shrub.

MACE (JAVITRI): The outer skin of the nutmeg seed dried into hard, reddish-brown, aromatic shavings. Mace has a less intense, fruitier profile than nutmeg, but in a pinch you could substitute one for the other.

MAKRUT LIME LEAVES: See headnote on page 151.

MANGO PICKLE: A condiment made with green mango, fenugreek, mustard seeds, chili powder, garlic, and oil and which can be found in varying degrees of pungency. Commercial mango pickle is available in stores.

MANGO POWDER (AMCHOOR): Dried green mango, ground into powder, used in Indian cooking as a souring agent.

MASALA: *Masala* means "a blend." It is a generic term that can mean:

1. A blend of aromatic dried spices, often toasted and ground, that is also known as a **dry masala**. Some common masalas sold premade include garam masala, *pav bhaji* masala, and chaat masala.
2. Masala can also refer to a **wet masala**, a common base of many dishes that is a paste or sauce in which spices are cooked with ingredients such as onions, garlic, ginger, fresh chilies, and tomatoes.

MUSTARD SEEDS (RAI): The seeds of the mustard plant, from the cabbage family. Indians favor the use of black mustard seeds (*Brassica nigra*) or brown mustard seeds (*Brassica juncea*) over the white (actually yellow) mustard seeds (*Brassica hirta*) commonly used in Europe and America. If you can't find black mustard seeds, brown are fine. (Brown are often sold as black anyway.) Mustard seeds are usually popped in hot oil before being added to dishes, which diminishes their pungency and gives them a nutty profile. They are often found in South Indian dishes.

NIGELLA SEEDS (KALONJI): Black, highly aromatic, slightly bitter seeds that resemble onion seeds in appearance. (They are often called onion seeds, but this is a misnomer.) They are one of the five types of seeds in *panch phoran* masala and are also often used in pickles.

NUTMEG (JAIPHAL): Dried seed from an evergreen tree indigenous chiefly to Indonesia. It has an aromatic, sweet, and nutty profile.

PANCH PHORAN: A masala also known as Bengali five-spice. (*Panch* means "five" and *phoron* means "spices.") The spices are nigella seeds, cumin seeds, fenugreek seeds, fennel seeds, and black mustard seeds.

PAV BHAJI MASALA: A prepared spice mix made with coriander, cumin, chili powder, mango powder, cardamom, ginger, black pepper, cloves, bay leaves, star anise, caraway, nutmeg, and mace. Specifically used to make *pav bhaji,* a popular Mumbai street food of mashed vegetables served on fluffy yeast rolls: Pao Bhaji (page 47) and Ladi Pao (page 252).

RED CHILI FLAKES: Dried and crushed hot red chili peppers and their seeds.

ROSE SYRUP: A bright-red, rose-flavored sugar syrup, similar in appearance to grenadine.

SAFFRON THREADS (KESAR): The stigmas of the saffron crocus. Saffron has a distinct perfume profile and just a little provides a rich, yellow-orange tint to foods, so use it sparingly. It is usually best to bloom saffron in liquid before adding it to foods. If you must, use a bit of turmeric as a substitute for coloring, but you'll give up the trademark flavor of the spice.

SESAME SEEDS (TIL): In Indian cooking, sesame seeds, usually white (*safed til*), are used for texture and nuttiness, especially when toasted.

STAR ANISE (CHAKRA PHOOL): Dried, star-shaped, licorice-flavored pods from the *Illicium verum* evergreen tree.

TAMARIND (IMLI): A leguminous tree whose dried pods, high in tartaric acid, are used to create a brown pulp that adds sourness, and a touch of sweetness, to dishes. See page 14.

TURMERIC (HALDI): Turmeric is a staple of Indian cooking, used as a food coloring and spice, but is also an anti-inflammatory. It is a powder ground from steamed, dried roots (rhizomes) of a plant in the ginger family. The steaming/drying/grinding process is done regularly in India, so turmeric there has a much more intense flavor than the bottled turmeric sitting on shelves for ages that we are used to in the United States. The powder, which is added in small quantities, provides an intense yellow-orange color and has a bitter, sour profile, which is why it is often used in pickling and to make mustard. Cooking it,

especially in oil, diminishes its astringency and enhances its quality as a colorant.

URAD DAL: See page 15.

VARK: Edible silver or gold foil used to garnish certain dishes and confections and, according to Ayurvedic principles, for antimicrobial (silver) and aphrodisiac (gold) qualities.

WHITE PEPPERCORNS (SAFED MIRCH): White pepper is less full-bodied and spicy than black pepper. Pepper loses its pungency quickly after being ground, so it is best to grind only the amount you need for a recipe.

WHITE POPPY SEEDS (KHUS KHUS): Seeds from the opium poppy. White poppy seeds are slightly milder than black poppy seeds and are sometimes toasted, ground, and used as a thickening agent.

A LIST OF SPICES, DRIED HERBS, PACKAGED SPICE BLENDS, MINERALS, FLAVORINGS, AND ELEMENTS USED IN OUR RECIPES

The number of recipes in this book that call for the ingredients listed here is provided in parentheses to give the reader a sense of each one's prevalence. That's not to say that spices used less frequently are less important, though; they are all essential. Keep in mind when stocking the spice pantry that whole spices, such as cumin seeds, black peppercorns, fenugreek seeds, green cardamom pods, mace, and cloves,

Asafetida (10)

Black cardamom pods (2)

Black cumin seeds (4)

Black or brown mustard seeds (13)

Black peppercorns (8), ground black pepper (8)

Black salt (3)

Black tea, such as Assam or Darjeeling (1)

Chana dal (8)

Charoli seeds (1)

Cinnamon stick (14), ground cinnamon (1)

Citric acid powder (1)

Cloves: whole (15), ground (1)

Coriander seeds (6), ground coriander (15)

Cumin seeds (41), ground cumin (1)

Deggi mirch (40)

Edible silver or gold foil (1)

Fenugreek leaves, dried (1), fenugreek leaf powder (7)

Fenugreek seeds (8), ground, toasted fenugreek (1)

Green cardamom pods (15), ground green cardamom (6), Mace-Cardamom Powder (6)

Ground ginger (2)

Indian bay leaves (6)

Kewra water (3)

Kashmiri chilies (8), Kashmiri chili paste (8)

Mace (3), Mace-Cardamom Powder (6)

Mango pickle (1)

Mango powder (1)

Nigella seeds (5)

Nutmeg, grated (1)

Packaged: Chaat masala (6)

Packaged: Garam masala (14)

Packaged: Pav bhaji masala (1)

Red chili flakes (5)

Roses: edible dried buds and petals (1), rose syrup (1)

Saffron threads (11)

Sesame seeds (1)

Star anise (2)

Tamarind block (2)

Turmeric, ground (63)

Vanilla beans (3)

White peppercorns, ground (1)

can be ground into powder at home, so there is no need to buy both whole and ground versions. Freshly ground spices are always more vibrant than store-bought ground spices.

NOTES ON SOME ESSENTIAL INGREDIENTS

SALT

The salt we use at Rasika is table salt. Feel free to use fine sea salt if you wish. Always check dishes for salt at the end and adjust accordingly. This especially applies to food that has been cooked ahead and reheated.

THE CORE QUINTET OF FRESH VEGETABLES

Onions, garlic, ginger, fresh green chili peppers, and tomatoes—either separately, in some combination, or, very frequently, all together—are found in nearly every savory recipe in *Rasika*. These ingredients are as essential to Indian cooking as mirepoix is to French cooking or the holy trinity of onions, celery, and bell peppers is to New Orleans cuisine. Chili peppers, garlic, and ginger add pungency. Onions and tomatoes often act as thickening agents and give dishes body, which is why when a recipe calls for them to be finely chopped, they really must be. It's best to chop by hand, but you can use a food processor. Cut the onions or tomatoes into small, uniform pieces first, then make sure to use very short pulses so you get even chopping, scraping down the bowl and removing any big pieces from time to time. With tomatoes, some recipes call specifically for either a blender or for a food processor. Follow the directions because those machines yield two different results: A blender liquefies and a food processor leaves more body and texture.

CHILI PEPPERS (MIRCH)

Guess which country grows and exports the most chilies in the entire world? Yes, India, which is also the world's greatest consumer of chilies. Fresh, dried, or ground into powder, chilies are cornerstones of Indian cooking. They came to India via the Americas. Columbus discovered them there when he was trying to find India at the end of the fifteenth century and brought them back to Europe. Portuguese and Spanish traders introduced them to the Middle East and Asia, where they were hugely embraced.

There are three chili ingredients used in the recipes in *Rasika,* all of which are considered staples: fresh, hot, green chilies; dried Kashmiri chilies; and deggi mirch (ground chili powder).

FRESH THAI GREEN CHILIES: There are many varieties of fresh green chilies (*hara mirch)* grown in India. Among the most widely used are long, thin, wrinkly *jwala*

("volcano" in Hindi) finger peppers and smaller bird's eye chilies. The most readily available comparable substitute in the United States is the Thai green chili, which is probably a bit hotter than a jwala. On a scale of 1 to 10, with 1 being the mildest, I'd put jwalas at 7 and Thai green chilies at 8. By contrast, serrano peppers and jalapeños are around 6.

It is important to note that the heat of chilies varies from pepper to pepper. The larger and thicker ones tend to be less hot than smaller, thinner ones. The heat comes largely from the white pithy part inside the chili and from the seeds. So if you want to adjust the heat downward, you can start by removing those. Or use a smaller total amount than the recipe calls for. Also, the more finely chopped the peppers are, the hotter they will be, because chopping releases more capsaicin, the compound that makes peppers hot.

The recipes in this book that use chopped Thai green chili give the measurement in teaspoons. That is more accurate than saying "medium Thai green chili," a more subjective description. In this book, a medium Thai green chili pepper is roughly 2 inches long and ¾ inch wide. Two finely chopped Thai green chilies is equal to 1 teaspoon.

DRIED KASHMIRI OR BYADGI CHILIES: These are both dried red chili peppers (*laal mirch).* There can be confusion about which of these peppers is which because often what are being sold as Kashmiri chilies are, in fact, the more abundant byadgi chilies. Kashmiri chilies are grown mostly in the small state of Jammu and Kashmir in the very north of India, near the Himalayas. Byadgi peppers are grown in the state of Karnataka in Southern India. Byadgis are long, narrow, pointy, shriveled peppers; Kashmiris are smaller, a little wider, less wrinkly, and conical. Both are a vibrant red when ground and have midlevel heat, with Kashmiris a little less. For the purposes of *Rasika*'s recipes, use these peppers interchangeably.

DEGGI MIRCH: A bright red chili powder made from a mix of ground Kashmiri and other dried red chili peppers. It is used as much for its vibrant, crimson-orange color as for its heat, which can range anywhere from low to midlevel. There are many brands of deggi mirch and their heat levels vary because you're never sure exactly what the blend of chilies includes. MDH brand, which I use at Rasika and in recipes in this book, is close to 5 on a scale of 1 to 10. Often deggi mirch is referred to as paprika, but I think it is much more vibrantly colored and flavorful than what is sold as paprika in the States. Do not substitute a mix of paprika and cayenne for deggi mirch, as I've seen suggested. This is such a vital ingredient in so many recipes that you should buy the real thing. Kashmiri chili powder is a fine substitute. It is made from ground Kashmiri chilies and imparts the vibrant red color you want, but is slightly milder in heat than deggi mirch. It is fine to use the two interchangeably.

COOKING OILS

The recipes in *Rasika* use five cooking oils. **CANOLA OIL,** made from a rapeseed crossbreed, is by far the most prevalent cooking oil called for in the book. You can use other neutral oils, such as peanut oil, sunflower oil, or vegetable oil, instead, or use olive oil; it really doesn't affect the flavor all that much.

GHEE is unsalted butter that has been clarified slowly over low heat to the point where its milk solids coagulate and fall to the bottom of the pot, brown, and create a nutty flavor. It's used in recipes calling for the extra richness and the fuller flavor it offers.

COCONUT OIL is most prevalent in the dishes from the southern regions of India.

MUSTARD OIL is especially popular in certain northern and eastern parts of India, where mustard is grown. You'll find it in many tandoori marinades or used as a cooking oil, especially in the Bengali dishes of Eastern India. Before frying spices in mustard oil, you must first heat it to the smoking point and let it cool slightly before proceeding. This removes its caustic property and brings its pungency forward.

EXTRA-VIRGIN OLIVE OIL is used in only two recipes: Black Pepper Crab Napoleon with Curry Oil (page 81) and Griddled Eggplant and Potato Stacks with Jaggery Peanut Sauce (page 73).

YOGURT

Full-fat cow's (or buffalo's) milk yogurt is a basic building block of the Indian diet.

It thickens curries and sauces, serves as a tenderizer in marinades, appears in cooling raitas to counterbalance a meal's heat, acts as a souring agent, lends richness, and provides protein for vegetarian diets.

Do not use anything but plain whole-milk yogurt in these recipes. If you do, sauces may break and be too tart, marinades would be too thin, and richness would disappear. We use Axelrod yogurt at Rasika. After trying many brands, this was the closest one we could find to Indian yogurt.

PANEER

Paneer is a fresh cheese made from cow's milk that has been curdled through the introduction of an acid (such as lemon juice or vinegar), drained and squeezed to rid it of whey, and pressed into a solid block. It is an important part of the Indian diet, especially to India's large vegetarian population, because it is loaded with protein, has a neutral flavor that balances boldly flavored foods, and has a firm texture that becomes creamy when cooked without melting or falling apart. That's why you'll find it in dishes such as curries and kebabs, including Paneer Makhani (page 129) and Paneer Shashlik (page 143).

TAMARIND

Tamarind pulp is widely used in Indian cooking as a souring agent. It is made from the brown pods of the *Tamarindus indica* tree indigenous to Africa and long ago introduced to India. Inside the pods are

seeds surrounded by stringy brown pulp, all of which is dehydrated (sun-dried) and sold in a dense, tar-like block. Pieces of that block are rehydrated in warm water and then squeezed and strained in order to extract all the pulp (see Tamarind Pulp, page 24). The result looks like a thin puree of dried prunes and water, but is sour, like lemon juice.

JAGGERY

Jaggery is unrefined sugar, made from sugarcane juice or palm sap boiled down and dried into solid blocks or large balls. Its color can range from pale gold to deep golden brown because the molasses has not been removed from it. Jaggery's flavor profile is butter, caramel, vaguely licorice, and slightly salty, and it adds much more depth than sugar or honey, especially to chutneys. The closest substitute would be panela, which can be found in Latino grocery stores.

FRESH CURRY LEAVES

Curry leaves (*kadi patta*) are the leaves of a curry tree (this has nothing to do with curry powder, which is a blend of various dried spices). They impart a lemon-lime profile to dishes, with the fresh leaves adding a bright, herbaceous, grassy quality that comes to the forefront, especially when cooked in hot oil with mustard seeds, a common finishing flourish to many South Indian dishes. We use them frequently in our dishes at Rasika and in numerous recipes in this book, among them chutneys, curries, vegetables, grain, and rice dishes, and even the zesty popcorn we serve with our cocktails. In an airtight container, curry leaves will last 2 to 3 weeks in the refrigerator. They can also be wrapped tightly in plastic wrap and frozen. Do not substitute with dried curry leaves.

LEGUMES, PULSES, GRAM, BESAN, AND DAL

Legumes are vital sources of protein around the world and hugely important to Indian cooking. Getting the English and Indian terms straight, though, can be challenging: *Legumes,* which include pulses and dal, are pod plants in the family Fabaceae, also known as the legume, pea, and bean family. It includes plants grown for use as forage, as vegetables, and for their dried edible seeds.

Pulses are legumes grown for their dried edible seeds (lentils, chickpeas). *Dal* technically refers to split pulses, although the word is sometimes used generally to describe any dish made with pulses, split or not. To make matters even more confusing, many cooks use the word *lentil* to mean any kind of split pulse, even though it technically refers to a specific species of the Fabaceae family known as *Lens culinaris.* None of the pulses in this book are true lentils.

Gram (a word derived from the Portuguese word for "grain") is a general term for a variety of different whole, dried pulses, including chickpeas.

Bengal gram is a small chickpea with dark husks, also known as *desi* chickpeas. The dried chickpeas familiar to Americans (garbanzo beans) are *kabuli* chickpeas. They are larger than desi chickpeas and have beige husks and interiors.

Chana dal is Bengal gram that has been husked and split. Chana dal that is toasted and ground into flour is known as *besan.* The common English translation for besan is "chickpea flour", which is misleading because chickpea flour in American stores is usually garbanzo flour, not Bengal gram flour. Garbanzo flour is made from untoasted ground kabuli chickpeas and is finer and more silken than gram flour. The recipes in this book call for gram flour, not garbanzo flour. I don't suggest substituting.

Here are the legumes used in *Rasika,* listed by how they are identified in the ingredient lists. The parenthetical explanations do not appear in the recipes.

BLACK GRAM (whole black gram; *urad sabut*)

CHANA DAL (husked and split small yellow chickpeas; known as Bengal gram)

DRIED CHICKPEAS (*kabuli chana*)

DRIED RED KIDNEY BEANS (*rajma*)

ROASTED CHANA DAL (whole Bengal grams roasted in their skins and then husked and split)

VATANA (whole dried yellow peas)

URAD DAL (husked and split black grams, which are white when husked; *urad dhuli*)

MOONG DAL (husked and split green mung beans, which are yellow when husked, *moong dhuli dalhl*)

ABOUT SOURCING

Excellent sources for the ingredients used in this book, including all spices listed in the Rasika spice pantry (page 11) and items not typically found in the American pantry or grocery store, such as fresh curry leaves, fresh Makrut lime leaves, ghee, paneer, guava paste and nectar, jaggery, mustard oil, mango pickle, Alphonso mango pulp, and everything outlined earlier in this chapter are www.ishopindian.com, www.kalustyans .com, and www.amazon.com.

GETTING ORGANIZED

The recipes in *Rasika* aren't difficult; they require organizational skills more than advanced culinary ones.

Chefs always emphasize the importance of *mise en place*—the French term for having everything set up and in its place before you start cooking—but for Indian cooking, it is critical. You don't want to be collecting spices, searching around for the ½-teaspoon measuring spoon, or finely chopping a pound of tomatoes while your onions and ginger-garlic paste are burning.

Here's a useful strategy:

Read through the recipe and make sure you have all of the necessary ingredients. These may include some of the basic flavorings and sauces from Chapter 2, such as Ginger-Garlic Paste, Kashmiri Chili Paste, or Korma Sauce.

See if the dish requires or suggests that you start the day before, especially if a marinade is involved. (See Marinating, page 139.)

Determine what can be prepared ahead of time and what needs to be finished just before serving.

Set up the mise en place: Prep all of the vegetables and proteins. Measure out all of the spices and flavorings, grouping those that are added to a dish at the same time in separate, small containers. (A masala *dabba* comes in handy for this. See the utensil list in the next section.)

On the counter next to the stove, line up all of the components for the dish in their order of inclusion.

Many dishes not only can be prepared a day or two before and reheated, but should be. Curries especially fall into this category. Marinades, sauces, desserts, and some breads can be made ahead, as can rice and *pulaos* (except for biryani). Most chutneys can be made weeks in advance.

Most curries in *Rasika* can be frozen, including kormas, because their sauces have been cooked with nuts and stabilized. Do not freeze Kadi Sauce (page 33), because that sauce has not been stabilized enough to withstand freezing and thawing.

That being said, dishes lose some boldness in the freezer. Thaw in the refrigerator, not the microwave. Then reheat over medium heat, stirring frequently until warmed through. Adjust the seasoning.

USEFUL UTENSILS

You are perfectly able to cook Indian food without acquiring all kinds of special equipment. Here is a list of necessary and recommended items and a list of small appliances and cookware used in this book's recipes.

NECESSARY ITEMS

A 10-INCH CAST IRON SKILLET OR GRIDDLE, for making breads.
AN ELECTRIC SPICE OR COFFEE GRINDER, essential for grinding whole spices.
A NUTRIBULLET (16- to 24-ounce capacity), or similar small blender with a powerful motor (at least 250W).
This is crucial for making pastes and chutneys where the size of the batch is too small for the blades of a full-size blender to work effectively. (Some full-size blenders come with 1-cup and/or 2-cup blender jar attachments. They work well, too.)
A PIZZA STONE, if you plan to bake naan.

RECOMMENDED ITEMS

A DIGITAL KITCHEN SCALE, for accuracy.
AN INDIAN *BELAN* AND *CHAKLA*: A narrow rolling pin and a circular, raised wooden board used to roll flatbreads, such as chapati and paratha. A regular cutting board and rolling pin are fine, but marking out 6-inch, 7-inch, 8-inch, 9-inch, and 10-inch circles with an indelible marker on the chakla as templates means not having to use a ruler for accuracy.

the various spices and flavorings of a dish you are preparing. It's an excellent tool for getting organized before you start cooking.

PLENTY OF FOOD STORAGE CONTAINERS in ¼-cup, ½-cup, and 1-cup sizes, for pastes and chutneys.

SILICONE ICE CUBE TRAYS with 1-ounce (2-tablespoon) cubes, for freezing apportioned pastes and flavorings.

A SPIDER STRAINER or mesh skimmer, for frying.

A TORTILLA WARMER, for breads.

A WOK, for frying. Or the Indian version, a *kadai.*

OTHER SMALL APPLIANCES AND COOKWARE

Baking dishes
Baking racks
Baking sheets
Box grater
Cake pans
Colander
Cotton kitchen towels
Cutting boards
Fine-mesh, regular, and coarse sieves
Food processor
Full-size blender
Grater/zester, for grating nutmeg and citrus zest
Ladles: 2-ounce and 4-ounce
Measuring cups
Mixing bowls
Pastry brush
Ramekins

AN INSTANT-READ THERMOMETER.

A KEBAB GRILLING SET that includes a metal rack and ½-inch-wide skewers, for tandoori-style grilling. The rack suspends skewers above the grill so the proteins and vegetables don't come into contact with the grate. Wide, flat skewers hold the foods threaded on them securely and prevent them from twisting.

A MASALA DABBA is a round, lidded, stainless-steel container with seven canisters fitted inside to hold spices. In Indian households, these would be filled with the spices most commonly used. That's a good idea if you plan to cook Indian food often, but I suggest you use it for apportioning

Rolling pin

Ruler or tape measure

Saucepans, skillets, and pots or Dutch
ovens, with lids

Spatulas: rubber, silicone, wide, offset

Spoons: measuring, mixing, wooden,
slotted

Stand mixer

Tongs

Whisks

A variety of sharp kitchen knives, especially
a chef's knife and a paring knife

Vegetable peeler

EQUIVALENTS

1 cup raw basmati rice = 6 ounces

10 medium (1½-inch) curry leaves cut into
thin strips = 1 tablespoon, packed

3 medium cloves garlic = ½ ounce =
1 generous tablespoon finely chopped

1-inch cube ginger = 1 tablespoon finely
chopped

1 medium fresh Thai green chili =
roughly 2 inches long and ¾ inch wide

2 medium fresh Thai green chilies,
finely chopped = 1 teaspoon

1 piece (2 x 1 x 1-inch) jaggery = 1 ounce

1 small onion = 6 ounces

1 medium onion = 9 ounces

1 large onion = 14 ounces

4½ ounces peeled, trimmed onion =
1 cup finely chopped

1 medium baking potato = ½ pound

1 medium tomato (about the size of a
lemon) = 5.3 ounces = ⅔ cup finely
chopped

3 medium tomatoes = 1 pound =
2 cups finely chopped

2

BASIC FLAVORINGS AND SAUCES

The basic flavorings and sauces in this chapter are used more than once in this book; in the list that follows, the number next to each item indicates the number of recipes in which it appears. It is a good idea to carve out time one day to make some or all of these flavorings and sauces and freeze them, especially Ginger-Garlic Paste, Kashmiri Chili Paste, and Tamarind Pulp, because they are used so frequently. See the recipes for freezing instructions. Having any of these on hand saves time down the road and gives you greater flexibility.

Toasted Cumin Powder (11)
Mace-Cardamom Powder (6)
Tamarind Pulp (8)
Crispy Fried Onions (5)

Caramelized Onion Paste (3)
Ginger-Garlic Paste (39)
Kashmiri Chili Paste (8)
Peri-Peri Paste (3)
Balchão Masala (2)

A Tomato Masala (2)
Korma Sauce (3)
Kadi Sauce (2)
Makhani Sauce (2)

TOASTED CUMIN POWDER

MAKES ABOUT 3 TABLESPOONS ⚙ This is a commonly used flavoring for chaats, *tikkis,* and other dishes. Toasting the seeds enhances and deepens their flavor. Many people make the mistake of using a hot pan to toast spices—all this does is blacken and ruin them. Take your time and toast them over medium heat, as we do here.

¼ cup cumin seeds

1 Put the cumin seeds in a small, cold skillet. Cook over medium heat, shaking the pan often, until the aromas are released along with a light smoke and the seeds are darkened but not black, about 6 minutes. Remove from the heat and let the seeds cool.

2 Transfer to a spice grinder and pulse into a fine powder. Store in an airtight container at room temperature for up to 1 month.

MACE-CARDAMOM POWDER

MAKES ABOUT 3 TABLESPOONS ⚙ This is a very fragrant blend, used especially in kormas. Use it sparingly if you add it to your own dishes as too much of it will be overpowering.

2 tablespoons whole green cardamom pods
2 tablespoons mace (javitri)

In a spice grinder, grind the cardamom pods and mace into a powder. Store in an airtight container at room temperature for up to 1 month.

TAMARIND PULP

MAKES 3 CUPS ❁ This pulp is made from dried tamarind pods sold in block form (see Tamarind, page 14). In my opinion, it's much better to make your own tamarind pulp than to use store-bought paste or concentrates that are reconstituted with water. They tend to be too dark in color and have much less body than homemade pulp does.

Once the tamarind has softened, really get in there with your hand to break it all up and separate as much of the pulp and strings as you can from the seeds. This will make the work of forcing the pulp through a sieve a lot easier.

If you're making the pulp just to have on hand for future use, store in ½-cup containers or in silicone ice cube trays. (See Freezing in Silicone Ice Cube Trays, page 27.) The recipe halves easily.

8 ounces dried tamarind block, such as Laxmi brand

1 quart warm water

1 In a large glass bowl, microwave the tamarind and water on high for 3 minutes to soften the tamarind. (Or cook in a saucepan over medium heat for about 6 minutes.) Let it soak for 1 hour, until very soft.

2 Use your hand to break up the pieces and squeeze them through your fingers. You are separating the stringy pulp and seeds and extracting juice.

3 Transfer everything to a coarse sieve set over a large bowl. Using the back of a spoon (a flat-edged wooden spatula also works well), press and scrape the pulp and seeds to extract as much liquid as you can. Scrape off and add to the bowl any pulp clinging to the bottom of the sieve. Discard the stringy solids and seeds. Store the pulp in an airtight container in the refrigerator for up to 3 weeks or in the freezer for up to 1 year.

CRISPY FRIED ONIONS

MAKES 2 1/2 TO 3 CUPS ◈ Biryanis, including the Goat Biryani (page 210) and Vegetable Biryani (page 133) found in this book, are usually garnished with fried onions. These onions are also used to make a paste with yogurt or some other liquid to thicken and stabilize sauces.

1 quart canola oil	1½ pounds yellow onions, halved and cut into ¼-inch-thick half-moon slices

Line a baking sheet with paper towels and have at the ready. Pour the oil into a wok or *kadai* and heat over high heat to 375°F. Add half the onions—the water in them will create steam and make the oil bubble up—and cook, stirring frequently, until they are deep golden brown, 10 to 15 minutes. Use a spider strainer or mesh skimmer to transfer them to the paper towels. Return the oil to 375°F and fry the rest of the onions. Let cool and store in an airtight container in the refrigerator for up to 3 weeks. Strain the cooled oil and reuse.

CARAMELIZED ONION PASTE

MAKES ABOUT 2 1/4 CUPS ⚙ Indian cooks always have this on hand as a kitchen staple. This paste acts as a thickener for sauces while adding body and deep, rich, aromatic flavor. When you mix it with yogurt, the paste acts as a stabilizer that keeps the yogurt from breaking. It is used in three recipes in this book: Jalapeño in Gravy (page 124), Stuffed Saffron and Almond Chicken (page 187), and Lamb and Pineapple Korma (page 204).

If you're making the paste just to have on hand for future use, freeze in ¼-cup or ½-cup containers or in a silicone ice cube tray. (See Freezing in Silicone Ice Cube Trays, opposite.) The recipe halves easily.

1½ pounds yellow onions, halved and
    thinly sliced

1 quart canola oil
2 cups water

1 Line a baking sheet with paper towels and have at the ready. Pour the oil into a wok or *kadai* and heat over high heat to 375°F. Add half the onions and cook, stirring frequently, until they are golden brown, not dark brown, about 8 minutes. (How long it will take for the onions to caramelize depends on their age and how much water is in them.) Use a spider strainer or mesh skimmer to transfer the onions to the paper towels. Return the oil to 375°F, then fry the remaining onions.

2 In a blender, puree the onions and water until smooth. It will resemble thick brown gravy. Store in an airtight container in the refrigerator for up to 1 week or in the freezer for up to 3 months.

GINGER-GARLIC PASTE

MAKES 2 CUPS ❁ This flavorful paste is one of the building blocks of Indian cooking and therefore used often in Rasika's recipes. It's a good idea to make a 2-cup batch; it keeps well. Freeze in ¼-cup containers or in a silicone ice cube tray. (See Freezing in Silicone Ice Cube Trays, below.) The recipe halves easily.

½ cup (2 ounces) chopped unpeeled
    fresh ginger
1½ cups (½ pound) medium garlic cloves

¾ cup water

In a NutriBullet or small blender, puree all the ingredients on high speed until smooth, about 3 minutes. Store in an airtight container in the refrigerator for up to 1 week. It also freezes well and will keep for up to 3 months.

FREEZING IN SILICONE ICE CUBE TRAYS

Silicone ice cube trays in 2-tablespoon (1-ounce) portions are useful for freezing certain flavorings, such as tamarind pulp, ginger-garlic paste, Kashmiri chili paste, peri-peri paste, and caramelized onion paste. A tray that yields 16 (1-ounce) cubes holds 2 cups. For a recipe that makes just a little more than 2 cups, distribute it evenly among the other cubes.

To freeze, wrap the ice cube tray well in plastic wrap and place it in a freezer-safe storage bag. If you're freezing a pungent mixture, like one containing garlic or Kashmiri chilies, you won't want to use the tray for anything else; the oil, flavor, and odor may be hard to get out. You don't want to put the tray in your dishwasher for the same reason.

Once the cubes are frozen, you can pop them out as needed or transfer them to a freezer-safe ziptop bag to store them; just make sure to remove as much air from the bag as possible before returning the cubes to the freezer.

Before use, thaw whatever amount you need in the refrigerator or microwave for several seconds.

KASHMIRI CHILI PASTE

MAKES 1 CUP ✦ Use a NutriBullet-type blender for best results. Puree for the full amount of time called for and scrape down often. It takes the seeds longer to break down than the rest of the chili. Most of the seeds won't, though, so you will have to strain the mixture to achieve a fine paste. We use an Indian wet spice grinder at Rasika that produces a fine paste so we don't have to strain it.

If you're making the paste just to have on hand for future use, freeze in ¼-cup containers or in a silicone ice cube tray. (See Freezing in Silicone Ice Cube Trays, page 27.)

2 cups (about 2 ounces) stemmed, coarsely chopped dried Kashmiri chilies, with seeds

1¼ cups water

1 In a small blender or NutriBullet, combine 1 cup of the chilies and all the water and puree on high speed for 1 minute. Add the remaining 1 cup chilies and puree for 5 minutes.

2 Pass the puree through a sieve into a bowl, pressing on the solids with a rubber spatula until mostly what are left in the sieve are seeds. (This takes a bit of time.) Rinse off the spatula to clean it before scraping off any paste on the underside of the sieve and add it to the bowl. Discard the solids. Store in an airtight container in the refrigerator for up to 1 week or in the freezer for up to 3 months.

RASIKA

PERI-PERI PASTE

MAKES 1 CUP ❁ The Portuguese introduced this preparation of vinegar and hot chili peppers (peri-peris are chili peppers) when they occupied the western coast of India in the sixteenth century. It became part of the culinary lexicon and is a hallmark of many Goan dishes. Peri-peri paste is the base for the Balchão Masala (page 30) used for Calamari Balchão (page 85), Pan-Seared Red Snapper with Shrimp Balchão (page 159), and the vindaloo sauce in Smoked Rack of Pork Vindaloo (page 194).

We suggest that you make a double or triple batch of peri-peri paste and freeze it. You need a single batch to make Balchão Masala and a double batch to make the Smoked Rack of Pork Vindaloo. It's certainly useful to have on hand.

In Goa, they use palm vinegar. You can substitute red wine vinegar for malt vinegar; in some ways it's closer to palm vinegar than malt vinegar.

If you're making the paste just to have on hand for future use, freeze in ¼-cup containers or in a silicone ice cube tray. (See Freezing in Silicone Ice Cube Trays, page 27.)

1½ teaspoons cumin seeds
1½ teaspoons black peppercorns
8 whole cloves
5 green cardamom pods
1-inch cinnamon stick, crushed

¾ ounce (about 1 cup) stemmed dried Kashmiri chilies, with seeds
5 medium garlic cloves
1 cup malt vinegar or red wine vinegar

1 In a spice grinder, grind the cumin seeds, peppercorns, cloves, cardamom pods, and cinnamon into a powder. Transfer it to a NutriBullet or small blender.

2 Add the Kashmiri chilies, garlic, and vinegar. Blend for 10 full minutes, shaking the container or scraping it down every now and then. The paste should be a deep adobe red, smooth, and the texture of thick tomato sauce. Store in an airtight container in the refrigerator for up to 1 month or in the freezer for up to 1 year.

BALCHÃO MASALA

MAKES ABOUT 1¹/₂ CUPS ⚙ The Portuguese introduced this red-chili-and-vinegar-based method of food preservation to India in the sixteenth century. It is used in India today to pickle seafood, such as shrimp and mackerel. At Rasika, we make the masala days in advance and allow it to mature, refrigerated. It mellows over time. Balchão masala is used for Calamari Balchão (page 85) and Pan-Seared Red Snapper with Shrimp Balchão (page 159).

¼ cup canola oil
2 cups finely chopped yellow onions
2 tablespoons finely chopped garlic
1 cup finely chopped tomato
10 (1½-inch) fresh curry leaves (more
    if smaller), cut into thin strips
¼ teaspoon ground turmeric

¼ teaspoon deggi mirch
1 cup Peri-Peri Paste (page 29)
2 tablespoons malt vinegar
6 tablespoons Tamarind Pulp (page 24)
2 teaspoons salt
1½ teaspoons sugar

1 In a large saucepan, heat the oil over medium-high heat until it shimmers. Stir in the onions and garlic and cook, stirring occasionally, until lightly browned, about 15 minutes. Add the tomato, curry leaves, turmeric, and deggi mirch and cook until the tomatoes are softened and all their liquid has evaporated, about 6 minutes.

2 Reduce the heat to medium and stir in the peri-peri paste, vinegar, and tamarind pulp. Cook, stirring occasionally, until the masala is a thick paste, about 15 minutes. Stir in the salt and sugar. If not using immediately, cool to room temperature. Store in an airtight container in the refrigerator for up to 2 weeks or in the freezer for up to 3 months.

A TOMATO MASALA

MAKES ABOUT 2 CUPS ❂ This masala, a simple tomato-based sauce, is used in Gujarati Eggplant and Sweet Potato "Lasagna" with Kadi Sauce (page 127) and Masala Corn and Peanuts (page 107).

1½ pounds tomatoes, coarsely chopped
3 tablespoons canola oil
½ teaspoon black or brown mustard seeds
½ teaspoon cumin seeds
¼ teaspoon fenugreek seeds
⅛ teaspoon asafetida
½ teaspoon ground turmeric
1 teaspoon deggi mirch

1½ teaspoons ground coriander
¾ teaspoon ground cumin
1½ teaspoons finely chopped fresh ginger
½ teaspoon finely chopped fresh Thai green chili
2 tablespoons tomato paste
2 teaspoons salt
1 tablespoon sugar

1 In a food processor, puree the tomatoes.

2 In a heavy-bottomed pot or Dutch oven, heat the oil over medium-high heat until it shimmers. Add the mustard seeds, cumin seeds, fenugreek seeds, and asafetida and let the seeds crackle. Stir in the pureed tomatoes, turmeric, deggi mirch, coriander, cumin, ginger, and green chili. Simmer vigorously for 15 minutes, stirring occasionally, to reduce the mixture to the consistency of thick marinara sauce.

3 Reduce the heat to medium and stir in the tomato paste, salt, and sugar. Cook for 5 minutes, stirring occasionally, to make the masala a little thicker. If not using right away, cool to room temperature. Store in an airtight container in the refrigerator for up to 3 days or in the freezer for up to 3 months.

KORMA SAUCE

❁ I consider this an Indian version of béchamel sauce, but made with yogurt and cashew paste instead of milk and flour, which makes it gluten-free.

Kormas are generally associated with the rich, braised meat dishes of Northern India, introduced to the region by the Moghuls, via Persia. (*Korma* means "braise" in Hindi.) They tend to be mild and flavorful from warm heat, but you can spice them up by adding chopped Thai green chilies.

We use this korma sauce at Rasika as the base for many dishes and in this book for the Cremini Mushroom and Artichoke Korma (page 120), Chicken Pista Korma (page 181), and Lamb and Pineapple Korma (page 204).

2 cups diced yellow onion
3 cups water
1 cup chopped unsalted raw cashews
1 cup whole-milk yogurt

2 tablespoons canola oil
2 tablespoons Ginger-Garlic Paste
   (page 27)

1 In a medium saucepan, combine the onions and water and bring to a boil over medium-high heat. Cover and cook until the onions are soft, about 10 minutes.

2 Transfer the onions and water to a blender. Add the cashews and puree until smooth, starting on low speed and slowly increasing to high speed to allow the steam to escape. Blend for at least a full minute. Transfer to a medium bowl and whisk in the yogurt.

3 In a large saucepan, heat the oil over medium heat until it shimmers. Stir in the ginger-garlic paste and cook for 30 seconds, stirring constantly. Stir in the yogurt mixture. Cook until the sauce is very thick and the cashews no longer taste raw, about 20 minutes. (It will come to a boil around the 9-minute mark.) Stir frequently (it will spatter) to keep the sauce from sticking to the bottom of the pan. If not using right away, let cool. Store in an airtight container in the refrigerator for up to 3 days or in the freezer for up to 1 month.

KADI SAUCE

MAKES 2 1/2 CUPS ❀ This particular kadi sauce is based on the Gujarati (Western India) version of a yogurt-based sauce thickened with gram flour (besan). (See Legumes, Pulses, Gram, Besan, and Dal, page 15.) In that region, the sauce is sweet and sour. There is also a Northern Indian version, which is spicier and even more sour. They never add sugar to their kadi as Gujaratis do.

A traditional kadi would consist of gram flour dumplings served in the sauce. Our Rasika version is Kale Fritters Kadi (page 112). The sauce also serves as the accompaniment for Gujarati Eggplant and Sweet Potato "Lasagna" with Kadi Sauce (page 127).

2 cups whole-milk yogurt
2 tablespoons gram flour (besan)
2 cups water
½ teaspoon ground turmeric
2 teaspoons finely chopped fresh ginger
1 teaspoon finely chopped fresh Thai
    green chili
2 tablespoons canola oil

1 teaspoon black or brown mustard seeds
2 large dried Kashmiri chilies, halved
10 (1½-inch) fresh curry leaves (more if
    smaller)
¼ teaspoon asafetida
1 tablespoon sugar
1½ teaspoons salt

1 In a small saucepan, combine the yogurt, gram flour, water, turmeric, ginger, and green chili. Cook over medium heat, stirring constantly, until the mixture comes to a boil, 10 to 12 minutes. (Once the sauce comes to a boil, it is stabilized and the yogurt is no longer in danger of breaking.) Continue to cook, stirring occasionally, until the sauce thickens and coats the back of the spoon, about 15 minutes. Remove from the heat.

2 In a small skillet, heat the oil over medium heat until it shimmers. Add the mustard seeds and let them crackle. Stir in the Kashmiri chilies, curry leaves, and asafetida. Scrape all of the pan's contents into the yogurt sauce. Stir in the sugar and salt. If not using immediately, let cool. Store in an airtight container in the refrigerator for up to 2 days.

MAKHANI SAUCE

MAKES 5 1/2 CUPS ✼ *Makhani* is Hindi for "with butter." A lot of recipes for this classic butter-and-cream-based tomato sauce call for sugar and honey. Ours doesn't do that. We cook the tomatoes slowly, simmering them to bring out their sweetness and reduce the acidity of the fruit. Use the ripest tomatoes you can find; this will give the sauce a brighter, redder appearance. If you find the finished sauce too acidic because of your tomatoes, add a tablespoon of honey at the end.

This sauce always comes in handy, so make a double batch and freeze it, but omit the salt and cream. To use, thaw the sauce and reheat it over medium heat. When it comes to a boil, stir in the salt and cream. Then the sauce is ready to add to Paneer Makhani (page 129) or Chicken Makhani (page 186).

RASIKA

1½ pounds medium tomatoes, quartered
8 medium garlic cloves
4 medium fresh Thai green chilies
1-inch piece fresh ginger, coarsely
    chopped
½ cup dried fenugreek leaves
1 quart water

1 cup tomato paste
1 stick (4 ounces) unsalted butter,
    cut into 1-inch cubes
1 tablespoon salt
¾ cup heavy cream

1 In a large saucepan, combine the tomatoes, garlic, green chilies, ginger, fenugreek leaves, and water and bring to a boil over medium-high heat. Reduce the heat to medium and simmer for 30 minutes, stirring occasionally. Remove from the heat and let cool for 10 minutes (this step reduces the amount of steam that builds up during blending).

2 Transfer the pan's contents to a blender and puree until smooth, starting on low speed and gradually increasing it to allow the steam to escape.

3 Clean out the saucepan and strain the sauce through a coarse sieve back into it. Using a wooden spoon, press down on the solids and extract as much liquid from them as possible. Discard the solids.

4 Return the pan to medium heat. Add the tomato paste and butter and bring to a rolling simmer, stirring occasionally. Simmer for 30 minutes, stirring from time to time. (If you're freezing the sauce for later, stop here and freeze for up to 1 month. The salt and cream will be added when you reheat the sauce.)

5 Stir in the salt and cream. Return the sauce to a boil and remove from the heat. If not using right away, let cool completely. Store in an airtight container in the refrigerator for up to 2 days.

Divya (page 41)

3

COCKTAILS AND MOCKTAILS

The cocktail culture was just beginning to take hold in Washington when we were developing the Rasika concept, so the same kind of thought and effort had to go into the development of our drinks as into that of our food. Ginger, chilies, pomegranate, passion fruit, mango, lime, cardamom, honey, cinnamon, and star anise are some of the Indian flavors with which we infuse our cocktails, perfect ingredients to prime the palate or act as foils to our cuisine. We make a point to offer mocktails as nonalcoholic options, along with fresh fruit juices we make every day, such as watermelon juice spiked with black-pepper-and-green-cardamom-laced cantaloupe juice.

ATUL NARAIN

In 2002, I went to New Delhi looking for managerial candidates for The Bombay Club. A friend suggested I consult Atul Narain, who was the food and beverage manager for the Taj Palace Hotel, thinking he would surely have some leads. An introduction was made and the two of us met. Atul made several suggestions, but by the end of the meeting the choice was clear to me. "What about you?" I asked.

He accepted my invitation to join the company, eventually becoming manager of The Bombay Club, where his commitment to hospitality was apparent in the rapport he built with our clientele, many of whom come from the neighboring World Bank, Chamber of Commerce, and White House.

Atul has vast knowledge of Indian food and a real passion for team building. People enjoy working with him. Not only did he lead the team at Rasika Penn Quarter, but he encouraged me, along with Vikram, to open Rasika West End, where he has been the general manager since day one. In 2012, we promoted him to group general manager, overseeing both Rasikas. He is dedicated to maintaining the highest standards and to our success, in which he plays a key role.

—Ashok

RASIKA COCKTAIL

MAKES 1 DRINK

½ ounce passion fruit puree
¼ ounce Domaine de Canton ginger
   liqueur

4 ounces chilled sparkling wine

Stir all of the ingredients in a mixing glass to combine and strain into a Champagne flute.

KAMINEE COCKTAIL

MAKES 1 DRINK

1 ounce Pimm's No. 1 Cup
1 ounce chili-infused gin*
1 ounce Ginger Syrup (page 40)

1 ounce fresh lime juice
Thin unpeeled cucumber round,
   for garnish

To infuse gin with chilies, split 3 large fresh Thai green chilies and let them sit in a 750 ml bottle of London dry gin for 3 days.

In an ice-filled cocktail shaker, shake the Pimm's, gin, ginger syrup, and lime juice. Strain into a beer goblet or highball glass filled with ice. Slice a radius into the cucumber round so you can twist it into an S-shape as a garnish.

GINGER POM PISCO SOUR

MAKES 1 DRINK

2 ounces pisco
1 ounce Domaine de Canton ginger
   liqueur
¾ ounce fresh lemon juice

½ ounce Pom pomegranate juice
½ ounce Ginger Syrup (recipe follows)
1 large pasteurized egg white
Angostura bitters, for garnish

In a cocktail shaker, dry-shake the pisco, ginger liqueur, lemon juice, pomegranate juice, ginger syrup, and egg white for several shakes. Add ice and shake some more. Strain into a coupe and garnish with a few drops of Angostura bitters.

RASIKA

GINGER SYRUP MAKES 2½ OUNCES

2 tablespoons ginger juice*
2 tablespoons water

¼ cup sugar

*Grate the flesh from a large chunk of fresh ginger and squeeze the juice from it.

In a small saucepan, combine all of the ingredients. Stir over medium heat until the sugar is dissolved, about 2 minutes. Store in an airtight container in the refrigerator for up to 1 month.

DIVYA

MAKES 1 DRINK

1 ounce gin, preferably Beefeater's
½ ounce apricot liqueur, such as The
    Bitter Truth brand
½ ounce Honey Spice Syrup (recipe
    follows)

½ ounce fresh lemon juice
Chilled sparkling wine, for topping
Lemon twist, for garnish

In an ice-filled cocktail shaker, shake the gin, apricot liqueur, honey spice syrup, and lemon juice. Double strain into a Champagne flute. (To double strain, use a bar sieve to strain the contents from the cocktail shaker through a mesh sieve held over the Champagne flute.) Top with sparkling wine and garnish with the lemon twist.

HONEY SPICE SYRUP   MAKES 6 OUNCES

½ cup honey
⅓ cup water
½ star anise

1-inch cinnamon stick, crushed
1 whole clove
1 green cardamom pod

In a small saucepan, combine all of the ingredients and bring to a boil over medium-high heat, stirring to dissolve the honey. Reduce the heat to medium and simmer the ingredients for 10 minutes. Strain. Store in an airtight container in the refrigerator for up to 1 month.

PRIYANKA COCKTAIL

MAKES 1 DRINK

¾ ounce Amrut Fusion Indian Single
    Malt Whisky
¾ ounce VSOP Cognac
½ ounce sweet vermouth, preferably
    Dolin Rouge

¼ ounce Benedictine liqueur
1 dash Peychaud's bitters
1 dash Angostura bitters
Lemon twist, for garnish

In an ice-filled mixing glass, stir together all of the ingredients except the lemon twist. Strain into a rocks glass with one jumbo ice cube in it. Garnish with the lemon twist.

MANGO MOCKTAIL

MAKES 1 DRINK

¾ ounce canned Alphonso mango pulp,
    such as Ratnā or DEEP brand
¼ ounce fresh lime juice

¼ ounce grenadine syrup
Club soda, for topping
Lime wheel, for garnish

In an ice-filled cocktail shaker, shake the mango pulp, lime juice, and grenadine. Strain into a highball glass filled with ice. Top with club soda and garnish with the lime wheel set on the edge of the glass.

PASSION FRUIT PUNCH

MAKES 1 DRINK

¾ ounce passion fruit puree
¼ ounce grenadine syrup

¼ ounce simple syrup*
Club soda, for topping

*To make simple syrup, heat equal parts sugar and water until the sugar is dissolved.

In an ice-filled cocktail shaker, shake the passion fruit puree, grenadine, and simple syrup. Strain into a highball glass filled with ice and top with club soda.

Rice and Dal Pancakes with Asparagus (page 65)

4

APPETIZERS

VEGETARIAN

PAO BHAJI 47

MASALA POPCORN 50

CRISPY FRIED SPINACH WITH TOMATO, ONION,
TAMARIND, AND YOGURT (PALAK CHAAT) 53

ROASTED STUFFED DATES WITH SAFFRON-CHILI
BEURRE BLANC 56

AVOCADO CHAAT WITH BANANA 59

SPICY FRIED CAULIFLOWER FLORETS
(CAULIFLOWER BEZULE) 62

RICE AND DAL PANCAKES WITH ASPARAGUS
(ASPARAGUS UTTAPAM) 65

BEET AND GOAT CHEESE TIKKI
WITH RHUBARB CHUTNEY 67

SWEET POTATO SAMOSA PURSES WITH
CRANBERRY CHUTNEY 70

GRIDDLED EGGPLANT AND POTATO STACKS
WITH JAGGERY PEANUT SAUCE
(TAWA BAINGAN) 73

POTATO PATTIES WITH SPICED YELLOW PEAS
(RAGDA PATTIES) 76

NONVEGETARIAN

CLAMS CALDINE 79

BLACK PEPPER CRAB NAPOLEON
WITH CURRY OIL 81

CALAMARI BALCHÃO 85

GINGER SCALLOPS 86

SEA BASS IN BANANA LEAF CHUTNEY WALA 89

CHICKEN 65 (INDIAN CHICKEN NUGGETS) 91

LAMB KATHI ROLL 93

LAMB PATTIES (SHAMMI KEBAB) 96

Many of the appetizers at Rasika satisfy the dual trends of small plates and street foods, such as kathi rolls, samosas, and tikki, but people really go crazy for chaats.

Chaats are street food snacks widely found in India. They are hard to describe. The word *chaat* in Hindi means "to lick," so a chaat is a combination of ingredients so delightful that it grabs your attention on the first bite and then leaves you wanting more and more.

Chaat stalls are to Indians what hot dog stands are to Americans. People will eat chaats for lunch, as snacks, before dinner, or bring the chaatwalla to their home to make chaats there. You'll find hundreds of these stalls all over India.

What chaats have in common is that they are flavor-packed and have sweet, tangy, salty, and spicy elements and often a crunchy component. There is some kind of main ingredient, be it a protein, dal, chickpeas, diced vegetables or fruits, as well as a spice mixture (say red chili, cumin, black salt) and something to balance the spice, such as yogurt or a chutney that can be sweet, tangy, or both. Ingredients such as tamarind chutney, mint chutney, black salt, mango powder, chilies, and, of course, spices are commonly found in chaats.

PAO BHAJI

SERVES 6 ❁ *Pao bhaji* is a thick, savory, buttery vegetable mash served with airy yeast rolls known as *pao*. It's a Mumbai street food eaten at any time of the day, really, but we have it on our brunch menu at Rasika because it makes a nice, wholesome, vegetarian lunch. Indians use the bread as a scoop for the stew, or they spoon stew onto the bread as they go along. It is worth the effort to make *ladi pao*, but you can substitute Texas toast or brioche rolls griddled with butter for them.

VEGETABLES
1 cup coarsely chopped carrots
1 cup cauliflower florets
¼ teaspoon ground turmeric
1 teaspoon salt
2 medium russet (baking) potatoes,
    boiled, cooled, and peeled
    (see Step 1, page 67)

MASALA
3 tablespoons canola oil
½ teaspoon cumin seeds
2 cups finely chopped yellow onions
2 cups finely chopped tomatoes
¼ teaspoon ground turmeric
4 teaspoons pav bhaji masala,
    such as MDH brand

2 teaspoons finely chopped fresh ginger
1 teaspoon finely chopped fresh Thai
    green chili
¼ medium green bell pepper, finely
    chopped
¼ medium red bell pepper, finely
    chopped
½ cup green peas, fresh or frozen
5 tablespoons unsalted butter
3 tablespoons fresh lemon juice
2 teaspoons salt
1 cup water
2 tablespoons chopped cilantro

6 Ladi Pao (page 252), for serving
Kachumber (page 268), for serving

1 PREPARE THE VEGETABLES: Bring a medium saucepan of water to a boil over high heat. Add the carrots, cauliflower, turmeric, and salt. Cook for 3 minutes. Drain the vegetables and let them cool. Chop them finely by pulsing them in a food processor. Coarsely grate the potato and set aside with the other vegetables.

2 MAKE THE MASALA: In a large saucepan, heat the oil over medium-high heat until it shimmers. Add the cumin seeds and let them crackle. Add the onions and cook, stirring often, for 4 minutes. Reduce the heat to medium and cook, stirring occasionally, until lightly browned and soft, about 5 minutes.

3 Stir in the tomatoes. Increase the heat to high and cook, stirring, until the tomatoes have turned into a mash and most of the liquid has evaporated, about 5 minutes.

4 Reduce the heat to medium and add the turmeric, *pav bhaji* masala, ginger, green chili, bell peppers, peas, chopped cauliflower/carrot mixture, and grated potatoes. Stir to combine well. Cook for 5 minutes, stirring occasionally.

5 Add the butter, lemon juice, salt, and water and cook for 5 minutes. Add the cilantro.

6 Serve hot in bowls with ladi pao and kachumber on the side.

RASIKA

NERAJ GOVIL

When I was planning to open the second location of Rasika, I needed to bring in a chef to run the kitchen at the flagship restaurant so that Vikram could oversee both of them. Vikram recommended Neraj Govil. The two had met in London when Neraj had come there from Mumbai to run a food festival at Selfridge's department store. Another friend of mine in the restaurant business also suggested Neraj, so I went to Mumbai to interview him. He had excellent credentials, having worked his way up to the Taj group's prestigious Taj Mahal Palace Hotel from chef-trainee to department chef to senior sous-chef over an eighteen-year career. He joined us at Rasika in 2012 and now creates dishes under Vikram's supervision and oversees the day-to-day operations of the kitchen, proving himself an invaluable asset.   —Ashok

MASALA POPCORN

VEGAN

MAKES ABOUT 6 CUPS ⬡ This popcorn, which we offer with drinks in Rasika's cocktail lounge, is a take on the Indian snack *chiwda,* a sweet and savory mix often made with fried *poha* (puffed rice), dried fruit, nuts, spices, and herbs. There are many ways to make it and people add whatever they like—maybe corn flakes, coconut chips, chana dal. It's a mainstay during Diwali, much like you'd have Chex Mix during the American holiday season.

If you don't want to use microwave popcorn, make it the old-fashioned way, following directions on the package of kernels to make 6 cups of popcorn.

One 3.2-ounce bag microwave popcorn (movie theater butter flavor or plain and salted), popped according to package directions
2 tablespoons canola oil
1 teaspoon fennel seeds
1 teaspoon coriander seeds
1 teaspoon cumin seeds
1 teaspoon coarsely chopped fresh Thai green chili

10 (1½-inch) fresh curry leaves (more if smaller), whole or cut crosswise into thin strips
¼ teaspoon Kashmiri chili powder
¼ teaspoon ground turmeric
⅛ teaspoon asafetida
¼ teaspoon sugar
¼ teaspoon salt

1 Place the popcorn in a large bowl.

2 In a small saucepan, heat the oil over medium-high heat until it shimmers. Add the fennel seeds, coriander seeds, and cumin seeds and let them crackle. Stir in the green chili, curry leaves, Kashmiri chili powder, turmeric, and asafetida. Pour the mixture over the popcorn. Add the sugar and salt and stir or toss to coat evenly. (Keep tossing as you eat it to distribute the spice.)

CRISPY FRIED SPINACH WITH TOMATO, ONION, TAMARIND, AND YOGURT (PALAK CHAAT)

VEGAN (WITHOUT THE YOGURT SAUCE)

SERVES 6 ❃   When Vikram had *palak chaat* (crispy fried spinach with sweet yogurt and tamarind sauce) on the menu at Bombay Brasserie in London, it wasn't so popular. But Americans love spinach and they went crazy for palak chaat from the very first day we opened Rasika. It soon became our signature dish. We sell over a hundred orders a day now and we wouldn't dare take it off the menu. —ASHOK

I took the essence of fritters, very common in Indian and other Asian cultures, and "deconstructed" it—before anyone really ever used that term. Rather than make a thick gram (besan) batter to bind spinach together as you would for a fritter, I made a batter thin enough to just barely coat the leaves so they would remain individual and delicate, like a very light Japanese tempura. (See Legumes, Pulses, Gram, Besan, and Dal, page 15.)

   The garnishes, a dusting of deggi mirch, black salt, and Toasted Cumin Powder, plus two sauces, red onion, chopped tomato, and chopped cilantro, all make each bite explode with texture and flavor—exactly what a chaat is supposed to do.

   At Rasika, we fry the spinach to order, but at home you can do the frying up to an hour before you plan on serving the dish and just leave the assembly to the last minute.

   Here are some useful pointers:

- The sauces and the garnishes can be done up to a day ahead of time and refrigerated.
- Be organized. Set up a complete mise en place before you start frying, including mixing bowls, a colander, and two baking sheets lined with paper towels. Because you have to fry the spinach in four batches, weigh out four equal piles before you start.
- A spider strainer is a good tool to use to keep the spinach moving around in the wok so it fries evenly and the leaves remain separate and beautiful. A 2-ounce ladle portions out the correct amount of batter for each batch.
- You absolutely MUST return the oil to 400°F for each batch. Use a thermometer for accuracy, and be patient.

—VIKRAM

½ cup whole-milk Greek yogurt

2 tablespoons water

¼ teaspoon Toasted Cumin Powder
(page 23)

4½ teaspoons sugar

¼ teaspoon salt

TAMARIND SAUCE

4 tablespoons Tamarind-Date Chutney
(page 258)

2 tablespoons water

BATTER

1 cup gram flour (besan)

¼ teaspoon deggi mirch

¼ teaspoon ground turmeric

¼ teaspoon salt

1 cup water

CHAAT

8 ounces fresh baby spinach leaves

6 cups canola oil, for deep-frying

½ teaspoon Toasted Cumin Powder
(page 23)

½ teaspoon deggi mirch

½ teaspoon black salt

½ cup finely chopped red onion

2 medium tomatoes, center pulp and
seeds removed, finely chopped
(½ cup)

¼ cup chopped fresh cilantro

1 MAKE THE YOGURT SAUCE: In a small bowl, whisk together the yogurt, water, cumin powder, sugar, and salt. Cover and refrigerate.

2 MAKE THE TAMARIND SAUCE: In a small bowl, thin the tamarind chutney with the water. Cover and refrigerate.

3 MAKE THE BATTER: In a NutriBullet or small blender, blend the gram flour, deggi mirch, turmeric, salt, and water until smooth. It will have the consistency of crepe batter. Pour into a small bowl.

4 PREPARE THE CHAAT: Have ready two large bowls, a colander set over a plate or bowl, and two baking sheets lined with paper towels. Divide the spinach into four 2-ounce piles.

5 Pour the oil into a wok or *kadai* and heat to 400°F.

6 In a large bowl, coat all the leaves of one pile of spinach with ¼ cup (a 2-ounce ladle) of batter. You can use a rubber spatula to fold the batter over the leaves, but your hand is a more efficient tool. (Have a towel handy to wipe it on as you work.)

7 Drop the leaves in the oil, covering the entire surface area rather than just clumping everything in the center of the wok. (The leaves will spatter and emit steam as the water in them comes in contact with the oil and evaporates.) Working

quickly, use a spider strainer or a skimmer to circulate the leaves and keep them from sticking to each other as best you can. Fry until the leaves look crisp and the batter lightly browned, 60 to 80 seconds. Using the spider strainer, transfer the spinach to the colander, tilting it to let excess frying oil drain. Then transfer the spinach to the paper towels.

8   Repeat with the remaining three batches of spinach and batter, allowing the oil to return to 400°F each time and using the spider strainer or a skimmer to remove as many particles of fried batter from the oil as you can. Discard any leftover batter.

9   Place all of the fried spinach in the second large bowl. Sprinkle the cumin powder, deggi mirch, and black salt over it and toss the leaves gently to distribute the spices evenly.

10   To serve, pile the spinach on six serving plates and drizzle with yogurt sauce and tamarind sauce. Garnish with the red onion, tomatoes, and cilantro. Serve immediately so the leaves don't get soggy.

ROASTED STUFFED DATES WITH SAFFRON-CHILI BEURRE BLANC

SERVES 4 ✦ Warm mascarpone-stuffed dates had become all the rage; we often featured them on the menu at Bibiana, the Italian restaurant in downtown D.C. that I opened in 2009. It seemed natural to come up with an Indian version of them because Indians love dates; in the wintertime, the street stalls in India are rife with them. —ASHOK

The dates would also make an excellent hors d'oeuvre for passing at a cocktail party, served with the saffron beurre blanc on the side. I use Medjool dates because they are large enough to leave ample room for the stuffing once you take the pits out. Deggi mirch in the paneer stuffing and red chili flakes in the sauce add a touch of heat to offset the sweetness of the dates.

You can stuff the dates the day before and have them ready to go into the oven, but don't make the sauce until you need it. —VIKRAM

STUFFED DATES
16 large Medjool dates
3 ounces paneer, finely shredded
¼ teaspoon deggi mirch
¼ teaspoon Toasted Cumin Powder
   (page 23)
¼ teaspoon chaat masala
⅛ teaspoon salt
2 tablespoons heavy cream

SAUCE
2 tablespoons unsalted butter
2 tablespoons finely chopped red onion
2 teaspoons finely chopped garlic
1 cup heavy cream
⅛ teaspoon red chili flakes
⅛ teaspoon saffron threads
⅛ teaspoon salt

1 Preheat the oven to 375°F. Line a small baking sheet with foil.

2 MAKE THE STUFFED DATES: Slit a date down the center just enough to spread it open and expose its pit. Remove and discard the pit and repeat with all the dates.

3 In a medium bowl, combine the paneer, deggi mirch, toasted cumin powder, chaat masala, salt, and cream.

4 Roll the paneer mixture into 16 marble-size balls between the palms of your hands. Stuff each date with one of them, encasing the cheese inside. Transfer them to the baking sheet and bake for 10 minutes to warm through.

5 MEANWHILE, MAKE THE SAUCE: In a small saucepan, heat the butter over medium-high heat until it sizzles. Add the onion and garlic and reduce the heat to medium. Cook, stirring frequently, to soften the onions, about 1½ minutes. Add the cream, red chili flakes, saffron, and salt. Bring the sauce to a boil and stir constantly for 1 to 2 minutes to thicken the sauce. Remove from the heat.

6 To serve, spoon some sauce on each of four salad plates. Top with 4 dates and finish with a drizzle of sauce on top. Serve warm.

AVOCADO CHAAT WITH BANANA
VEGAN

SERVES 8 ❁ It's always important to keep an eye on trends. Americans love avocadoes—look at the popularity of guacamole. But that had been done, so Vikram and I went around to other restaurants to see the various dishes that were being made with avocado. That's when we hit on the idea of doing an avocado chaat. What could be better than tamarind and chili with avocado? Now it's one of our most sought-after dishes. —ASHOK

Avocadoes are not necessarily widely used in India, but they are used in the United States. I love their bold green color, their texture, and their richness. They lend themselves perfectly to a chaat because their mild flavor serves as a perfect canvas for Indian spice and heat and for tamarind's tanginess. We serve this chaat with bananas because they add a touch of sweetness and the texture complements that of the avocadoes.

If the avocadoes are too ripe, this dish won't work. They will be too soft and become a mish-mash when you mix them with the seasonings. At Rasika, we mold the avocado mixture into a small cake ring and then lift it off to form a neat cylinder. That gives the dish a polished appearance. You can easily do the same at home with a 2-inch or 2½-inch ring, which can be purchased at stores that sell cake-baking supplies. Food-grade PVC pipe also works well as a mold. Hardware stores will often cut them to the length you want.

You can sauté the bananas a couple of hours ahead of time. Have all of the components in Step 3 ready to go, but fold them together as close to serving them as possible so the avocado retains its brightness. —VIKRAM

1 tablespoon canola oil
2 just-ripe bananas, halved lengthwise
  and then crosswise
Salt and freshly ground black pepper
4 just-ripe avocadoes
½ cup Tamarind-Date Chutney
  (page 258), chilled

1 teaspoon fresh lemon juice
2 tablespoons chopped fresh cilantro
½ teaspoon finely chopped fresh Thai
  green chili
¼ teaspoon Toasted Cumin Powder
  (page 23)
¼ teaspoon deggi mirch

1 Line a plate with paper towels. In a nonstick skillet, heat the oil over medium-high heat until it shimmers. Add the banana slices and cook until just golden, but not mushy, 2 to 3 minutes per side. Transfer them to the plate. Season with salt and freshly ground pepper.

2 Halve the avocadoes lengthwise and discard the pits. Using a paring knife and slicing down to the skin but not through it, cut ¾-inch-wide vertical rows and ¾-inch-wide horizontal rows in each avocado half to form cubes. Use a large spoon to scoop all of the cubed avocado flesh into a bowl.

3 Gently fold in the Tamarind-Date Chutney, lemon juice, cilantro, green chili, toasted cumin powder, deggi mirch, and ¼ teaspoon salt with a rubber spatula. Take care to keep the avocado cubes as intact as possible.

4 On each of eight salad plates, neatly spoon a mound of the avocado chaat and lay a slice of banana on top.

SPICY FRIED CAULIFLOWER FLORETS (CAULIFLOWER BEZULE)

SERVES 4 ⊛ *Bezule* is a South Indian dish, a Mangalorean street food dish usually made with chicken or shrimp. We like to make it with cauliflower so that it's vegetarian. Mustard seeds, Thai green chilies, and curry leaves tempered in hot oil provide extra dimension to the chili-coated florets when they come out of the wok, and a final tossing with lemon juice adds a bit of tang. In India, yogurt is often used instead of lemon juice at the end. Feel free to do that if you'd like; it's just as tangy, but less acidic than lemon juice.

Double-frying the cauliflower makes it crispier. You can make the batter and do the first frying of the cauliflower through Step 4 earlier in the day, then do the second frying (Step 5) and finish the dish (Step 6) when ready to serve. Having your mise en place set up ahead of time for that will make the job easier.

BATTER
2 cups cornstarch
1 tablespoon Ginger-Garlic Paste (page 27)
3 tablespoons Kashmiri Chili Paste (page 28)
2 teaspoons salt
1 large egg
¾ cup cold water

CAULIFLOWER
1 small (1½-pound) head cauliflower, cored and broken into small florets the size of large olives (about 4 cups)

6 cups canola oil, for deep-frying, plus 2 tablespoons
1 tablespoon black or brown mustard seeds
4 medium fresh Thai green chilies, thinly sliced on an angle
15 (1½-inch) fresh curry leaves (more if smaller)
¼ cup fresh lemon juice

1 MAKE THE BATTER: In a large bowl, whisk together the cornstarch, ginger-garlic paste, Kashmiri chili paste, salt, egg, and water to form a smooth batter.

2 PREPARE THE CAULIFLOWER: Add the cauliflower to the batter and stir to coat the florets evenly. Let stand for 10 minutes so that the batter permeates into the florets.

3 Have ready next to the stove a wire rack set over a baking sheet. Pour the 6 cups of oil into a wok or *kadai* and heat over medium-high heat to 350°F.

4 Work in three batches to keep from overcrowding the pan. Fold the batter over the cauliflower, then, with your hand, carefully place one-third of the florets in the oil one at a time. (Do this close to the oil so it doesn't splash you.) Cook, stirring with a spider strainer so the pieces cook evenly, until lightly browned, about 2 minutes. Transfer the florets to the rack with the spider strainer. Between batches, remove and discard any bits of fried batter floating on the oil and allow the oil to return to 350°F. With each batch, give the batter a good stir to coat the cauliflower just before frying.

5 Once all the cauliflower has been fried, return the oil to 350°F. Add all of the cauliflower at once and fry, stirring, until it gets extra crispy and golden brown, about 2 minutes. Transfer the cauliflower to the rack again. Discard the remaining batter.

6 In a large skillet, heat the remaining 2 tablespoons oil over medium-high heat until it shimmers. Add the mustard seeds and let them crackle. Stir in the green chilies and curry leaves. Add the cauliflower and lemon juice and toss to coat evenly. Serve hot.

RICE AND DAL PANCAKES WITH ASPARAGUS (ASPARAGUS UTTAPAM)

VEGAN (SUBSTITUTE CANOLA OIL FOR GHEE)

MAKES SIX 6-INCH UTTAPAM ✺ This thick, topped pancake is made from a fermented batter of rice and dal. It is a popular southern dish, particularly in Tamil Nadu, where people eat it for breakfast or with afternoon tea. Chopped onions and tomatoes are a common topping that we sometimes add at Rasika. We've also made uttapam with fava beans when in season and asparagus, as we have here.

You need to prepare a bit in advance to make this dish. The rice and urad dal need to soak overnight and then the batter you make from them needs to ferment overnight. Fermenting the batter makes the flavor profile more interesting by virtue of the sourness, as with sourdough bread.

You drizzle oil around the outside edge of the pancake while it's cooking to keep it moist and to achieve a nice golden color.

It's best to make uttapam when you want to eat it, although I can't say it's exactly bad if you were to reheat leftovers.

BATTER
1 cup basmati rice
¼ cup parboiled (converted) rice, such as Uncle Ben's or Mahatma brand
½ cup urad dal
1 tablespoon chana dal
¼ teaspoon fenugreek seeds
1 tablespoon ghee, melted
1 teaspoon sugar
1 teaspoon salt

TOPPING
Salt
1 pound asparagus, tough ends trimmed
3 tablespoons canola oil
1 teaspoon black or brown mustard seeds

1 teaspoon chana dal
1 teaspoon urad dal
1 cup finely chopped yellow onion
2 tablespoons finely chopped fresh ginger
1½ teaspoons finely chopped fresh Thai green chili
10 (1½-inch) fresh curry leaves (more if smaller), coarsely chopped
¼ teaspoon ground turmeric
¼ teaspoon asafetida

UTTAPAM
6 teaspoons canola oil
Coconut Chutney, for serving (page 259)

1 MAKE THE BATTER: In a bowl, combine the basmati rice, parboiled rice, urad dal, chana dal, and fenugreek seeds. Pour in enough water to cover them well and leave them on the counter to soak overnight uncovered. The next day, drain them and puree them in a blender with 1½ cups water until smooth. Pour the liquid into a bowl, cover it, and let it ferment overnight. Stir in the ghee, sugar, and salt.

2 PREP THE ASPARAGUS FOR THE TOPPING: Set up a large bowl of ice and water. Bring a pot of water to a boil and add 1 tablespoon salt. Add the asparagus and cook for 1 minute. Transfer the asparagus spears to the ice water. Once they are completely cool, drain them and blot dry on paper towels. (Don't let them languish in the water.) Cut the spears on the diagonal into ¼-inch slivers.

3 MAKE THE TOPPING: In a large nonstick skillet, heat the oil over medium-high heat until it shimmers. Add the mustard seeds, chana dal, and urad dal. Once the dals turn golden brown, about 30 seconds, add the onion, ginger, green chili, and curry leaves. Sauté, stirring frequently, until the onions are soft but not at all browned, about 4 minutes. Stir in the turmeric, asafetida, and 1 teaspoon salt. Add the asparagus and mix well. Portion the filling into six equal piles on a plate.

4 Preheat the oven to 175°F. Line a baking sheet with parchment and put it in the oven.

5 MAKE THE UTTAPAM: Heat a large nonstick skillet over medium-high heat until a drop of water spatters—you want the pan hot but not scorching. Using a 4-ounce ladle, pour ½ cup of batter into the center of the pan. Use the bottom of the ladle to spread it from the center and coax it into a 6-inch round. (This is so it won't be too thick in the center.)

6 Drizzle ½ teaspoon oil around the outside edge of the pancake. Sprinkle the entire surface of the pancake with one of the piles of asparagus filling. (Your hand is the best tool.) With a wide spatula, gently press the filling into the batter. Cook for a minute, then flip the uttapam over. Drizzle another ½ teaspoon oil around the outside edge. Let the filling heat through, 1 to 2 minutes. Flip again and transfer the uttapam to the oven.

7 Repeat with the remaining batter and topping, wiping out the pan after each one with a wad of paper towels and letting the pan get hot again. Serve warm with coconut chutney on the side.

Pictured on page 44.

BEET AND GOAT CHEESE TIKKI WITH RHUBARB CHUTNEY

SERVES 4 ❁ Beets are not widely eaten in India, but Americans love them. Beet salads are everywhere, especially with goat cheese. I took Vikram on one of our many restaurant outings so he could see what other people were doing with beets. That's how this dish came about. —ASHOK

This is really an interpretation of beet and goat cheese salads you see on so many restaurant menus, but turned into *tikki,* like the potato patties (*aloo tikki*) that are so typical of Indian street food. In this case, a beet patty is formed around a nugget of goat cheese. The magenta hue of the tikki resting on rhubarb chutney the color of a sunset and the surprise of a white fluff of creamy goat cheese inside make this dish so intriguing. The sweetness of the beets and the tang of rhubarb and goat cheese are nicely balanced, plus there's a nice little kick of heat at the end.

You may want to use gloves to keep the beets from staining your hands while making this dish. —VIKRAM

2 medium russet (baking) potatoes
Salt
2 pounds (4 medium) red beets, trimmed and washed
2 teaspoons ghee
2 teaspoons finely chopped fresh ginger
1 teaspoon finely chopped fresh Thai green chili

1⅛ teaspoons Toasted Cumin Powder (page 23)
½ teaspoon freshly ground black pepper
1 teaspoon chaat masala
2 ounces goat cheese
⅛ teaspoon deggi mirch
¼ cup canola oil
4 tablespoons Rhubarb Chutney (page 266)

1 Place the potatoes in a saucepan large enough to hold them in a single layer. Add 1½ teaspoons salt and cover well with water. Bring to a boil over high heat and cook until a knife inserts easily into the potatoes, 25 to 30 minutes. Drain and cool the potatoes completely, preferably refrigerating them overnight.

2 Preheat the oven to 375°F. Line a small rimmed baking sheet with foil.

3 Trim the beets so they lie flat and place on the lined baking sheet. Cover the pan with foil and bake until a knife inserts easily into the beets, about 45 minutes. When cool enough to handle, peel the beets. Using a box grater, coarsely shred the beets. You should have about 3 cups. (If you have a little more or less than 3 cups, not to worry.)

4 In a medium skillet, heat the ghee over medium-high heat until it shimmers. Add the ginger, green chili, and beets. Cook, stirring occasionally, until most of the beets' moisture has leached out and evaporated, 13 to 15 minutes. Transfer them to a large bowl to cool completely.

5 Peel the potatoes and coarsely shred them, enough to make 2 cups (save any leftover potato for another use). Add them to the beets, along with 1 teaspoon of the toasted cumin powder, the black pepper, chaat masala, and ¾ teaspoon salt. Mix well. Form the beet mixture into eight lime-size balls. (The most precise way to do this is to weigh the mixture, divide by eight, and weigh out portions of that number.)

6 For the stuffing, in a bowl, mix together the goat cheese, deggi mirch, remaining ⅛ teaspoon toasted cumin powder, and ⅛ teaspoon salt. Form into eight marble-size balls and refrigerate them for a few minutes to firm them up a bit.

7 To form a patty, place a beet ball in the palm of your hand and make a large thumbprint impression in it. Press one of the balls of goat cheese into the well you just created and cup your hand so that the beet mixture envelops the cheese completely. Using the palms of your hands, gently roll the beet mixture back into a ball, then press the ball into a patty roughly ¾ inch thick. Repeat the process to make eight patties.

8 To cook the tikki, have ready a large plate lined with paper towels. In a large nonstick skillet, heat the oil over medium-high heat until it shimmers. Place the patties in the pan and reduce the heat to medium. Sauté until golden brown, 3 minutes per side. Transfer the patties to the paper towels.

9 To serve, spread 1 tablespoon rhubarb chutney into a wide circle on each of four salad plates and top with two patties.

SWEET POTATO SAMOSA PURSES WITH CRANBERRY CHUTNEY

VEGAN

MAKES 8 SAMOSAS ❁ We put these on the menu in the fall close to Thanksgiving and Christmas because sweet potatoes and cranberries are so much a part of the American table at that time of year. In the summer, we may fill the samosas with corn and fava beans.

Samosas are the traditional, pyramid-shaped fried pastries common in India, especially in the northern part. They are usually filled with potatoes and peas and served with mint-cilantro chutney and tamarind chutney.

We use square spring roll pastry sheets instead of a heavy dough because it makes the samosas lighter and crispier. Also, it's a lot easier to use. These are wheat-flour-based and made without eggs, so they are vegan. Do not confuse them with egg roll wrappers, which are thicker than spring roll sheets and made with eggs, or with rice paper, which is used for Vietnamese spring rolls.

Assembled samosas freeze well, so you can make these through Step 5 up to a month ahead, provided they are wrapped well. Thaw them before baking.

1 green onion, dark green tops only, cut lengthwise into 8 strips (½ inch wide)

1 pound sweet potatoes, peeled and cut into 1-inch cubes

¼ cup canola oil, plus 6 cups for deep-frying

½ teaspoon cumin seeds

1-inch piece fresh ginger, finely chopped

1 teaspoon finely chopped fresh Thai green chili

½ teaspoon chaat masala

¼ teaspoon deggi mirch

½ teaspoon salt

1 tablespoon fresh lemon juice

8 (6 x 6-inch) spring roll pastry sheets, such as Spring Home brand

½ cup Cranberry Chutney (page 260)

1 Set up a small bowl of ice and water. Bring a small saucepan of water to a boil. Dip the green onion strips into the boiling water, then transfer them to the ice water. Drain them and blot them dry on paper towels. You will use these as "strings" to tie the purses.

2 Preheat the oven to 375°F. Line a small baking sheet with foil or parchment.

3 Coat the sweet potatoes with 2 tablespoons of the oil and spread them on the baking sheet. Bake until soft, about 20 minutes. Remove the pan from the oven and mash the potatoes with a potato masher. (You can do this right on the pan.)

4 In a medium skillet, heat 2 tablespoons of the oil over medium-high heat until it shimmers. Add the cumin seeds and let them crackle. Add the ginger, green chili, chaat masala, deggi mirch, and salt, stirring to combine. Sauté for 1 minute, then mix in the mashed sweet potatoes and lemon juice. Cook for 2 minutes, stirring constantly. Remove from heat and let the filling cool.

5 Lay the spring roll wrappers on the counter. Place a heaping tablespoon of filling in the center of each. Join two opposite corners, then bring up the other two to create a purse and hold it together by tying a green onion string around it with a double knot.

6 Line a plate with paper towels. Pour the 6 cups of oil into a wok or *kadai* and heat to 350°F. Fry the samosas until golden, 2 to 3 minutes. Turn them constantly with a spider strainer or skimmer so they brown evenly. Transfer to paper towels to blot them and serve with cranberry chutney.

GRIDDLED EGGPLANT AND POTATO STACKS WITH JAGGERY PEANUT SAUCE (TAWA BAINGAN)

VEGAN

SERVES 4 ❖ *Aloo baingan* (potatoes and eggplant) is a common dish in India, especially in the North. I didn't want to do it the traditional way because it's not attractive—the eggplant and potatoes are cooked in a tomato and onion masala until they turn soft. It's delicious, to be sure, but just isn't pretty. Vikram came up with this delightful interpretation, a tower of eggplant slices interspersed with a flavorful potato filling and topped with a sweet jaggery and peanut sauce. It's a dish that is very pleasing to the eye. —ASHOK

Look for eggplants that are about 2½ inches in diameter and about 7 inches long so your stacks will be just the right size. We use European eggplant (they are actually called Italian eggplant) because they have fewer seeds.

The assembled stacks and the sauce can be made a day ahead and reheated. The eggplant needs to marinate for at least 2 hours, but is even better if marinated overnight, so factor that into your timing if you wish to do that. —VIKRAM

EGGPLANT
1½ cups extra-virgin olive oil
2 tablespoons finely chopped garlic
½ teaspoon freshly ground black pepper
½ teaspoon salt
2 medium Italian eggplants (about 1 pound total), trimmed

POTATO FILLING
2 medium russet (baking) potatoes, boiled, cooled, and peeled (see Step 1, page 67)
2 tablespoons canola oil
½ teaspoon cumin seeds
¾ cup finely chopped red onion
¾ cup finely chopped tomato
¼ teaspoon deggi mirch
¼ teaspoon ground turmeric

2 teaspoons finely chopped fresh ginger
1 teaspoon finely chopped fresh Thai green chili
½ teaspoon chaat masala
4 teaspoons fresh lemon juice
1¼ teaspoons salt

SAUCE
2½ ounces jaggery
½ cup unsweetened coconut milk
⅛ teaspoon red chili flakes
1 teaspoon fresh lemon juice
¼ cup finely chopped unsalted roasted peanuts
⅛ teaspoon salt

2 teaspoons chopped cilantro, for garnish (optional)

1 MARINATE THE EGGPLANT: In a large bowl, mix together the olive oil, garlic, black pepper, and salt. Cut the eggplant crosswise into ½-inch-thick slices and place the 16 largest slices in the marinade. Stir to coat well. Cover and marinate for 2 hours at room temperature or overnight in the refrigerator.

2 MAKE THE POTATO FILLING: Coarsely shred the potatoes. In a large skillet, heat the canola oil over medium-high heat until it shimmers. Add the cumin seeds and let them crackle. Stir in the onion and sauté for 1 minute to soften. Add the tomato, deggi mirch, and turmeric and cook, stirring occasionally, until the tomatoes are very soft, about 3 minutes. Add the ginger, green chili, and potatoes and mix well. Add the chaat masala, lemon juice, and salt and mix well.

3 MAKE THE SAUCE: Place the jaggery in a sturdy plastic ziptop bag. Seal it and use a mallet to break it up into small bits. Transfer to a small saucepan and melt over medium heat, stirring constantly. Continue cooking and stirring until the jaggery is caramelized and the color of dark brown sugar, about 4 minutes. Stir in the coconut milk. (It will bubble up as it releases steam.) Add the chili flakes, lemon juice, peanuts, and salt. Remove from the heat.

4 Preheat the oven to 350°F. Line a small baking sheet with paper towels. Spoon 1 tablespoon of oil from the marinating eggplant into a large skillet. Heat over medium-high heat until it shimmers. Place half the eggplant slices in the pan and cook until golden brown, 4 to 5 minutes. Flip them over and cook until golden brown on the second side, another 3 to 4 minutes. Transfer the slices to the lined baking sheet. Repeat with the remaining eggplant slices. (Don't add more oil to the skillet. There will be enough already.)

5 To assemble the stacks, spread about 2 tablespoons of potato filling on each of twelve eggplant slices. Stack three slices per serving, then top each stack with a final (untopped) slice of eggplant. Place the finished stacks on a baking sheet (you can use the same one on which you blotted the eggplant, but remove the paper towels first). Bake for 5 minutes to warm the stacks through. While the stacks are in the oven, reheat the sauce to warm it through.

6 Serve the eggplant stacks warm, drizzling each one with 2 tablespoons of sauce. Garnish with chopped cilantro, if using.

POTATO PATTIES WITH SPICED YELLOW PEAS (RAGDA PATTIES)

VEGAN

SERVES 6 ⚙ Potato patties are a traditional Northern Indian street food. You see vendors with enormous cast iron skillets on the streets with heaps of *ragda* patties waiting to be fried and the peas in large bowls next to them.

The peas make a great side dish on their own. You can make them up to 2 days in advance and reheat them, or freeze them. You can also make the patties a day in advance and have them ready for the sauté pan.

PEAS

2 cups vatana (whole dried yellow peas), rinsed
1 teaspoon salt
1 pound tomatoes, coarsely chopped
2 tablespoons canola oil
½ teaspoon cumin seeds
2 teaspoons Ginger-Garlic Paste (page 27)
½ teaspoon deggi mirch
½ teaspoon ground turmeric
½ teaspoon Toasted Cumin Powder (page 23)
½ teaspoon freshly ground black pepper
½ teaspoon black salt

PATTIES

4 medium russet (baking) potatoes, boiled, cooled, and peeled (see Step 1, page 67)
½ teaspoon deggi mirch
½ teaspoon freshly ground black pepper
½ teaspoon black salt
1 teaspoon Toasted Cumin Powder (page 23)
½ teaspoon salt
¼ cup canola oil

GARNISH

6 tablespoons Tamarind-Date Chutney (page 258)
6 tablespoons Mint-Cilantro Chutney (page 257)
6 tablespoons finely chopped red onion

1 START THE PEAS: Place the peas in a large bowl. Pick them over, discarding any stones or dirt. Pour in water to cover by at least 4 inches. Soak them uncovered at room temperature overnight. (Or use the quick-soak method; see Note.) Drain.

2 In a medium saucepan, combine the drained peas, 2½ cups water, and the salt and bring to a boil over medium-high heat. Skim off any foam that rises to the top. Reduce the heat to medium, adjusting it to maintain a vigorous simmer. Cover and cook until the peas are soft, about 40 minutes.

3 Meanwhile, in a food processor, puree the tomatoes.

4 In a large saucepan, heat the oil over medium-high heat until it shimmers. Add the cumin seeds and let them crackle. Add the ginger-garlic paste and cook for 1 minute, stirring constantly. Add the pureed tomatoes, deggi mirch, and turmeric. Cook the tomatoes for 8 minutes, stirring occasionally, until you have a soupy sauce. Add the peas and their cooking liquid.

5 Reduce the heat to medium and cook the peas, stirring occasionally, for 8 minutes. Add the toasted cumin powder, black pepper, and black salt. The peas should have the consistency of chili. Keep warm over very low heat.

6 MAKE THE PATTIES: Use a box grater to coarsely shred the potatoes until you get 4 cups (reserve any leftover potato for another use) and transfer to a large bowl. Add the deggi mirch, black pepper, black salt, toasted cumin powder, and salt and mix well. Shape the potato mixture into six flat patties, 2½ inches in diameter and 1 inch thick.

7 Line a large plate with paper towels. In a large nonstick skillet, heat the oil over medium-high heat until it shimmers. Place the patties in the pan and reduce the heat to medium. Cook until nicely golden brown, about 5 minutes on each side. Transfer the patties to the lined plate.

8 To serve, spread ½ cup peas into a round on each of six dinner plates and top with a patty. Garnish each with 1 tablespoon tamarind-date chutney spread over one half of the patty and 1 tablespoon mint-cilantro chutney spread over the other half. Sprinkle each plate with chopped red onion.

NOTE: *To quick-soak beans, peas, or other legumes, put them in a pot with water to cover by at least 2 inches and bring to a boil. Boil for 1 minute and remove from the heat. Cover the pot and let soak for 1 hour.*

CLAMS CALDINE

SERVES 4 ⚙ This dish is from Goa, on the west coast of India, which was a Portuguese colony. *Caldine* is a derivative of the Portuguese word *caldeirão*, which is a cooking vessel similar to a Dutch oven. Caldine is often a nonspicy, yellow fish curry, but clams, being so meaty, call for a bolder sauce, in my opinion. That's why I prefer this spicy green curry.

At Rasika, we have a machine that removes the flesh from a fresh coconut half by pressing it against stone grinder blades, much like you would press an orange half into an automatic juicer. It removes the flesh, but leaves the skin behind. We then take the flesh and put it in another grinder with herbs and spices to make a paste, adding water as required.

I've provided a much easier method here for home cooks, using coconut milk. Lemon juice, in addition to adding acidity, maintains the bright green color of the cilantro and mint, keeping them from turning brown.

Serve with Plain Basmati Rice (page 217) to make this a main course. And Naan (page 247).

One 13½-ounce can unsweetened
    coconut milk
4 medium fresh Thai green chilies
2 x 1-inch piece fresh ginger, coarsely
    chopped
8 medium garlic cloves
2 cups coarsely chopped cilantro,
    including stems
½ cup packed mint leaves
1 tablespoon coriander seeds
1 teaspoon cumin seeds

½ teaspoon ground turmeric
3 tablespoons fresh lemon juice
2 tablespoons canola oil
½ medium yellow onion, halved and
    thinly sliced
¼ cup Tamarind Pulp (page 24)
½ cup water
1 teaspoon salt
1 teaspoon sugar
32 middleneck clams, scrubbed

1 In a blender, puree the coconut milk, green chilies, ginger, garlic, cilantro, mint, coriander seeds, cumin seeds, turmeric, and lemon juice until smooth.

2 In a large sauté pan or deep straight-sided skillet, heat the oil over medium-high heat until it shimmers. Add the onion and reduce the heat to medium. Cook, stirring occasionally, until it is soft but not browned, about 4 minutes. Stir in the

tamarind pulp and cook for 1 minute. Stir in the coconut mixture. Swirl the water around the blender container to clean it out as best you can and add that liquid to the pan. Add the salt and sugar. Increase the heat to high and bring to a boil. Add the clams. Cover the pan and cook until the clams open fully, 8 to 10 minutes. Serve hot in soup plates or pasta bowls and pour the cooking liquid over them.

BLACK PEPPER CRAB NAPOLEON WITH CURRY OIL

SERVES 6 ❀ The inspiration for this dish comes from a restaurant in Mumbai called Mahesh Lunch Home, which is famous for their seafood and coastal fare. They have a very popular dish called butter pepper garlic crab.

In Mumbai, crabs are abundant and a favorite preparation is to sauté the cut-up crustaceans in their shells in a peppery masala. My interpretation is a lot less messy—no need to pick the crabmeat out of the shells. Layering the crab between squares of crisped phyllo dresses up the dish, offers a nice crunch, and provides a great backdrop for the wonderful product we get from the Chesapeake, blue crabs.

The black pepper really must be ground just before you make the dish so the spice is at its freshest and hottest.

4 tablespoons unsalted butter
3 sheets (16 x 13-inch) phyllo dough
2 teaspoons freshly ground black pepper, plus more for sprinkling
3 tablespoons finely chopped garlic
2 cups finely chopped yellow onions
¼ teaspoon ground turmeric
1 tablespoon finely chopped fresh ginger

1 teaspoon finely chopped fresh Thai green chili
1 teaspoon salt
½ pound fresh jumbo lump crabmeat, preferably from Maryland
2 tablespoons fresh lemon juice
6 teaspoons Curry Oil (recipe follows)

1 Preheat the oven to 375°F. Line a baking sheet with parchment paper.

2 Melt 2 tablespoons of the butter. To make the phyllo squares, place 1 sheet of phyllo on the parchment and brush with the melted butter. Sprinkle with black pepper. Repeat with another phyllo sheet. Top with the remaining sheet of phyllo and brush with butter. Using a paring knife, trim the stacked phyllo into a 15 x 12-inch rectangle and discard the excess dough. With a long edge of the rectangle facing you, slice it vertically into five 3-inch strips and then crosswise into four 3-inch rows to make twenty 3-inch squares. Bake until golden brown, about 7 minutes.

3 For the crab filling, heat the remaining 2 tablespoons butter in a medium skillet over medium-high heat until it sizzles. Add the garlic and cook, stirring,

until lightly browned, about 2 minutes. Stir in the onions and cook until they are soft but not browned, about 7 minutes. Reduce the heat to medium and add the turmeric, ginger, green chili, and salt. Cook for 1 minute. Add the crabmeat, 2 teaspoons black pepper, and lemon juice and cook briefly, just until the crab is warmed through.

4 To assemble, place 2 heaping tablespoons crab mixture in the center of each of six plates. Top each with 1 square of phyllo. Top the phyllo with another 2 heaping tablespoons of crab mixture and another phyllo square. Drizzle ½ teaspoon curry oil around the stack. (There will be some phyllo squares left over to snack on.)

CURRY OIL

MAKES ABOUT 1/2 CUP ❁ If you make any less than the amount here, it will not be enough for the processor to run smoothly. Save any unused curry oil to use in a marinade or salad dressing.

½ cup packed fresh curry leaves
½ cup extra-virgin olive oil

In a small food processor, puree the curry leaves and oil for 1 minute. Strain through a fine-mesh sieve, pressing on the leaves with the back of a spoon to extract all of the oil. Discard the leaves.

CALAMARI BALCHÃO

SERVES 4 ❀ *Balchão* is a traditional method of preparation in Goa. Its trademark is a hot and sour vinegar-and-red-chili-based masala that goes well with seafood. Indians use balchão to pickle things such as shrimp and mackerel.

At Rasika, we use only the bodies of the calamari for this dish, cutting them into rings, but there is no reason why you can't use the tentacles as well, if you wish.

The recipe calls for Balchão Masala, which is made with Peri-Peri Paste (page 29). If you make the masala days in advance, putting together this dish will be a snap.

1½ cups Balchão Masala (page 30)
1¼ pounds clean calamari tubes, cut into
    ½-inch-thick rings

½ teaspoon salt
Chopped cilantro, for garnish

In a wok, *kadai,* or large skillet, bring the balchão masala to a simmer over medium-high heat. Add the calamari and salt and cook, stirring occasionally, until the calamari is white and no longer translucent, 2 to 3 minutes. Divide the calamari evenly among four soup plates and garnish with chopped cilantro. Serve hot.

GINGER SCALLOPS

SERVES 4 ○ Fresh ginger juice has a distinctly hot profile, so we use it to marinate the scallops in this easy-to-prepare dish. The ginger and hint of deggi mirch serve as good counterpoints to the sweetness of the honey and bell peppers in the sauce.

SCALLOPS

4 to 6 ounces fresh ginger
1 tablespoon fresh lemon juice
¼ teaspoon ground turmeric
¼ teaspoon deggi mirch
½ teaspoon salt
12 medium (U12 to U14) dry-packed sea scallops (1 pound), small side muscles removed
2 tablespoons canola oil

SAUCE

2 tablespoons unsalted butter
6 large garlic cloves, thinly sliced
1 large red bell pepper, diced
1 tablespoon honey
½ teaspoon salt

Chopped chives, for garnish

1 MARINATE THE SCALLOPS: Finely grate the ginger into a fine-mesh sieve set over a medium bowl. Press the grated ginger against the sieve to extract all of its juice. This should yield about 6 tablespoons of juice, depending on how fresh your ginger is. If it doesn't, grate a little more ginger. Discard the solids.

2 Add the lemon juice, turmeric, deggi mirch, salt, and scallops, stirring to coat the scallops well. Cover and refrigerate for 30 minutes.

3 MEANWHILE, MAKE THE SAUCE: In a medium saucepan, melt the butter over medium-high heat. Add the garlic and cook, stirring often, until the garlic is dark brown and the butter is nutty, about 3 minutes. Add the bell pepper and cook, stirring often, for 2 minutes to soften. Transfer the mixture to a NutriBullet or mini food processor. Add the honey and salt and puree until smooth, stopping to scrape down the sides a couple of times.

4 In a nonstick medium skillet, heat the oil over medium-high heat until it shimmers. Place the scallops in the pan directly from the marinade (no need to drain them) and cook until golden brown, 1 to 2 minutes. Flip and cook for another 30 seconds.

5 To serve, spread 2 tablespoons sauce in the center of each of four salad plates. Top each with 3 scallops and garnish with chopped chives.

SEA BASS IN BANANA LEAF CHUTNEY WALA

SERVES 4 ❁ This is a traditional Parsi dish called *patra ni machhi,* which means "fish in a leaf." The fish of choice is pomfret, which is abundant in India. Cooks swathe fillets in a chutney made with mint, cilantro, and coconut to lend sweet and sour notes, then steam them in banana leaf packets. The leaves help keep the fish moist.

At Rasika, we use sea bass because it is widely available in our region, but you can use any thin fillet, like flounder or sole, or even skate. We also cook the packets on a flat top grill, instead of in a pan.

For the chutney, making a paste out of grated coconut first and then adding the herbs preserves its vibrant green color. It is also excellent as a dipping sauce or spread on sandwich bread (or baguette that you cut into rectangles) that you top with thinly sliced cucumber for open-faced sandwiches.

You can make the chutney a day in advance.

CHUTNEY
½ cup grated coconut, fresh or frozen
1 teaspoon Ginger-Garlic Paste
   (page 27)
1 teaspoon finely chopped fresh Thai
   green chili
½ teaspoon cumin seeds
½ teaspoon ground turmeric
⅓ cup fresh lemon juice
¼ cup packed mint leaves, coarsely
   chopped
½ cup coarsely chopped cilantro,
   including stems

¾ teaspoon salt
1 tablespoon sugar

FISH
4 sea bass fillets (3½ to 4 ounces each),
   skinned, pin bones removed
¼ teaspoon ground turmeric
¼ teaspoon salt
2 teaspoons fresh lemon juice
4 banana leaves, roughly 9 inches square
   (see Note)
½ cup canola oil

1 MAKE THE CHUTNEY: In a NutriBullet or small blender, combine the coconut, ginger-garlic paste, green chili, cumin seeds, turmeric, and lemon juice. Blend for 3 minutes, shaking the jar or scraping it down from time to time, to make a thick, fairly smooth puree. Add the mint leaves and puree until smooth. Add the cilantro, salt, and sugar and puree until smooth.

2 PREPARE THE FISH: In a medium bowl, coat the sea bass fillets with the turmeric, salt, and lemon juice.

3 Microwave 2 of the banana leaves for 15 seconds to soften them and put them on a large cutting board. Lay a fish fillet on the bottom half of each leaf. Spread 1½ tablespoons of chutney over each fillet, then flip them and spread another 1½ tablespoons chutney on the other sides of the fillets. Fold the leaves in half over the fillets. Starting and ending at the fold, use a sharp paring knife to trim each packet, leaving a 1-inch border around the fish on three sides. Transfer the packets to a baking sheet. Repeat with the remaining 2 banana leaves, sea bass fillets, and chutney. Refrigerate the packets for 1 hour.

4 Preheat the oven to 200°F. Have ready another large baking sheet.

5 In a large skillet, heat ¼ cup of the oil over medium-high heat until it shimmers. Reduce the heat to medium and place two packets of fish in the pan side by side. Cook for 3 minutes on each side. Transfer the packets to the baking sheet and put them in the oven to keep warm. Wipe the pan out with a wad of paper towels and repeat with the remaining ¼ cup oil and two packets of fish. Serve immediately.

NOTE: *The banana leaves need to be squares large enough to encase a piece of fish completely when folded in half, plus a 1-inch border around it so the chutney doesn't ooze out. Measure the longest fillet and cut the leaves into squares that size. Banana leaves are available at stores specializing in Asian or Latin foods.*

CHICKEN 65 (INDIAN CHICKEN NUGGETS)

SERVES 4 ✿ I call these Indian Chicken Nuggets with a kick. Pieces of chicken tenders are marinated with Kashmiri chili paste and other seasonings, coated with rice flour, and fried until crispy and bright red. There are lots of theories about the name, like they're made with 65 ingredients or 65 chilies or the chicken is 65 days old, but the most widely accepted one is that they were created at the Buhari Hotel in Chennai, Tamil Nadu, and named after the year they were introduced: 1965.

Whatever the origin, it's hard to stop eating them. To me, the curry leaves really make them pop. If you don't have any, I'd consider making another dish.

When you add the rice flour to the chicken, it creates a paste that makes the pieces stick together. The best way of frying them is to grab a small clump and pinch off coated pieces fairly close to the oil—not so close that you come into contact with it and not so far above it that you'd get spattered when chicken pieces drop into the oil. Do smaller batches if you need to until you get the hang of it.

You can marinate the chicken several hours in advance, but it's best to fry it to order.

1 pound chicken tenders, center tendons removed, cut into ½-inch cubes
2 teaspoons Ginger-Garlic Paste (page 27)
3 tablespoons Kashmiri Chili Paste (page 28)
4 teaspoons fresh lemon juice

12 (1½-inch) fresh curry leaves (more if smaller), cut into thin strips
1 teaspoon salt
1 teaspoon black peppercorns
1 teaspoon coriander seeds
6 cups canola oil, for deep-frying
6 tablespoons rice flour

1 In a bowl, combine the chicken, ginger-garlic paste, Kashmiri chili paste, lemon juice, curry leaves, and salt. In a spice grinder, grind the peppercorns and coriander seeds into a powder and add it to the bowl. Stir to coat the chicken well. Cover and refrigerate for at least 2 hours.

2 Line a small baking sheet with paper towels. Pour the oil into a wok or *kadai* and heat to 350°F.

3 Add the rice flour to the chicken and use your fingers to mix it into the chicken and create a paste around the pieces.

4 Fry the chicken in three batches. Grab a mound of it with your hand and use your thumb and forefinger to pinch separate pieces into the oil. (A couple of pieces may stick together; that's fine.) Cook, stirring with a skimmer or spider strainer, until crispy and reddish gold all around, 2 to 3 minutes. Drain on paper towels. Return the oil to 350°F between batches. Serve hot.

LAMB KATHI ROLL

MAKES 6 ROLLS ✿ This rolled street food is popular in Northern India. It started off as kebabs of meat (*kathi* means "stick" in Hindi) rolled in flatbread, such as chapati or paratha, kind of an Indian version of souvlaki or doner kebab. Now kathi rolls can have all kinds of fillings, be it meat, vegetables, or fish. Some people make them without the scrambled egg coating on the bread that we use at Rasika, which helps keep the bread soft.

Kathi rolls originated in Calcutta. In Mumbai, they are called frankies, and the most well known are Tibb's frankies. They are attributed to Amarjit Tibbs, an entrepreneur who adapted them from pita rolls he ate on a trip to Lebanon in the sixties.

At Rasika, we marinate cubes of lamb leg, grill them in the tandoor, and dice them. The method provided here is easier for the home cook because it leaves out the grilling part. (You could certainly do it that way if you want.) We also use whole wheat flour tortillas instead of chapatis for convenience. (If you prefer to make chapatis, there's a recipe for them on page 237.)

Make the filling earlier in the day or the day before and reheat it when you need it. You may substitute chicken (or cubed paneer to make it vegetarian), but reduce cooking times accordingly.

We serve kathi roll with Kachumber (page 268), a salad-like side dish made with cucumber, tomatoes, and red onion, but feel free not to.

FILLING
¼ cup canola oil
½ teaspoon cumin seeds
2 cups finely chopped red onions
¼ cup Ginger-Garlic Paste (page 27)
2 cups finely chopped tomatoes
½ teaspoon ground turmeric
½ teaspoon deggi mirch
2 teaspoons ground coriander
1 pound boneless leg of lamb, all fat and
    sinew removed, cut into ¼-inch dice
1 teaspoon finely chopped fresh Thai
    green chili
1 teaspoon salt

1 teaspoon garam masala
1 teaspoon chaat masala
1 tablespoon fresh lemon juice
2 tablespoons chopped fresh cilantro

FOR THE ROLLS
6 large eggs
¼ teaspoon salt
1½ tablespoons chopped fresh cilantro
Six 8-inch whole wheat flour tortillas
Canola oil, for brushing

Mint-Cilantro Chutney (page 257),
    for serving

1 MAKE THE FILLING: In a heavy-bottomed pot or Dutch oven, heat the oil over medium-high heat until it shimmers. Add the cumin seeds and let them crackle. Add the onions and sauté, stirring occasionally, until soft but not browned, about 5 minutes. Stir in the ginger-garlic paste. Reduce the heat to medium and cook, stirring, until the odor of raw garlic dissipates, about 3 minutes.

2 Add the tomatoes and increase the heat to high. Stir in the turmeric and cook until the water has evaporated from the tomatoes and the mixture looks mushy, about 5 minutes. Add the deggi mirch and coriander and cook for 2 minutes. Stir in the lamb and cook for 5 minutes, stirring occasionally. Reduce the heat to medium, cover, and cook until the lamb is tender, 10 to 12 minutes. Add the green chili, salt, garam masala, chaat masala, lemon juice, and cilantro. Set aside.

3 START THE ROLLS: In a medium bowl, beat together the eggs, salt, and cilantro. Keep by the side of the stove.

4 Preheat the oven to 180°F. Heat a large nonstick skillet over medium-high heat until very hot. Working with one at a time, warm a tortilla on each side for about 30 seconds. Brush each side with oil and brown on each side for 30 seconds. Spread 2 tablespoons of egg mixture on the entire surface of the tortilla. Flip it over (some egg will come off) and spread 2 tablespoons of egg on the other side. Flip it over and let the egg cook for several seconds. Keep warm on an ovenproof plate in the oven while you repeat with the other 5 tortillas.

5 To assemble the rolls, warm the filling and keep it warm over very low heat. Take 3 tortillas from the oven and place them on a cutting board. Spread ½ cup filling on the bottom half of each tortilla. Starting with the bottom edge, roll each tortilla into a log. Halve them and transfer them to the oven while you roll the others. Serve warm with mint-cilantro chutney.

LAMB PATTIES (SHAMMI KEBAB)

SERVES 6 ✿ This kebab is made by cooking the lamb with spices and chana dal and processing it into a smooth mixture that gets formed into patties and sautéed. Black cardamom gives the meat a smoky and earthy quality while fried onions lend sweetness.

At Rasika, we sometimes jazz up shammi kebab by embedding a frozen, marble-size piece of foie gras in the center, which melts into the meat when it is sautéed and adds an extra dimension of richness.

You can form the patties the day before.

SPICE MIX
1-inch cinnamon stick, crushed
5 whole cloves
5 green cardamom pods
2 black cardamom pods
1 large dried Indian bay leaf, torn into
    pieces
¼ teaspoon black cumin seeds
¼ teaspoon cumin seeds
½ teaspoon mace (javitri)
½ teaspoon black peppercorns

PATTIES
1 pound boneless leg of lamb, trimmed of
    fat and sinew, cut into 2-inch pieces
¼ cup chana dal
2 tablespoons Ginger-Garlic Paste
    (page 27)

1 medium fresh Thai green chili,
    coarsely chopped
¼ teaspoon ground turmeric
2 teaspoons ground coriander
2 dried Kashmiri chilies, stemmed,
    broken into pieces
¼ teaspoon deggi mirch
½ cup Crispy Fried Onions (page 25)
1 teaspoon salt
2 cups water
1 large egg, beaten
¼ cup canola oil

1 small red onion, very thinly sliced
6 lemon wedges
Mint-Cilantro Chutney (page 257)

1 MAKE THE SPICE MIX: In a spice grinder, grind the cinnamon stick, cloves, green and black cardamom pods, bay leaf, black cumin seeds, cumin seeds, mace, and black peppercorns to a powder.

2 MAKE THE PATTIES: In a large saucepan, combine the lamb, chana dal, ginger-garlic paste, green chili, turmeric, coriander, dried chilies, deggi mirch, fried onions, salt, and water. Cover and bring to a boil over medium-high heat.

3 Reduce the heat to medium and cook, stirring occasionally, until the lamb is tender and the liquid has reduced to a thick sauce, about 45 minutes. Stir in the spice mix and cook for 2 minutes. Remove from the heat and let cool.

4 Transfer the cooled lamb mixture to a food processor and process until smooth, scraping down the sides of the bowl a couple of times. Transfer the mixture to a bowl and add the beaten egg, stirring to combine it well.

5 Form the lamb into twelve golf ball–size balls, then press each into a 2-inch-wide patty between the palms of your hands.

6 In a large nonstick skillet, heat the oil over medium-high heat until it shimmers. In two batches, sauté the patties until golden brown, 2 minutes on each side.

7 Serve with sliced red onion, lemon wedges, and mint-cilantro chutney.

Green Beans Chili Garlic (page 110)

5

VEGETABLES

CREATING A SIGNATURE DISH

I had the privilege of being asked by the U.S. State Department to prepare a lunch there in honor of Indian prime minister Narendra Modi's visit to Washington, D.C., in September 2014. They requested a menu that reflected Indo-American cuisine and asked me to create a vegetable-based dish especially for the occasion, because the prime minister is a vegetarian. I was happy to comply.

When I sat down to design the dish, lasagna came to mind. Even though it is Italian in origin, it is something that has truly been Americanized.

I based the "noodles" on a classic Gujarati snack called *khandvi*. To make khandvi, you cook a yellow batter made with besan (chickpea flour), yogurt, turmeric, and other seasonings and spread it onto the counter in a thin layer. When the dough cools, you cut it into long strips, roll them up into bite-size pieces, and top them with mustard seeds and curry leaves fried in hot oil.

So, for the lasagna, I cut that dough instead into rectangular sheets and layered them in baking pans with a filling made of tiny cubes of eggplant, zucchini, sweet potatoes, and bell peppers bound with a zesty tomato masala.

Lunch began with Crispy Fried Spinach with Tomato, Onion, Tamarind, and Yogurt (page 53) and proceeded to the lasagna, cut into individual portions and topped with a besan-and-yogurt-based kadi sauce to which we added asparagus. Puffed golden tomato and spinach puris accompanied the meal.

Dessert was a parfait served in two glasses. One represented the colors of the American flag with layers of strawberries, creamy thickened vanilla-cardamom yogurt (called *shrikhand*), and blueberries. The other glass had three layers of shrikhand—one colored orange with saffron, the middle one white, and the third layer green from pistachio paste—to represent the colors of the Indian flag.

The lunch was a resounding success, especially the lasagna, and a signature dish was born. Gujarati Eggplant and Sweet Potato "Lasagna" with Kodi Sauce (page 127) is now on the menu permanently at Rasika Penn Quarter.

PLANTAIN DUMPLINGS IN TOMATO SAUCE (KELA TAMATAR KUT)

VEGAN

SERVES 6 ✿ Since plantains are plentiful in the southern part of India, we thought of pairing these dumplings with a tomato sauce popular in the southern city of Hyderabad.

Before frying spices in mustard oil, you must first heat it to the smoking point and let it cool slightly before proceeding. This removes its caustic property and brings its pungency forward.

You can make the sauce a day or two before and reheat it. Once you form the dumplings, they should be fried. If they sit too long, they will fall apart in the fryer. If you want to make them ahead, fry them several hours in advance and reheat them in the oven before serving.

SAUCE

2 pounds tomatoes
1½ cups water
½ teaspoon nigella seeds
½ teaspoon black or brown mustard seeds
½ teaspoon cumin seeds
¼ teaspoon fenugreek seeds
2 tablespoons mustard oil
2 teaspoons Ginger-Garlic Paste (page 27)
½ teaspoon ground turmeric
2 teaspoons deggi mirch
2 teaspoons ground coriander
¼ cup tomato paste
2 teaspoons salt
2 teaspoons sugar

DUMPLINGS

2 large plantains, unpeeled, tops and bottoms trimmed, and halved crosswise
½ teaspoon ground turmeric
3 teaspoons salt
1 medium russet (baking) potato, boiled, cooled, and peeled (see Step 1, page 67)
2 tablespoons canola oil, plus 1 quart for deep-frying
1 teaspoon cumin seeds
1 tablespoon finely chopped fresh ginger
1 teaspoon finely chopped fresh Thai green chili
¼ cup golden raisins
1 tablespoon cornstarch, for dusting

Naan (page 247), for serving

1 MAKE THE SAUCE: Set up a large bowl of ice and water. Bring a large pot of water to a boil over high heat. Use a sharp paring knife to remove the cores from the stem ends of the tomatoes and cut a shallow "X" into the skin at the bottom of

each tomato. Blanch the tomatoes for 2 minutes, until the skins begin to peel back where the Xs are cut. Transfer the tomatoes to the ice bath to cool them. (Leave them in the water just long enough to cool them down.) Remove and discard their skins. Quarter them and place them in a blender. Add the 1½ cups water and puree on high speed until smooth. You'll have about 1 quart of puree.

2 In a small bowl, combine the nigella seeds, mustard seeds, cumin seeds, and fenugreek seeds.

3 In a large saucepan, heat the mustard oil over medium-high heat until it smokes. Remove the pan from the heat and let it cool until the oil stops smoking, about 1 minute. Return the pan to the heat, add the seed mix and let it crackle. Stir in the ginger-garlic paste and cook for 30 seconds.

4 Add the pureed tomatoes, turmeric, deggi mirch, and coriander. Cook for 5 minutes, stirring occasionally. (It will be boiling.) Stir in the tomato paste and reduce the heat to medium. Cook for another 9 to 10 minutes, stirring occasionally, to thicken. (It should resemble marinara sauce.) Add the salt and sugar. Remove from the heat.

5 MAKE THE DUMPLINGS: Place the plantains in a large saucepan and cover with water. Add the turmeric and 1 teaspoon of the salt. Cover the pan and bring to a boil over high heat. Reduce the heat to medium and cook until the plantains feel soft when you insert the tip of a knife into them, like cooked potatoes do, about 20 minutes. Transfer them to a bowl to cool.

6 Peel the plantains and discard the skins. Coarsely shred the flesh into a large bowl. Then coarsely shred the potato into the same bowl.

7 In a small skillet, heat 2 tablespoons of the canola oil over medium-high heat until it shimmers. Add the cumin seeds and let them crackle. Add the ginger and green chili and cook for 30 seconds. Transfer the contents of the pan to the shredded plantains and potato. Add the raisins and remaining 2 teaspoons salt and mix well. The mixture will have the texture of stiff cookie dough.

8 Rolling between the palms of your hands and applying a fair amount of pressure (so the balls hold their shape), form the dough into twelve firm dumplings the size of golf balls.

9 Place the cornstarch in a small bowl and roll the balls in it one at a time. Transfer each dusted ball to a plate.

10 Reheat the tomato sauce and keep warm over low heat.

11 Have ready a plate lined with a double thickness of paper towels. Pour 1 quart of the canola oil into a wok or *kadai* and heat over high heat to 375°F. Working in two batches, fry the balls until lightly browned, about 2 minutes, using a spider strainer or slotted spoon to turn them often so they cook evenly. Transfer the dumplings to the lined plate. Return the oil to 375°F between batches.

12 Place the dumplings in a serving bowl and spoon the tomato sauce over them. Serve warm, two per serving, with naan.

BUTTERNUT SQUASH BHARTA
VEGAN

SERVES 4 ⬡ A *bharta* is a roasted vegetable mash traditionally made with eggplant (*baingan bharta*). We thought of using butternut squash in the fall and winter seasons because that vegetable is so popular and prevalent in the States. This makes a terrific Thanksgiving side dish—in fact, we introduced this dish on the Thanksgiving menu at Rasika.

The tenderness of butternut squash can vary, so start checking your roasting time at the 20-minute mark. That may be enough time for the cubes to soften. Or it may take up to 30 minutes.

The same holds true for the cooking time in Step 4, when you want the finished squash to be dry rather than loose. Some squash have more moisture in them than others, so this step could perhaps take an extra minute or two.

You could also smoke the bharta after you've finished making it by removing it from the heat and employing the same smoking method as for Smoked Dal (page 228).

2½-pound butternut squash, peeled, seeded, and cut into 1-inch cubes (about 6 cups)
6 tablespoons canola oil
1 teaspoon cumin seeds
2 cups finely chopped yellow onions
2 cups finely chopped tomatoes
½ teaspoon ground turmeric
1 tablespoon finely chopped fresh ginger

1 teaspoon finely chopped fresh Thai green chili
½ teaspoon deggi mirch
1 teaspoon salt
½ teaspoon Toasted Cumin Powder (page 23)
2 teaspoons fresh lemon juice
Chopped cilantro, for garnish

1 Preheat the oven to 350°F.

2 In a bowl, coat the squash cubes with 2 tablespoons of the oil. Spread them on a baking sheet in a single layer and bake, stirring occasionally, until soft, 20 to 30 minutes. Transfer the squash to a large bowl and mash it with a potato masher. (It will be quite lumpy.)

3 In a heavy-bottomed pot or Dutch oven, heat the remaining 4 tablespoons oil over medium-high heat until it shimmers. Add the cumin seeds and let them crackle. Add the onions and cook, stirring occasionally, until lightly browned, about 7 minutes. Add the tomatoes and turmeric. Cook, stirring occasionally, until

the tomatoes are completely broken down and their moisture has evaporated, about 7 minutes.

4 Reduce the heat to medium. Stir in the ginger, green chili, and deggi mirch and sauté for 1 minute, stirring occasionally. Add the squash and the salt and cook, stirring constantly, until the mixture leaves the sides of the pan and is dry rather than loose, about 5 minutes (or more, depending on the moisture in the squash).

5 Finish the dish by adding the toasted cumin powder and lemon juice. Garnish with chopped cilantro.

VARIATION

BAINGAN BHARTA

To make the eggplant version of this bharta, start with an amount of eggplant equal in weight to the butternut squash. Cook the eggplant using the method in Eggplant and Ginger Chutney (page 264). When you peel the eggplant, mash it with a potato masher as you would the squash. The eggplant bharta will be a bit looser than the squash bharta.

MASALA CORN AND PEANUTS (MAKKI MOONGPHALI MASALA)

VEGAN

SERVES 6 ❀ We get wonderful corn in the mid-Atlantic region in the summer, so we often offer this dish in that season. I love the combination of crunchy peanuts and corn, whose sweetness is perfectly balanced by the acid in the tomato masala. It reflects the sweet and sour flavor profile of many Gujarati dishes.

You can make the tomato masala a day ahead, but the corn and peanuts are best added just before serving.

3 large or 4 medium ears of corn, husked, all silk removed

A Tomato Masala (page 31)
1 cup chopped unsalted roasted peanuts

1 Bring a large pot of salted water to a boil. (It should taste like seawater.) Cook the ears of corn uncovered (weight them down with a plate) for 10 minutes. Remove from the water, cool slightly, and cut the kernels off the cob. You want 3 cups of them.

2 In a large saucepan, bring the masala to a simmer over medium heat. Add the corn and peanuts and cook for 2 minutes to heat the corn through. Serve hot.

OKRA WITH MANGO POWDER (BHINDI AMCHOOR)

VEGAN

SERVES 4 ❖ This dish has been on the menu at Rasika since we opened. We tried to take it off once and so many people complained that we had to put it back on. *Amchoor* (dried mango) powder gives the okra a pleasant tang.

At the restaurant, we blanch the okra in 375°F oil for a couple of minutes to retain the vegetable's bright green color and cut the pods into julienne strips. We've altered the process here for ease of preparation.

Use young okra pods that feel soft when you squeeze them between your fingers and are not hard and fibrous. (The tip at the end of the pod should snap off easily.)

You can make the dish several hours in advance and reheat it.

¼ cup canola oil
1 teaspoon cumin seeds
1½ cups finely chopped yellow onions
¼ teaspoon ground turmeric
2 teaspoons finely chopped fresh ginger
1 teaspoon finely chopped fresh Thai
    green chili

1½ teaspoons salt
1½ pounds okra pods, ends trimmed
    and cut into ½-inch pieces
1 tablespoon mango powder
1 tablespoon fresh lemon juice

1 In a heavy-bottomed pot or Dutch oven, heat the oil over medium heat until it shimmers. Add the cumin seeds and let them crackle. Add the onions and cook, stirring occasionally, until they are soft and only lightly browned, about 10 minutes. Reduce the heat to medium-low. Stir in the turmeric, ginger, green chili, and salt.

2 Stir in the okra. Cover the pot and cook, stirring occasionally, until the okra is soft but still a nice green color, about 15 minutes. Add the mango powder and lemon juice. Serve warm.

GREEN BEANS CHILI GARLIC

VEGAN

SERVES 4 ✽ This is a quick stir-fry that's packed with flavor, thanks to fresh and dried chilies, lots of onions, and ginger. Have everything ready to go and make the beans when you're ready to serve them. They are at their best when eaten immediately.

You can use regular green beans for this recipe instead of the thinner French beans, but you may have to cook them a few minutes longer. Okra, broccoli, and cauliflower are also excellent prepared in this fashion.

RASIKA

2 tablespoons plus 1 teaspoon salt
1¼ teaspoons ground turmeric
¾ pound haricots verts (French green beans), trimmed on both ends and cut into 1-inch pieces
¼ cup canola oil
½ teaspoon cumin seeds

2 cups finely chopped yellow onions
2 tablespoons finely chopped garlic
2 teaspoons finely chopped fresh ginger
1 teaspoon finely chopped fresh Thai green chili
½ teaspoon red chili flakes
1 tablespoon fresh lemon juice

1 Set up a large bowl of ice and water. Bring a medium pot of water to a boil. Stir in 2 tablespoons of the salt and 1 teaspoon of the turmeric. Add the beans and cook until crisp-tender but still bright green, about 4 minutes. Drain the beans and submerge them in the ice water, stirring until they're cooled. Remove any ice floating in the bowl before draining the beans. Blot the beans on paper towels.

2 In the same pot, heat the oil over medium-high heat until it shimmers. Add the cumin seeds and let them crackle. Stir in the onions and garlic. Cook, stirring occasionally, until the onions are dark brown, about 10 minutes.

3 Reduce the heat to medium-low. Stir in the ginger, green chili, chili flakes, and the remaining ¼ teaspoon turmeric and 1 teaspoon salt. Add the beans and lemon juice and cook until the beans are warmed through.

Pictured on page 98.

BROCCOLI PORIYAL

VEGAN

SERVES 4 ❖ A *poriyal* is a South Indian dish, especially popular in Tamil Nadu. The word *poriyal* means "wet fry," basically a vegetable stir-fry. In Tamil Nadu, grated coconut is invariably a component of a poriyal. Try the dish with various vegetables, such as carrots, beans, asparagus, butternut squash, and Brussels sprouts, of course adjusting blanching times accordingly.

You can make the poriyal a day ahead and warm it up in a Dutch oven over medium-low heat or in the microwave. The flavor actually improves because it deepens.

2 tablespoons plus 1 teaspoon salt
1¼ teaspoons ground turmeric
¾ pound broccoli florets, cut roughly into 1 x 1-inch pieces
2 tablespoons coconut oil
1 teaspoon black or brown mustard seeds
1 teaspoon chana dal
1 teaspoon urad dal
2 cups finely chopped yellow onions

12 (1½-inch) fresh curry leaves (more if smaller)
2 teaspoons finely chopped fresh ginger
1 teaspoon finely chopped fresh Thai green chili
⅛ teaspoon asafetida
6 tablespoons grated coconut, fresh or frozen

1 Set up a large bowl of ice and water. Bring a medium pot of water to a boil. Stir in 1 tablespoon of the salt and 1 teaspoon of the turmeric. Add the broccoli and cook until crisp-tender but still bright green, about 3 minutes. Drain the broccoli and transfer to the ice bath, stirring just until the broccoli is cooled. Remove any ice floating in the bowl before draining the broccoli. Blot on paper towels. (If you don't drain the broccoli as soon as it has cooled, it will become waterlogged.)

2 Using the same pot, heat the coconut oil over medium-high heat until it shimmers. Add the mustard seeds, chana dal, and urad dal and cook until the dals are golden brown and nutty, about 1 minute. Add the onions and curry leaves and sauté, stirring occasionally, until the onions are softened but not browned, about 4 minutes.

3 Stir in the ginger, green chili, asafetida, the remaining ¼ teaspoon turmeric, and remaining 1 teaspoon salt. Add the broccoli and cook for 2 to 3 minutes to heat through. Stir in the grated coconut and serve hot.

KALE FRITTERS KADI

MAKES 12 FRITTERS (SERVES 4) ❀ In this dish, *kadi* really refers to the sauce, which is yogurt-based and thickened with gram flour (besan). (See Legumes, Pulses, Gram, Besan, and Dal, page 15.) In Northern India, the sauce tends to have a sour and spicier profile, whereas in Gujarat (Western India), it is sweeter.

Often there will be some kind of fritter or pakora paired with this sauce. Kale became so wildly popular in the States a few years ago that it seemed a natural choice to make fritters out of them for a kadi.

You could make these fritters as a cocktail party hors d'oeuvre by serving them crisp out of the fryer with a cold dipping sauce made with yogurt and the same spices and seasonings as the sauce in this dish. Kadi sauce would be too thin as a dip, however.

¼ pound kale, well washed, center ribs removed
2½ cups Kadi Sauce (page 33)
2 teaspoons finely chopped fresh ginger
1 teaspoon finely chopped fresh Thai green chili
½ teaspoon cumin seeds
¼ teaspoon ground turmeric

½ cup gram flour (besan)
¼ teaspoon baking soda
¼ teaspoon salt
¼ cup water
1 quart canola oil, for deep-frying
Plain Basmati Rice (page 217), for serving

1 Stack the kale leaves and roll tightly, like a cigar. With a chef's knife, slice the roll into very thin strips to shred the kale. You need 2 cups packed.

2 In a small saucepan over medium-low heat, heat the kadi sauce through (if it isn't already) and keep it warm over very low heat.

3 In a large bowl, combine the kale, ginger, green chili, cumin seeds, turmeric, gram flour, baking soda, and salt. Stir in the water. (The mixture will seem like it isn't bound, but if you squeeze some in the palm of your hand, it will hold together.) Using the palms of your hands, lightly roll the batter into twelve balls the size of cherry tomatoes.

4 Have ready a plate lined with paper towels. Pour the oil into a wok or *kadai* and heat over high heat to 350°F.

5 Fry the balls until the kale is dark green and crispy, about 3 minutes. Use a spider strainer or slotted spoon to stir them gently while they cook so they brown evenly. Transfer them to the paper towels to drain.

6 Place the fritters in a serving bowl. Pour the warm kadi sauce over them and serve hot with basmati rice.

CAULIFLOWER AND PEAS WITH CUMIN (JEERA GOBI MATTAR)

VEGAN

SERVES 4 ⚬ This combination of cauliflower and peas is made in every Indian household, but with regional variations, such as, say, mustard seeds and curry leaves in the south and this northern preparation from Rasika. Basically, you cook the cauliflower in its own moisture. In India, people cook the vegetables until they are very soft, whereas the fashion in the States these days is to cook them more on the al dente side.

¼ cup canola oil
1 teaspoon cumin seeds
2 cups finely chopped yellow onions
2 tablespoons finely chopped fresh ginger
1 teaspoon finely chopped fresh Thai green chili

½ teaspoon ground turmeric
1 teaspoon salt
1 large (2-pound) head cauliflower, cored and cut into 2-inch florets
1 cup frozen green peas, thawed, or cooked fresh peas

1 In a heavy-bottomed pot or Dutch oven, heat the oil over medium-high heat until it shimmers. Add the cumin seeds and let them crackle. Add the onions and cook, stirring occasionally, until soft and beginning to brown, about 10 minutes.

2 Reduce the heat to medium-low. Stir in the ginger, green chili, turmeric, salt, and cauliflower. Cover the pot and cook, stirring occasionally, until the cauliflower is tender, about 30 minutes.

3 Increase the heat to medium and add the peas, stirring until they are hot.

GREEN PEA AND PANEER SCRAMBLE (PANEER MATTAR BHURJEE)

SERVES 4 ⚙ Scrambled eggs (*bhurjee* means "scrambled") with tomatoes and green chilies are a popular breakfast food in Northern India. Substituting shredded paneer makes it suitable for vegetarians who don't eat eggs, while maintaining an appearance similar to them. We like to make this version with peas in the spring when they come into season.

Add the paneer just before you're ready to serve the dish; otherwise the water will leach from it and make it soggy. I've filled mini tart shells with this mixture and served them as hors d'oeuvres.

RASIKA

2 tablespoons canola oil
½ teaspoon cumin seeds
2 cups finely chopped yellow onions
2 teaspoons finely chopped fresh ginger
1 teaspoon finely chopped fresh Thai green chili
2 cups chopped tomatoes
½ teaspoon deggi mirch
½ teaspoon ground turmeric

1½ cups fresh green peas (or frozen)
1 teaspoon Toasted Cumin Powder (page 23)
1½ teaspoons salt
12 ounces shredded paneer (3 cups)
Chopped cilantro, for garnish
Naan (page 247) or Mint Paratha (page 242), for serving

1 In a large saucepan, heat the oil over medium-high heat until it shimmers. Add the cumin seeds and let them crackle. Add the onions and cook, stirring often, until they are translucent but not at all browned, about 6 minutes. Add the ginger and green chili and sauté for 1 minute.

2 Stir in the tomatoes, deggi mirch, and turmeric. Cook, stirring occasionally, until the tomatoes look mashed and all their water has been leached from them, about 10 minutes.

3 Stir in the peas, toasted cumin powder, and salt and cook until the peas are soft, about 6 minutes (2 minutes for frozen).

4 Add the paneer. Garnish with cilantro and serve hot with naan or mint paratha.

SAUTÉED MUSHROOMS AND GREEN ONIONS (KHUMB HARA PYAZ)

VEGAN

SERVES 4 ✸ We wanted to create a dish with mushrooms, so I came up with this—a quick stir-fry with green onions. Use a wok or *kadai* to make these mushrooms because both pans conduct heat well. Make sure to have your mise en place done so you can make fast work of this recipe.

You could make the masala a day ahead, reheat it in the wok, and add the mushrooms, green onions, lemon juice, and salt when you are ready to serve.

1½ pounds medium cremini mushrooms
¼ cup canola oil
1 teaspoon cumin seeds
1 cup finely chopped yellow onion
1 tablespoon finely chopped fresh ginger
1 teaspoon finely chopped fresh Thai
   green chili

2 cups finely chopped tomatoes
½ teaspoon ground turmeric
1 teaspoon deggi mirch
1½ teaspoons salt
2 bunches green onions, white and green
   parts, finely chopped
1 tablespoon fresh lemon juice

1 Trim the mushroom stems flush to the caps (discard the stems). Quarter the mushrooms and clean them in a large bowl of water. Transfer them to a colander.

2 In a wok or *kadai*, heat the oil over medium-high heat until it shimmers. Add the cumin seeds and let them crackle. Add the onion and cook until soft and just beginning to brown, about 3 minutes. Stir in the ginger, green chili, tomatoes, turmeric, and deggi mirch. Cook, stirring occasionally, to soften the tomatoes, about 3 minutes. Add the mushrooms and 1 teaspoon of the salt. Cook, stirring occasionally, for 5 minutes. Add the green onions, lemon juice, and remaining ½ teaspoon salt and serve.

CREMINI MUSHROOM AND ARTICHOKE KORMA

SERVES 6 ☺ Artichokes are very popular in French cooking, but they also sold very well on the menu at Bibiana, our Italian restaurant, whether as fried artichokes or in pasta or risotto. So we thought we'd give them the Indian treatment. Because they have a mild flavor, I decided to pair them with a rich korma sauce with hints of sweetness and spice to complement the artichokes instead of overwhelming them.

This is a very saucy dish, so make sure you have plenty of Plain Basmati Rice (page 217) or Jeera or Saffron Pulao (page 220) on hand, as well as Naan (page 247).

VEGETABLES
1 pound medium cremini mushrooms
1 lime, halved
6 large artichokes
1 tablespoon salt

SAUCE
4 tablespoons unsalted butter
1 teaspoon Ginger-Garlic Paste (page 27)
½ teaspoon deggi mirch

2 cups Korma Sauce (page 32)
½ cup water
1 cup guava nectar, such as Goya brand
¼ cup guava paste
½ cup heavy cream
2½ teaspoons salt
¾ teaspoon ground cardamom, preferably freshly ground*
¾ teaspoon freshly ground black pepper

Chopped cilantro, for garnish (optional)

Make ground cardamom by grinding whole green cardamom pods into powder in a spice grinder.

1 PREP THE VEGETABLES: Trim the mushroom stems flush to the caps (discard the stems). Quarter the mushrooms and clean them in a large bowl of water. Transfer them to a colander.

2 Fill a medium bowl with water and squeeze the lime into it. Discard the squeezed fruit.

3 Cut off the artichoke stems at the base where the leaves are. Hold an artichoke on its side and, using a bread knife, slice all the way through the globe about 1 inch above the bottom and discard the entire top portion. Dip the bottom in the lime water to keep it from discoloring. Using a sharp paring knife, cut around the base of the artichoke to remove whatever leaves remain and until you only see the white

flesh of the bottom. Using the tip of the paring knife, cut the cone of fuzzy choke from the center and discard it. Repeatedly plunge the bottoms in the lime water throughout the process. What you should have left is a scooped-out disk of artichoke bottom with no traces of the dark green, fibrous leaves. Repeat for all the artichokes.

4 Set up a bowl of ice and water. In a medium saucepan, bring 1 quart of water and the salt to a boil over medium-high heat. Add the artichoke bottoms and cook, stirring occasionally, until the tip of a paring knife inserts easily into them but they are still slightly firm, 6 to 8 minutes. Use a slotted spoon to transfer the artichokes to the ice water. Once they have cooled completely, drain them, pat them dry on paper towels, and cut them into sixths.

5 MAKE THE SAUCE: In a heavy-bottomed pot or Dutch oven, melt the butter over medium heat. Stir in the ginger-garlic paste and cook for 30 seconds. Stir in the deggi mirch, korma sauce, water, guava nectar, and guava paste. Bring the sauce to a boil and cook, stirring frequently, for 5 minutes to melt and incorporate the guava paste. Stir in the cream, mushrooms, and salt. Simmer for 5 minutes, stirring occasionally, to cook the mushrooms.

6 Add the artichoke bottoms, cardamom, and black pepper. Bring to a boil and cook for 5 minutes. Garnish with chopped cilantro, if desired. Serve hot.

CREAMED SPINACH (MALAI PALAK)
VEGAN (WITHOUT THE HEAVY CREAM)

SERVES 6 ❁ Creamed spinach (*malai* means "cream" and *palak* means "spinach") forms the base of other Indian dishes, such as Palak Paneer and Aloo Palak (variations follow). This is my version of it.

Blanching the spinach before pureeing it maintains its lovely bright green color. Notice that the dish uses a lot less cream than American versions often do (and no white sauce thickened with roux). It's just enough fat to convey richness while allowing the earthiness of the vegetable to predominate. If you want the dish to be vegan, just leave the cream out.

You can make the spinach 2 days ahead of time and store refrigerated. Reheat in the microwave or in a large saucepan over medium heat.

1 pound baby spinach
¼ cup canola oil
½ teaspoon cumin seeds
2 tablespoons finely chopped garlic
2½ cups finely chopped yellow onions
1 tablespoon finely chopped fresh ginger

1 teaspoon finely chopped fresh Thai
    green chili
½ teaspoon ground turmeric
¼ cup heavy cream
1 teaspoon salt
1 teaspoon fenugreek leaf powder*

To make fenugreek leaf powder, grind dried fenugreek leaves in a spice grinder, using enough so that the blades can pulverize them into a fine powder.

1 Set up a large bowl of ice and water. Bring a pot of water to a boil. In two batches, submerge the spinach in the boiling water, stirring well to just wilt it. Use a spider strainer or mesh spoon to transfer it to the ice water.

2 Drain the spinach well and transfer it to a blender. Add 1 cup water and blend into a fine, bright green puree.

3 In a large skillet, heat the oil over medium-high heat until it shimmers. Add the cumin seeds and garlic and let the garlic brown, about 30 seconds or less. Add the onions and cook, stirring occasionally, until soft but not browned, about 5 minutes. (The garlic will make the onions look browner than they really are.)

4 Stir in the ginger, green chili, and turmeric and cook for 30 seconds. Add the spinach puree and cook, stirring constantly, for 5 minutes. Be careful; it will sputter like bubbling lava.

5 Reduce the heat to medium and add the cream, salt, and fenugreek leaf powder. Return to a boil and cook for 5 minutes. Serve hot.

VARIATIONS

PALAK PANEER

Add 2 cups cubed paneer along with the cream, salt, and fenugreek leaf powder in Step 5.

ALOO PALAK

Add 2 cups cooked potatoes cut into ½-inch cubes along with the cream, salt, and fenugreek leaf powder in Step 5.

JALAPEÑO IN GRAVY (MIRCH KA SALAN)

VEGAN

SERVES 8 AS A GRAVY ⚙ *Mirch* is Hindi for "chili pepper"; *ka salan* means "in curry or gravy." Together they form a classic Hyderabadi dish, which is always served at festive occasions. It can be used simply as a side gravy to serve with biryanis or combined with paneer or potatoes to create full-on dishes. Variations for Paneer ka Salan and Aloo Mirch ka Salan follow this recipe.

1 tablespoon coriander seeds
1 teaspoon cumin seeds
2 tablespoons sesame seeds
1 teaspoon white poppy seeds
¼ teaspoon fenugreek seeds
2 tablespoons shredded unsweetened coconut
1¾ cups water
2 tablespoons canola oil
1 tablespoon Ginger-Garlic Paste (page 27)

1 large jalapeño, stemmed, quartered lengthwise, and cut into ¾-inch pieces (with seeds)
10 (1½-inch) fresh curry leaves (more if smaller)
¼ teaspoon ground turmeric
¾ cup Caramelized Onion Paste (page 26)
1 cup unsweetened coconut milk
½ cup Tamarind Pulp (page 24)
2 ounces jaggery, coarsely chopped
1 tablespoon salt

1 In a dry skillet, toast the coriander seeds, cumin seeds, sesame seeds, poppy seeds, fenugreek seeds, and coconut over medium heat, shaking the pan and stirring frequently, until the spices release their fragrance and the coconut is golden brown, 3 to 4 minutes.

2 In a NutriBullet or small blender, combine the toasted spices and 1¼ cups of the water and blend on high speed for a full 3 minutes. Strain the liquid into a bowl, stirring and then pressing down on the solids with a rubber spatula to extract as much liquid as you can. Return the solids to the blender with the remaining ½ cup water and blend for 1 full minute. Strain as before. Discard the solids. (You will have about 1½ cups of toasted seed liquid. If you have a little more or less, that's fine.)

3 In a large saucepan, heat the oil over medium-high heat until it shimmers. Add the ginger-garlic paste, jalapeño, and curry leaves and cook, stirring, for 1 minute.

4 Add the turmeric, toasted seed liquid, and caramelized onion paste. Bring to a boil. Add the coconut milk, tamarind pulp, and jaggery. Cook, stirring occasionally, until the jaggery is dissolved and the sauce thickens, about 5 minutes. Stir in the salt.

VARIATIONS

POTATOES IN JALAPEÑO GRAVY (ALOO MIRCH KA SALAN)

SERVES 6 ⚙ Boil, cool, and peel 2 russet (baking) potatoes (see Step 1, page 67). Bring the gravy to a boil over medium heat and add the potatoes, quartered. Cook, stirring occasionally, for 5 minutes to warm the potatoes through.

PANEER IN JALAPEÑO GRAVY (PANEER MIRCH KA SALAN)

SERVES 6 ⚙ Substitute 2½ cups (1-inch) cubed paneer for the potatoes in the preceding variation.

GUJARATI EGGPLANT AND SWEET POTATO "LASAGNA" WITH KADI SAUCE

SERVES 6 AS AN ENTRÉE ❀ I created this interpretation of vegetarian lasagna for a lunch in honor of Indian prime minister Narendra Modi's visit to Washington, D.C., in September 2014 (see page 100). Thin sheets made with gram flour (besan) batter stand in for lasagna noodles, which are then layered with Indian ratatouille and baked.

This is not a difficult dish, but it does require some extra work. You can make the Kadi Sauce and A Tomato Masala 2 days ahead. The day before, make the vegetable filling and the "lasagna sheets" and assemble the lasagna so it is oven-ready. Then all that is left to do is bake the lasagna and reheat the sauce. For the State Department lunch, we added thin diagonal slices of blanched asparagus to the sauce before serving.

FILLING
A Tomato Masala (page 31)
1 pound sweet potatoes, peeled
½ pound eggplant, unpeeled, ends trimmed
¾ pound zucchini, ends trimmed
½ large red bell pepper (4 ounces)
½ large green bell pepper (4 ounces)
¼ cup canola oil
½ cup chopped unsalted roasted peanuts
1 teaspoon salt

"LASAGNA"
1 cup gram flour (besan)
3 cups water
1 teaspoon finely chopped fresh ginger
½ teaspoon finely chopped fresh Thai green chili
½ teaspoon ground turmeric
1 tablespoon whole-milk yogurt
2 teaspoons salt
¼ teaspoon citric acid powder (see Note)
Cooking spray

Kadi Sauce (page 33), for serving

1 MAKE THE FILLING: Prepare the tomato masala and set aside.

2 Prep the vegetables for the filling, keeping all of them separate:

- Cut the sweet potatoes into ½-inch cubes.
- Cut the eggplant into ½-inch cubes.
- Halve the zucchini crosswise. Stand one of the halves up and cut four ½-inch slices of flesh from around the seeds in the center. Dice the flesh into ½-inch cubes (discard the seeds). Repeat with the other half.
- Cut the bell peppers into ½-inch squares.

3 In a large skillet, heat the oil over medium-high heat until it shimmers. Stir in the sweet potatoes and sauté, stirring occasionally, until parcooked and still a bit crunchy, about 5 minutes. Stir in the eggplant and cook for 4 minutes, stirring frequently. Add the zucchini and cook until the zucchini is soft, about 5 minutes. Add the bell peppers and sauté for 1 minute. Transfer the vegetables to a large bowl. Add the peanuts, tomato masala, and salt and mix well. (Makes about 5 cups.)

4 MAKE THE "LASAGNA" SHEETS: Have ready a wide expanse of very clean counter space.

5 In a medium saucepan, whisk together the gram flour and water until smooth. Add the ginger, green chili, turmeric, yogurt, salt, and citric acid. Cook over medium heat, stirring constantly with a silicone spatula or wooden spoon, until the batter is very thick, 9 to 10 minutes. (It will resemble thick pastry cream or cream puff dough.)

6 Turn the dough out onto the counter. Working quickly and using an offset spatula, spread it into a very thin (⅛-inch-thick) rectangular sheet roughly 24 x 20 inches. Use a paring knife to trim the rectangle to an 18-inch square. (Discard the trimmings or snack on them.) Then cut that square into four precise 9-inch squares. The dough cools and sets quickly so you will be able to peel each of the four squares off the counter easily as you need them.

7 Preheat the oven to 375°F. Grease a 9-inch square baking dish with cooking spray.

8 To assemble the lasagna, spread one-fourth of the vegetable mixture evenly into the bottom of the pan, pressing down lightly on it with the back of a spoon so it gets into the corners and is compact rather than loose.

9 Position one of the lasagna sheets over the vegetables so that it fits exactly in the pan. Repeat with the remaining three portions of vegetables and three lasagna sheets, ending with a lasagna sheet.

10 Cover the lasagna with a 9-inch square of parchment paper, then cover the dish with foil. Place it on a baking sheet and bake for 40 minutes.

11 Meanwhile, make (or reheat) the kadi sauce.

12 To serve, cut the lasagna into six rectangles. Serve in large pasta bowls with kadi sauce ladled over each portion.

NOTE: *If you can't find citric acid powder, substitute 1 tablespoon fresh lemon juice for it and subtract 1 tablespoon water from the 3 cups water called for in the gram flour dough.*

PANEER MAKHANI

SERVES 4 ✿ This combination of creamy, buttery, tomato-y makhani sauce and cubes of paneer is a rich dish that vegetarians love. If you have some Makhani Sauce in your freezer (always a good idea!), it's a snap to put this dish together in a hurry.

You can make the sauce up to 2 days ahead of time.

Makhani Sauce (page 34; see Note)
1 pound paneer, cut into 1 x 1 x ½-inch pieces

Salt
Jeera Pulao (page 220) and Naan (page 247), for serving

In a large saucepan, bring the makhani sauce to a boil over medium heat. Stir in the paneer cubes and return the sauce to a boil. Add salt if necessary. Serve hot with *pulao* and naan.

NOTE: *If you are using makhani sauce that you have made ahead and frozen (which you would have done without adding the heavy cream), when you bring it to a boil as directed, add the ¾ cup heavy cream at the same time that you add the paneer.*

MIXED VEGETABLE CURRY WITH MANGO

SERVES 6 AS AN ENTRÉE ❀ This is a South Indian version (from Tamil Nadu) of a *kadi,* a yogurt sauce thickened with gram flour/besan. (See Legumes, Pulses, Gram, Besan, and Dal, page 15.) I added mango to the sauce, flavored with coconut milk and curry leaves, mostly because I like it and it adds a nice sweetness to the dish.

In India and at Rasika we use a squash called bottle gourd. It resembles a large zucchini, but is light green in appearance and has a fibrous, seed-filled center. The flesh is a little bit denser than zucchini, which I've used in this recipe. You can find bottle gourd sometimes at Indian markets and some other Asian markets. I suggest you try it if you can find it.

Use any mixed blanched vegetables that you prefer in addition to, or instead of, the ones here, such as broccoli, snow peas, sugar snaps, or zucchini.

You can prep the vegetables and make the sauce the day before (Steps 1 to 6) and put the dish together (Step 7) when you are ready to serve.

VEGETABLES

1 small (6-ounce) zucchini, ends trimmed
Salt
¼ pound cauliflower florets, cut into roughly 1-inch chunks (1 heaping cup)
¼ pound carrots, cut into 1 x ½-inch batons (1 cup)
¼ pound green beans, ends trimmed, cut crosswise into 1-inch lengths (1 cup)
1 cup (5 ounces) frozen green peas, thawed (or cooked fresh peas)

SAUCE

3 cups whole-milk yogurt
One 13½-ounce can unsweetened coconut milk
1 tablespoon gram flour (besan)
¼ cup canola oil
1 teaspoon black or brown mustard seeds

½ teaspoon fenugreek seeds
3 dried red Kashmiri chilies, torn in half (with seeds)
10 (1½-inch) fresh curry leaves (more if smaller)
¼ teaspoon asafetida
½ large yellow onion, thinly sliced
2 teaspoons Ginger-Garlic Paste (page 27)
½ teaspoon ground turmeric
1½ teaspoons deggi mirch
1 tablespoon ground coriander
1 large (1-pound) just-ripe mango, peeled, pitted, and cut into ¾-inch cubes (1¾ cups)
4 teaspoons salt

Plain Basmati Rice (page 217) or Lemon Cashew Rice (page 224), for serving

1 PREPARE THE VEGETABLES: Halve the zucchini lengthwise and use a teaspoon to scoop out and discard the little seeds in the center of each half. Cut the halves crosswise into 1-inch sections, then cut each section into 1 x ½-inch batons, enough to yield 1 cup.

2 Set up a large bowl of ice and water. Bring a small stockpot of salted water to a boil. (It should taste like seawater.) Blanch the vegetables separately in the following order for the proscribed amount of time, using a spider strainer or slotted spoon to transfer them to the ice water when they are done. Return the water to a boil between vegetables:

> Zucchini: 2 minutes
> Cauliflower: 2½ minutes
> Carrot: 3½ minutes
> Beans: 2½ minutes

3 Drain the vegetables, blot them dry on paper towels, and transfer them to a bowl. Add the peas and set aside.

4 MAKE THE SAUCE: In a large bowl, whisk together the yogurt, coconut milk, and gram flour. Set aside.

5 In a large saucepan, heat the oil over medium-high heat until it shimmers. Add the mustard seeds, fenugreek seeds, dried chilies, curry leaves, and asafetida and let the seeds crackle. Stir in the onion and cook, stirring occasionally, until the onions are soft, about 5 minutes. Stir in the ginger-garlic paste and cook for 30 seconds. Stir in the turmeric, deggi mirch, and coriander. Add the mango and cook, stirring, for 2 minutes to begin to soften.

6 Stir in the reserved yogurt mixture. Bring to a boil and cook, stirring constantly, for 6 to 7 minutes to thicken the sauce.

7 Add the vegetables and salt and cook for 5 minutes. Serve hot with basmati rice or lemon cashew rice.

VEGETABLE BIRYANI

SERVES 8 ❂ Biryanis are for festive occasions and this recipe makes a sizeable amount. It is a terrific main dish to serve to vegetarians because it's hearty, full of complex flavors, and loaded with colorful vegetables. It is generally served with raita, such as Cucumber Raita or Tomato and Red Onion Raita, and a gravy or sauce, such as Jalapeño in Gravy (page 124). See On Biryanis, page 135.

You can make the vegetable masala (Steps 1 to 5) the day before and refrigerate it, then pick up the recipe from there the next day. (Bring the masala to room temperature first.)

VEGETABLE MASALA
1 quart whole-milk yogurt
½ teaspoon ground turmeric
1 teaspoon deggi mirch
1 tablespoon ground coriander
¼ cup canola oil
4 green cardamom pods
4 whole cloves
1-inch cinnamon stick
½ teaspoon cumin seeds
2 large dried Indian bay leaves
1 large yellow onion, quartered and thinly sliced
4 teaspoons Ginger-Garlic Paste (page 27)
5 cups mixed blanched vegetables (see Note)
1 teaspoon Mace-Cardamom Powder (page 23)
1 teaspoon garam masala
1 tablespoon salt
1 tomato (5 ounces), cut into ¾-inch cubes
4 medium fresh Thai green chilies, thinly sliced at an angle
2 x 1-inch piece fresh ginger, thinly sliced lengthwise and cut into thin julienne strips

½ cup loosely packed mint leaves
½ cup chopped cilantro, including stems

RICE
3 cups basmati rice
½ cup whole milk
½ teaspoon saffron threads
¼ teaspoon ground turmeric
1 tablespoon kewra water, such as Dabur brand
3 quarts water
¼ cup canola oil
2 teaspoons fresh lemon juice
4 green cardamom pods
4 whole cloves
1-inch cinnamon stick
½ teaspoon black cumin seeds
2 large dried Indian bay leaves
3 tablespoons salt

6 tablespoons ghee
Crispy Fried Onions (page 25), for garnish
Cucumber Raita (page 269) or Tomato and Red Onion Raita (page 269), for serving

1 MAKE THE VEGETABLE MASALA: In a medium bowl, whisk together the yogurt, turmeric, deggi mirch, and coriander. Set the yogurt mixture aside.

2 In a heavy-bottomed pot or Dutch oven, heat the oil over medium-high heat until it shimmers. Add the cardamom pods, cloves, cinnamon stick, cumin seeds, and bay leaves. Let the cumin seeds crackle. Add the onion and sauté, stirring occasionally, until golden brown, about 20 minutes. Reduce the heat to medium. Add the ginger-garlic paste and cook for 30 seconds.

3 Add the yogurt mixture to the onions and cook, stirring occasionally, for 15 minutes. The yogurt will appear curdled, as if it has broken. Don't worry about it.

4 Add the blanched vegetables, mace-cardamom powder, garam masala, and salt. Cook for 5 minutes, stirring once or twice.

5 Sprinkle the tomato, green chilies, ginger, mint leaves, and cilantro over the vegetables and remove from the heat.

6 Preheat the oven to 375°F.

7 MAKE THE RICE: Clean the rice by covering it with cool water in a very large bowl. Tip the bowl to drain as much water out as you can without letting any grains fall into the sink. Repeat three or four times, or until the water is clear. Once it is, cover the rice with water and let it soak for 30 minutes.

8 In a small glass bowl, microwave the milk, saffron, and turmeric for 1 minute to warm the milk. Stir in the kewra water. Let the saffron steep while you parboil the rice.

9 In a small stockpot, combine the 3 quarts water, oil, lemon juice, cardamom pods, cloves, cinnamon stick, black cumin seeds, bay leaves (see Note), and salt and bring to a boil over high heat. Drain the rice and stir it into the water. Return to a boil and cook, stirring once or twice, until the rice is partially cooked and al dente (when you bite into a grain you should definitely sense a bit of hardness in the center), 1 to 5 minutes. The cooking time depends on the age of the rice (and who knows how old it is) and how long it has been soaked. To be on the safe side, start checking it after 1 minute and keep checking until it is just right.

10 Drain the rice and cover the vegetables with half of it. Drizzle the steeped saffron milk all over, then top with the remaining rice.

11 In a small saucepan, heat the ghee over medium heat until it is hot. Drizzle it all over the rice.

12 Cover the pot with foil and a tight lid. Bake for 25 minutes. Remove from oven and let rest for 5 minutes.

13 Fluff the rice with a serving spoon to jumble the vegetables and rice. Serve hot directly from the pot or pile onto a serving platter. Garnish with crispy fried onions and serve with cucumber raita or tomato and red onion raita on the side.

NOTE: *The vegetables used in this biryani are the same as those used in the Mixed Vegetable Curry with Mango (page 131): zucchini, cauliflower, carrots, green beans, and peas. Follow the prep and blanching instructions (Steps 1 to 3). Feel free to substitute other blanched vegetables, such as broccoli, snow peas, or sugar snaps, as you wish.*

NOTE: *If you don't want whole spices in the rice, you can tie them up in a square of cheesecloth and remove it before serving.*

ON BIRYANIS

A biryani, which derives from the Persian word *beryan* (fried or roasted), is a layered rice dish, often made with meat and therefore substantial enough to be the centerpiece of a meal. The rice is often scented with a subtle flavoring, such as rose, saffron, or jasmine, but also bold spices, such as cinnamon, clove, cardamom, and mace.

Biryani, by the way, came to India via Persia. During the Mughal Empire in the sixteenth century, Muslims ruled Northern India and greatly influenced the Awadhi cuisine there, especially in Lucknow, the capital of Uttar Pradesh. That city is known for its *dum* cooking.

In dum cooking, a heavy clay pot (*handi*) is heated over an open fire and foods are sautéed in it to parcook them. Then a clay lid is put on top and the rim is sealed with dough made of flour and water. The flames are then extinguished and the handi cooks slowly over embers. The seal allows the juices released during slow-cooking to go back into the food.

Biryanis were, and sometimes still are, slow-cooked in this manner over a low fire in a sealed pot, allowing the mélange of flavors to develop and bloom. The common method nowadays is to parboil the rice before layering it and then cooking the assembled biryani in a covered pot in the oven.

Preparing biryanis can be an elaborate undertaking; they generally require many ingredients and steps, but the payoff in pleasure makes it worth the effort. Goat or Lamb Biryani (page 210) and Vegetable Biryani (page 133) certainly are.

Paneer Shashlik (page 143)

6

TANDOORI-STYLE GRILLING

ON TANDOORI-STYLE GRILLING

To me, there are few foods more alluring than skewers of fish, meat, or paneer fresh out of a tandoor. At Rasika, we use a cylindrical tandoori clay oven whose temperature is around 500°F. The intense heat of the enclosed environment lightly chars and deepens richly colored marinades on kebabs' exteriors while retaining moisture and tenderness on the interior, whether the kebabs are salmon, shrimp, swordfish, lamb, chicken, or paneer.

Marination is vital to tandoori cooking. (See Marinating, opposite.) We marinate overnight, in thick, yogurt-based mixtures that enrich, tenderize, and inject flavor. Common elements in these marinades are ginger-garlic paste, chili pepper, citrus, and, often, mustard oil; these ingredients add dimensions of heat and tang, doing the heavy lifting flavorwise rather than spices.

I have found that the best approximation of tandoori cooking at home requires two things: a charcoal (best) or gas grill and a kebab set comprising a notched rack and six ½-inch-wide flat skewers that rest on it. Oven-broiling just doesn't achieve a similar result. The marinade usually doesn't char fast enough, if at all, and you lose the depth of color and flavor that makes these dishes so appealing.

Using a kebab rack allows the protein to hover just over the grill grate without coming into contact with it. This is important because if you put the skewers directly on the grill grate, the marinade would stick to it. Then, when you try to turn the skewers over, the marinade would remain on the grill (and burn) and there would be little, if any, left on the protein.

Wide, flat skewers are essential, because you can thread items securely on them and they won't twist or rotate when you turn them over. When you thread the protein, the skewer should go right through the middle of each piece so they are secure. (Another option is to double-skewer your proteins, using two skewers spaced at least ½ inch apart, which can be tricky to do.) The pieces should not be scrunched close together; they should just barely touch so each piece can cook evenly and completely.

If you don't have a kebab rack, you can make one yourself. Take two long sheets of heavy-duty foil and crumple them into two fairly solid rods 1½ inches in diameter and 14 inches long. Place them on the grill parallel to one another and on either side of the direct heat, but close enough to one another that your skewers will be able to sit on them securely over the flame.

Figure all this out before you start the fire, keeping in mind that the number of skewers you can grill at one time will depend on how much real estate your fire covers. Thread all of your skewers and then position the rack (or rods) so that everything is where you want it to be and the skewers can rotate freely. If you need to crumple the foil rods a little more to get the protein closer to the fire, do it. If the pieces of protein on the skewers are so wide that the skewers cannot rotate 360 degrees unimpeded, grill in batches instead of overcrowding the grill.

Turn the skewers, in quarter-turns if possible, throughout the cooking process so they get color on them evenly all the way around. This applies to items that have four sides, like Creamy Tandoori-Style Chicken Kebabs (page 145), Kashmiri Cinnamon Salmon (page 148), and Paneer Shashlik (page 143). Flatter items, such as the Tandoori-Style Mango Shrimp (page 140) and Grilled Cashew Cardamom Lamb Chops (page 154), get turned only once.

Switch out skewers getting too much color for those from a cooler part of the grill. Do not walk away. You need to babysit the skewers and fuss over them, the way you do with anything you grill, be it barbecued chicken or a steak.

Total cooking times will vary from grill to grill because there are so many variables: the heat of your fire, how much of the grilling area the fire covers, where the hot spots are, the distance between the proteins and fire, etc. Also bear in mind that yogurt marinades contain fat; when they drip into the fire, the fat can cause flare-ups—this is another reason to move the skewers around during the process.

The process is really quite simple once you get the hang of it. A lot of the preparation, the marinating for example, can and should be done the day before. The actual cooking time, after the fire is ready, is minimal—barely enough to enjoy a cocktail!

MARINATING

Marination is often an essential element in Indian cooking when preparing protein, especially in the tandoor. In India, all chefs and cooks have their own recipes for marinades, which puts a personal stamp on their dishes. That goes for us at Rasika, too.

There are two kinds of marinating:

1. A quick marinade to impart bold flavor and salt directly on the surface of the protein. For me, this always includes salt, ginger-garlic paste, and citrus, usually lemon juice. I also add turmeric for color when it's called for.

2. A yogurt-based, flavorful marinade to help tenderize the meat. (Other acids in the marinade, such as lemon juice or ginger-garlic paste, also help to tenderize.) With the yogurt marinade, the flavoring in the marinade seeps into the meat, which tenderizes without becoming too denatured because the lactic acid in the yogurt is less potent than citric acid. The fat in the yogurt helps to keep the protein moist.

I usually recommend that food be marinated for at least 4 hours, but preferably overnight. This is what we do at Rasika and it makes a world of difference in terms of both prep and flavor.

Some recipes in this book only call for a quick marinade, others call for both, including all of the tandoori-style dishes in this chapter. The marinade used for Chicken Tikka Masala (page 177), by the way, is a typical tandoori marinade that creates the trademark red coloring that many tandoori dishes are known for. The color comes from Kashmiri Chili Paste (page 28).

TANDOORI-STYLE MANGO SHRIMP

SERVES 6 ❖ Mangoes are beloved in India and they must be in the United States, too, because these shrimp have always been a top seller at both The Bombay Club and Rasika. I'm pretty sure that we were the first to create this dish in Washington, if not the whole country, but don't hold me to it. —ASHOK

Before you begin to make this dish, read On Tandoori-Style Grilling (page 138) carefully. You will need a kebab rack and ½-inch-wide flat kebab skewers.

For best results and optimal flavor, marinate the shrimp the day before. (See Marinating, page 139.) —VIKRAM

MARINADE
½ cup unsalted raw cashew pieces
1 cup canned Alphonso mango pulp, such as Ratnā or Deep brand
1 tablespoon fresh lemon juice
2 teaspoons Ginger-Garlic Paste (page 27)
¼ teaspoon ground turmeric
1 teaspoon finely chopped fresh Thai green chili
1½ teaspoons salt

2 tablespoons canola oil
1 cup whole-milk yogurt

SHRIMP
24 (U16 to U20) shrimp, tails on, peeled and deveined
1 tablespoon fresh lemon juice
¼ teaspoon ground turmeric
½ teaspoon salt

Mint, Cilantro, and Yogurt Chutney (page 257), for serving

1 MAKE THE MARINADE: In a NutriBullet or small blender, puree the cashews, mango pulp, lemon juice, ginger-garlic paste, turmeric, green chili, and salt until smooth. Transfer to a large bowl and whisk in the oil and yogurt.

2 SEASON THE SHRIMP: Using a paring knife cut a ½-inch slit down the back of each shrimp where they were deveined. (This will allow the marinade to penetrate well.) Place the shrimp in a bowl and add the lemon juice, turmeric, and salt and coat the shrimp well.

3 Fold the mango mixture into the shrimp, coating them well. Cover and marinate in the refrigerator for at least 4 hours, but preferably overnight.

4 Line a baking sheet with foil. Thread four shrimp on a ½-inch-wide kebab skewer by starting at its thick end and running through its tail end just above the shell. The tails should all face the same direction. The shrimp should be very close to one another, but not touching. Repeat with five more skewers and the remaining twenty shrimp. Place the kebabs on the baking sheet. (There should be a good amount of marinade on them.)

5 Prepare a grill, preferably with charcoal, for direct-heat grilling. (See Note.) Center a kebab rack on the grill directly over the hot part of the grill. (If you don't have a kebab rack, you can jury-rig one; see page 138.)

6 Place the skewers on the rack so that the shrimp are above the coals but not touching the grate. Make sure you can rotate the skewers 360 degrees without the shrimp knocking into one another. You may have to cook in batches.

7 When you start to see small spots of char on the underside of a skewer, turn it over to let the other side char. If a skewer is charring too quickly, trade places with one that isn't. One note of caution: The fat in the marinade can cause flare-ups when it drips onto the fire—another good reason to pay attention and move the skewers around.

8 The shrimp is done when the flesh feels firm when you pinch it between your thumb and forefinger. Total cooking time should be around 8 minutes. It will vary depending on your grill and fire, so always keep your eye on the skewers.

9 Remove and discard the foil from the baking sheet and put the skewers on it as they come off the grill. Serve with mint, cilantro, and yogurt chutney.

NOTE: *To prepare a grill for direct-heat grilling: Fill a chimney starter with charcoal and light it. Let it burn until the flames subside and a light layer of ash covers it, 20 to 25 minutes. Dump it in the center of the grill to cover the expanse of the kebab rack. Place the grill grate on the grill. (Or turn a gas grill to medium-high or high, depending on how hot your grill runs.)*

PANEER SHASHLIK

SERVES 6 ❋ Paneer is fresh cow's milk cheese curds that have been pressed into a dense brick. Cubes cut from it hold their shape when cooked and soften, but don't melt. Paneer is very commonly eaten in Northern India. It's considered to be a meat substitute for vegetarians and always a part of a meal on festive occasions.

When grilled, the paneer cubes take on a nice color and char from the marinade. On the inside, they are creamy, provided you eat them right away. As they cool, the curds harden.

You want the paneer, peppers, and red onion pieces to be uniform in size to avoid having stray edges that will burn if they get too close to the fire. Plus, it looks neater when all the pieces are the same size. They don't have to be 100 percent exact, but you want everything to be roughly an inch all around.

Before you begin to make this dish, read On Tandoori-Style Grilling (page 138) carefully. You will need a kebab rack and ½-inch-wide flat kebab skewers. Mango pickle is a prepared jarred condiment available at Indian or other Asian markets.

For best results and optimal flavor, marinate the paneer for 24 hours, because the cheese is bland and needs a good amount of time to absorb the marinade's flavor. (See Marinating, page 139.)

MARINADE
1 cup whole-milk yogurt
¼ cup mango pickle, such as Priya brand
1 tablespoon Ginger-Garlic Paste
    (page 27)
¼ teaspoon ground turmeric
½ teaspoon deggi mirch
1 tablespoon mustard oil
¼ teaspoon nigella seeds
1 teaspoon salt

PANEER
1 pound paneer, cut into 18 (roughly
    1-inch) cubes
1 large red bell pepper
1 large green bell pepper
1 medium red onion, quartered

Mint, Cilantro, and Yogurt Chutney
    (page 257), for serving

1 MAKE THE MARINADE: In a NutriBullet or small blender, puree ¼ cup of the yogurt, the mango pickle, and ginger-garlic paste until smooth. Transfer to a large bowl and whisk in the turmeric, deggi mirch, mustard oil, nigella seeds, salt, and remaining ¾ cup yogurt.

2 MARINATE THE PANEER: Put the paneer in the marinade and coat all the pieces well. Cover and refrigerate for at least 12 hours, but preferably 24.

3 Halve the two bell peppers. Remove and discard their stems and seeds and any white membrane. Cut each bell pepper half into (1-inch) squares, six each. (You will have twelve red squares and twelve green squares.)

4 Separate the layers of the onion quarters. Take the twelve largest pieces and trim them into 1-inch squares. Reserve the rest of the onion for another use.

5 Line a baking sheet with foil. Thread each of six ½-inch-wide kebab skewers in this order: paneer, red pepper, green pepper, red onion; repeat; finish with a final cube of paneer. All of the pieces should be touching one another but not scrunched together. Place the kebabs on the baking sheet.

6 Prepare a grill, preferably with charcoal, for direct-heat grilling. (See Note, page 142.) Center a kebab rack on the grill directly over the hot part of the grill. (If you don't have a kebab rack, you can jury-rig one; see page 138.)

7 Place the skewers on the rack so that the paneer is above the coals but not touching the grate. Make sure you can rotate the skewers 360 degrees without the cubes knocking into one another.

8 When you start to see small spots of char on the underside of a skewer, turn it 90 degrees to let another side char. Repeat with the other two sides. The idea is to keep turning the skewers so they brown and cook evenly. If a skewer is charring too quickly, trade places with one that isn't. One note of caution: The fat in the marinade can cause flare-ups when it drips onto the fire—another good reason to pay attention and move the skewers around.

9 The paneer is done when a cube feels soft when you pinch it between your thumb and forefinger. Total cooking time should be between 6 and 14 minutes. It will vary depending on your grill and fire, so always keep your eye on the skewers.

10 Remove and discard the foil from the baking sheet and put the skewers on it as they come off the grill. Serve with mint, cilantro, and yogurt chutney.

Pictured on page 136.

CREAMY TANDOORI-STYLE CHICKEN KEBABS (MALAI CHICKEN TIKKA)

SERVES 4 TO 6 ❁ *Malai* means "cream," so it's a safe bet that these Northern Indian–inspired chicken brochettes are going to be rich.

In addition to yogurt, the marinade has cream, cream cheese, Boursin cheese, and cheddar cheese in it. The cheese helps get a nice char on the chicken cubes once they hit the grill and the fat in the marinade keeps the meat moist. If you want to be adventurous, experiment with using different kinds of cheese. One thing you won't see in the marinade: turmeric. You want to retain the whiteness and creamy appearance of the chicken, down to the ground pepper you use.

Before you begin to make this dish, read On Tandoori-Style Grilling (page 138) carefully. You will need a kebab rack and ½-inch-wide flat kebab skewers. For best results and optimal flavor, marinate the chicken the day before. (See Marinating, page 139.)

CHICKEN

1 pound boneless, skinless chicken breasts, cut into 18 or 24 (1-inch) cubes (see Note)
1 teaspoon fresh lemon juice
1 teaspoon Ginger-Garlic Paste (page 27)
¼ teaspoon salt

MARINADE

½ cup heavy cream
¼ cup whole-milk yogurt
¼ cup (2 ounces) cream cheese, at room temperature
2 tablespoons (½ ounce) finely shredded mild white cheddar cheese
2 tablespoons (1 ounce) Boursin cheese
2 teaspoons Ginger-Garlic Paste (page 27)
1 teaspoon fresh lemon juice
½ teaspoon finely chopped fresh Thai green chili
1 tablespoon finely chopped cilantro stems
¼ teaspoon salt
½ teaspoon freshly ground white pepper (or black pepper)
2 tablespoons unsalted butter, melted

Mint, Cilantro, and Yogurt Chutney (page 257), for serving

1 SEASON THE CHICKEN: In a small bowl, combine the chicken, lemon juice, ginger-garlic paste, and salt.

2 MAKE THE MARINADE: In a large bowl, whisk together the cream, yogurt, cream cheese, cheddar, Boursin cheese, ginger-garlic paste, lemon juice, green chili, cilantro, salt, white pepper, and melted butter until thick. Add the chicken and coat the pieces well. Cover and marinate in the refrigerator for at least 4 hours, but preferably overnight.

3 Line a baking sheet with foil. Thread the chicken cubes onto ½-inch-wide kebab skewers (see Note) and place them on the baking sheet. There should be a good amount of marinade on them.

4 Prepare a grill, preferably with charcoal, for direct-heat grilling. (See Note, page 142.) Center a kebab rack on the grill directly over the hot part of the grill. (If you don't have a kebab rack, you can jury-rig one; see page 138.)

5 Place the skewers on the rack so that the chicken is above the coals but not touching the grate. Make sure you can rotate the skewers 360 degrees without the cubes knocking into one another. You may have to cook in batches.

6 When you start to see small spots of char on the underside of a skewer, turn it 90 degrees to let another side char. Repeat with the other two sides. The idea is to keep turning the skewers so they brown and cook evenly. If a skewer is charring too quickly, trade places with one that isn't. One note of caution: The fat in the marinade can cause flare-ups when it drips onto the fire—another good reason to pay attention and move the skewers around.

7 The chicken is done when the flesh feels firm when you pinch it between your thumb and forefinger. Total cooking time should be between 7 and 10 minutes. It will vary depending on your grill and fire, so always keep your eye on the skewers.

8 Remove and discard the foil from the baking sheet and put the skewers on it as they come off the grill. Serve with mint, cilantro, and yogurt chutney.

NOTE: *If serving 4 or 5 people, cut the chicken into 20 pieces (5 or 4 per skewer). If serving 6, cut the chicken into either 18 pieces (3 per skewer) or 24 slightly smaller pieces (4 per skewer).*

KASHMIRI CINNAMON SALMON

SERVES 4 ◈ Salmon can be found in India, but all of it is imported, naturally. I like to use Scottish salmon because the fat content tends to be higher than in Atlantic salmon and therefore makes it moister.

The marinade I prefer here differs from what might traditionally be used for tandoori preparations. For example, I don't use mustard oil, I cook the Kashmiri chili paste, and I flavor the marinade predominantly with cinnamon. Kashmiri chilies provide a nice bright red color to the marinade and a good amount of heat without being too fiery.

Before you begin to make this dish, read On Tandoori-Style Grilling (page 138) carefully. You will need a kebab rack and ½-inch-wide flat kebab skewers.

For best results and optimal flavor, marinate the salmon the day before. (See Marinating, page 139.)

RASIKA

MARINADE

3 tablespoons canola oil
½ cup Kashmiri Chili Paste (page 28)
2 tablespoons Ginger-Garlic Paste
   (page 27)
½ cup water
1 teaspoon ground cinnamon
1 teaspoon salt
½ teaspoon freshly ground black pepper
1 cup whole-milk yogurt

SALMON

1½ pounds center-cut salmon, skin and
   pinbones removed
2 tablespoons fresh lemon juice
1 tablespoon Ginger-Garlic Paste
   (page 27)
¼ teaspoon ground turmeric
1 teaspoon salt

Mint-Cilantro Chutney (page 257),
   for serving
Lemon wedges, for serving
Garlic Naan with Cilantro (page 249),
   for serving

1 MAKE THE MARINADE: In a small saucepan, heat the oil over medium heat until it shimmers. Stir in the Kashmiri chili paste, ginger-garlic paste, and water. Bring to a boil and cook for 10 minutes, stirring occasionally, until you have a thick paste the color of tomato paste. Stir in the cinnamon, salt, and black pepper. Set aside to cool for a few minutes. Stir in the yogurt.

2 MARINATE THE SALMON: Trim the thin belly meat from the salmon so the fillet is of even thickness. Cut the fillets into twelve 3 x 1½-inch chunks. Place the salmon pieces in a bowl and coat them with the lemon juice, ginger-garlic paste, turmeric,

and salt. Fold the yogurt marinade into the salmon and coat the pieces well. Cover and marinate in the refrigerator for at least 4 hours, but preferably overnight.

3 Line a baking sheet with foil. Run a ½-inch-wide kebab skewer lengthwise through three pieces of salmon with their skinned sides all facing in the same direction (see Note). Make sure the pieces are very close to one another, but not touching. Repeat with the remaining three skewers and nine pieces of salmon. Place the skewers on the baking sheet. (There should be a good amount of marinade on them.)

4 Prepare a grill, preferably with charcoal, for direct-heat grilling. (See Note, page 142.) Center a kebab rack on the grill directly over the hot part of the grill. (If you don't have a kebab rack, you can jury-rig one; see page 138.)

5 Place the skewers on the rack so that the salmon is above the coals but not touching the grate. Make sure you can rotate the skewers 360 degrees without the cubes knocking into each other. You may have to cook in batches.

6 When you start to see small spots of char on the underside of a skewer, turn it 90 degrees to let another side char. (The skinned side will char faster because of its higher fat content.) Repeat with the other two sides. The idea is to keep turning the skewers so they brown and cook evenly. If a skewer is charring too quickly, trade places with one that isn't. One note of caution: The fat in the marinade can cause flare-ups when it drips onto the fire—another good reason to pay attention and move the skewers around.

7 The salmon is done when it is a deep orange all around and feels firm but slightly soft in the middle when you pinch a piece between your thumb and forefinger. Total cooking time should be between 10 and 15 minutes for medium. It will vary depending on your grill and fire, so always keep your eye on the skewers.

8 Remove and discard the foil from the baking sheet and put the skewers on it as they come off the grill. Serve with mint-cilantro chutney, lemon wedges, and garlic naan.

NOTE: *You want to thread the salmon with the fatty, grayish-brown skinned sides facing the same way. This will allow you to brown all the pieces evenly. The fat causes those sides to char more quickly due to flare-ups and you want all the pieces cooking at the same rate.*

TANDOORI-STYLE LIME SWORDFISH (NIMBOO SWORDFISH)

SERVES 4 ✿ Swordfish is such a dense fish that it really benefits from a long marination, which coaxes flavor out of it. This recipe relies on the tandoori marinating method of using yogurt to tenderize and enrich, and ginger, chili, garlic, and mustard oil to add heat, tang, and zip.

Lime is the citric acid used here instead of lemon (*nimboo* means both "lime" and "lemon" in Hindi) and to me it is lime leaves that really make the marinade come to life. They come from trees that produce the makrut lime, a bumpy-skinned lime grown in tropical Asia. The leaves have a concentrated lime flavor, and are much more floral, herbal, and aromatic than the Persian lime zest commonly used as a flavoring. Thai cooking features them prominently. You can usually find the leaves at Asian markets, so when you do find them, buy extra; they can be frozen if wrapped well in plastic wrap. (Makrut limes are known in much of the world as kaffir limes, but the word *kaffir* is considered by many people to be an ethnic slur, particularly in South Africa.)

Before you begin to make this dish, read On Tandoori-Style Grilling (page 138) carefully. You will need a kebab rack and ½-inch-wide flat kebab skewers.

For best results and optimal flavor, marinate the swordfish the day before. (See Marinating, page 139.) You need lime zest and juice for the double marinade in this recipe, so zest the lime before juicing it.

SWORDFISH

1½ pounds skinless swordfish fillet, ¾ inch thick, cut into 16 (roughly 2-inch) squares
½ teaspoon ground turmeric
1 tablespoon fresh lime juice
1 teaspoon Ginger-Garlic Paste (page 27)
1 teaspoon salt

MARINADE

1 cup whole-milk yogurt
10 fresh lime leaves, center veins removed, finely chopped (or enough to yield 1½ teaspoons; see Note)

2 teaspoons Ginger-Garlic Paste (page 27)
½ teaspoon ground turmeric
2 tablespoons mustard oil
1 teaspoon red chili flakes
1 teaspoon grated lime zest
2 tablespoons fresh lime juice
1 teaspoon salt

Mint, Cilantro, and Yogurt Chutney (page 257), for serving
Lemon Pickle (page 267), for serving

1 SEASON THE SWORDFISH: In a medium bowl, coat the swordfish pieces with the turmeric, lime juice, ginger-garlic paste, and salt.

2 MAKE THE MARINADE: In a large bowl, whisk together the yogurt, chopped lime leaves, ginger-garlic paste, turmeric, mustard oil, chili flakes, lime zest, lime juice, and salt. Add the fish and coat them well. Cover and marinate in the refrigerator for at least 4 hours, but preferably overnight.

3 Line a baking sheet with foil. Thread four pieces of swordfish on a ½-inch-wide kebab skewer by running it through the middle of each piece horizontally. The pieces should be just barely touching one another. Repeat with the three remaining skewers and twelve pieces of swordfish. Place the kebabs on the baking sheet. (There should be a good amount of marinade on them.)

4 Prepare a grill, preferably with charcoal, for direct-heat grilling. (See Note, page 142.) Center a kebab rack on the grill directly over the hot part of the grill. (If you don't have a kebab rack, you can jury-rig one; see page 138.)

5 Place the skewers on the rack so that the fish is above the coals but not touching the grate. Make sure you can rotate the skewers 360 degrees without the swordfish pieces knocking into one another. You may have to cook in batches.

6 When you start to see small spots of char on the underside of a skewer, turn it over to let the other side char. If a skewer is charring too quickly, trade places with one that isn't.

7 The fish is done when the flesh feels firm when you pinch it between your thumb and forefinger. Total cooking time should be 6 to 8 minutes. It will vary depending on your grill and fire, so always keep your eye on the skewers.

8 Remove and discard the foil from the baking sheet and put the skewers on it as they come off the grill. Serve with mint, cilantro, and yogurt chutney and lemon pickle.

NOTE: *If you come up short on the amount called for, double the lime zest and add an extra tablespoon of lime juice to the recipe.*

GRILLED CASHEW CARDAMOM LAMB CHOPS

SERVES 4 ✦ This white marinade is extra creamy thanks to the cashew paste you make as a foundation for it. Mustard oil adds tang that complements lamb well, especially when paired, as it is here, with mace and cardamom, aromatics that lend a hint of sweetness.

It is preferable to have the chops frenched by the butcher, meaning that they have been trimmed down to the loin eye and the ends of the bones have been scraped clean. This makes a nicer appearance and helps keep the bones from getting too charred on the grill.

Before you begin to make this dish, read On Tandoori-Style Grilling (page 138) carefully. You will need a kebab rack and ½-inch-wide flat kebab skewers.

For best results and optimal flavor, marinate the lamb the day before. (See Marinating, page 139.)

LAMB
12 rib lamb chops (2½ ounces each, ½ inch thick), trimmed of most fat and frenched (see headnote)
1 teaspoon fresh lemon juice
1 teaspoon Ginger-Garlic Paste (page 27)
½ teaspoon salt

MARINADE
2 cups whole-milk yogurt
2 tablespoons unsalted raw cashew pieces
2 tablespoons mustard oil
1 tablespoon fresh lemon juice

1½ tablespoons water
2 tablespoons Ginger-Garlic Paste (page 27)
½ teaspoon finely chopped fresh Thai green chili
1 teaspoon Mace-Cardamom Powder (page 23)
1½ teaspoons salt

Chopped mint, for garnish
Mint-Cilantro Chutney (page 257), for serving
Naan (page 247), for serving

1 SEASON THE LAMB: In a large bowl, coat the lamb chops with the lemon juice, ginger-garlic paste, and salt.

2 MAKE THE MARINADE: In a NutriBullet or small blender, puree ¼ cup of the yogurt, the cashews, mustard oil, lemon juice, and water until smooth. Transfer to a bowl and whisk in the remaining 1¾ cups yogurt, the ginger-garlic paste, green chili, mace-cardamom powder, and salt. Add the chops to the marinade and coat

them well. Cover and marinate in the refrigerator for at least 4 hours, but preferably overnight.

3 Line a baking sheet with foil. Thread two chops on a ½-inch-wide kebab skewer by running it through the middle of the length of the loin eye parallel to the rib. The chops should be very close to one another, but not touching. Only two will fit on a skewer. Repeat with the five remaining skewers and ten chops. Place the kebabs on the baking sheet. Dab the chops with marinade on both sides.

4 Prepare a grill, preferably with charcoal, for direct-heat grilling. (See Note, page 142.) Center a kebab rack on the grill directly over the hot part of the grill. (If you don't have a kebab rack, you can jury-rig one; see page 138.)

5 Place the skewers on the rack so that the lamb is above the coals but not touching the grate. Make sure you can rotate the skewers 360 degrees without the chops knocking into one another. You will have to cook in batches.

6 When you start to see small spots of char on the underside of a skewer, turn it over to let the other side char. If a skewer is charring too quickly, trade places with one that isn't. One note of caution: The fat in the marinade can cause flare-ups when it drips onto the fire—another good reason to pay attention and move the skewers around.

7 The lamb is done when the flesh feels firm on the outside but still a little soft on the inside when you pinch it between your thumb and forefinger. Total cooking time should be 8 to 10 minutes for medium. It will vary depending on your grill and fire, so always keep your eye on the skewers.

8 Remove and discard the foil from the baking sheet and put the skewers on it as they come off the grill. Garnish with chopped mint and serve with mint-cilantro chutney and naan.

Pan-Seared Red Snapper with Shrimp Balchão (page 159)

7

FISH AND SEAFOOD ENTRÉES

The Indian coast is so vast that it makes perfect sense that fish and seafood are so important to our cuisine. Along the western coast, from Mumbai down to Kerala, saltwater fish, such as tuna, mackerel, and pomfret, are abundant whereas in Northeastern India, such as West Bengal and Assam, freshwater fish, such as ilish, koi, and *bhetki*, which is like barramundi, are preferred. We've adapted recipes at Rasika to take advantage of the abundance we have available to us, such as black cod, red snapper, and trout.

MARIO VENTURA

Mario Ventura's first restaurant job was as a dishwasher at The Bombay Club in 1998. The chef at that time, Ramesh Kaundal, saw promise in him and started teaching him how to cook. It didn't take him long to rise up through the ranks. Within a year, he was dividing his time between The Bombay Club and another restaurant of mine, 701, working on the sauté station with then chef Trent Conry.

In the months before Rasika opened in 2005, Vikram worked on the dishes for the first menu out of The Bombay Club kitchen. He saw how good Mario was and asked if he could be on the Rasika team.

Thanks to Ramesh, Mario already had a good foundation. He started working at Rasika as a junior sous-chef and Vikram trained him on the curries. It turned out he had a natural palate and a real understanding of Indian cooking—we call him Indian Mario. Now he is the sous-chef of Rasika Penn Quarter. He trains the line cooks and is an expert in every station—curries, tandoori, chaats, bread—you name it. He is the backbone of the kitchen and plays a vital role at Rasika.

—Ashok

PAN-SEARED RED SNAPPER WITH SHRIMP BALCHÃO

SERVES 6 ❖ This dish is a riff on a classic Goan dish: stuffed pomfret, a fish that is abundant and loved there. (It's as close to Dover sole as you can get.) Cooks open the fish down the center between the tail and the head, bone it, and fill the pockets with shrimp stuffing. Then they marinate the pomfret in peri-peri masala and pan-fry it whole.

On the Rasika menu, we call the dish Snapper Rechad. *Rechad* comes from the Portuguese word *recheado,* which means "stuffed." Rechad masala, a paste made with red chili peppers, vinegar, garlic, and spices, is used as the spice base for fish and seafood stuffings. For our Red Snapper Rechad, we top the fish with shrimp *balchão* instead of stuffing it.

The recipe calls for peri-peri paste, made with Kashmiri chili peppers and malt vinegar, and a masala made from that paste—balchão masala. It is quite bold in its sweet, sour, and fiery profile.

To make putting together this dish fast and easy, you can prepare both the peri-peri paste and the balchão masala days, even weeks, in advance. The peri-peri paste recipe makes 1 cup, so freeze 2 tablespoons of it in one container (that's to marinate the snapper) and the rest of it (1 cup minus 2 tablespoons) in another for the masala. The balchão masala recipe yields 2½ cups, but you only need 1½ cups for this recipe. Freeze it in 2 containers (1½ cups and 1 cup) and use the 1-cup batch for another dish one day.

6 skin-on red snapper fillets (5 ounces each), pin bones removed
½ teaspoon ground turmeric
2 tablespoons malt vinegar
2¼ teaspoons salt
2 tablespoons Peri-Peri Paste (page 29)

3 tablespoons canola oil
1½ cups Balchão Masala (page 30)
1 pound peeled baby shrimp (or larger shrimp cut into small pieces)
Chopped cilantro, for garnish
Plain Basmati Rice (page 217), for serving

1 In a large bowl, coat the fish fillets with the turmeric, vinegar, 2 teaspoons of the salt, and the peri-peri paste. Cover and refrigerate for 30 minutes.

2 Preheat the oven to 450°F. In a large ovenproof skillet, heat the oil over medium-high heat until it shimmers. Place the red snapper fillets in the pan skin side down.

After 1 minute, flip the fillets over and put the pan in the oven. Bake until the fish is firm around the edges and set, but soft like custard when you poke the center with your finger, about 10 minutes.

3 Meanwhile, in a large skillet, bring the balchão masala to a simmer over medium-high heat. Add the shrimp and remaining ¼ teaspoon salt and cook, stirring occasionally, until the shrimp are cooked through, about 4 minutes.

4 When the fish is done, place each fillet skin side down on a warm plate and spoon the shrimp balchão over them. Garnish with chopped cilantro and serve with basmati rice.

Lobster Moilee (opposite)

LOBSTER MOILEE

SERVES 4 ✽ This dish is a curry from the southwestern state of Kerala, part of the Malabar Coast. Coconuts and fresh seafood are abundant there and find their way into many dishes, as do curry leaves.

This is an easy and quick dish to prepare à la minute, but you could make the sauce (Step 2) a day ahead, and then bring it to a boil before performing Step 3 the next day. We use Maine lobster tails for moilee at Rasika, but you could make the stew with any shellfish or fish or combination of them. At Sunday brunch we serve seafood stew made this way.

Four 8-ounce lobster tails (or thawed frozen tails)
2 tablespoons coconut oil
1 small (6-ounce) yellow onion, halved and thinly sliced
1 teaspoon Ginger-Garlic Paste (page 27)
10 (1½-inch) fresh curry leaves (more if smaller)
1½ cups finely chopped tomatoes

½ teaspoon ground turmeric
1-inch piece fresh ginger, cut into very thin julienne strips
2 medium fresh Thai green chilies, very thinly sliced on an angle
3 cups unsweetened coconut milk
1 tablespoon salt
Plain Basmati Rice (page 217) or Lemon Cashew Rice (page 224), for serving

1 Use sharp kitchen shears to cut the shell of the top side of each lobster tail down the middle, starting at the thick end and going all the way to the tail. Pry the shells open and extract the tail meat from them in one piece. Slice the tail meat in half lengthwise (remove any veins if there are any), then crosswise into 1-inch pieces.

2 In a large saucepan, heat the coconut oil over medium-high heat until it shimmers. Add the onion and cook, stirring occasionally, until soft and just beginning to brown, about 5 minutes. Stir in the ginger-garlic paste and cook for 30 seconds. Add the curry leaves, tomatoes, turmeric, ginger, and green chilies. Cook, stirring occasionally, until all of the liquid has evaporated from the tomatoes and they have disintegrated completely, about 3 minutes. Stir in the coconut milk. Bring the sauce to a boil.

3 Add the salt and lobster pieces and cook, stirring occasionally, until the lobster is cooked through, about 6 minutes. Serve hot with rice.

BENGALI SHRIMP CURRY

SERVES 4 ✿   I learned how to make this dish when I worked at Bombay Brasserie in London in the nineties. The chef was Udit Sarkhel, now deceased, who was from West Bengal in Northeastern India, noted for its freshwater shrimp and fish curries. You often find that this curry includes vegetables such as cauliflower and eggplant.

This dish incorporates the *panch phoron* masala popular in that region, a blend of mustard seeds, nigella seeds, fennel seeds, cumin seeds, and fenugreek seeds known as Bengali five-spice. It calls for frying the nigella seeds in mustard oil, which you must heat to the smoking point and let cool slightly before adding the seeds. This removes the oil's caustic property and brings its pungency forward.

You can make the sauce a day or two ahead through Step 4, then bring it to a boil and finish the dish.

2 cups diced yellow onions
2 cups diced tomatoes
2 cups water
2 teaspoons fennel seeds
1 teaspoon cumin seeds
2 teaspoons black or brown mustard seeds
½ teaspoon fenugreek seeds
2 tablespoons mustard oil
½ teaspoon nigella seeds
1 tablespoon Ginger-Garlic Paste (page 27)

2 medium fresh Thai green chilies, halved lengthwise
½ teaspoon ground turmeric
½ teaspoon deggi mirch
1 teaspoon ground coriander
1½ pounds (U16 to U20) shrimp, peeled and deveined, tails removed
1 teaspoon salt
2 tablespoons fresh lemon juice
2 tablespoons cilantro leaves
Plain Basmati Rice (page 217) and Naan (page 247), for serving

1 In a medium saucepan, combine the onions, tomatoes, and water and bring to a boil over high heat. Reduce the heat to medium and cook until the tomatoes and onions are soft, 10 to 12 minutes. Transfer to a blender and puree until smooth, starting on low speed and slowly increasing to high speed to allow the steam to escape.

2 In a spice grinder, grind the fennel seeds, cumin seeds, mustard seeds, and fenugreek seeds into a powder.

3 In a large skillet heat the mustard oil over medium-high heat, until it smokes. Remove from the heat and cool for several minutes. Return the pan to medium heat and add the nigella seeds, letting them crackle. Stir in the ginger-garlic paste and cook for 1 minute. Add the green chilies, then the tomato-onion puree.

4 Bring the mixture to a boil and stir in the turmeric, deggi mirch, and coriander. Cook for several minutes, stirring occasionally. Add the ground fennel/cumin/mustard/fenugreek powder.

5 Stir in the shrimp and salt. Cover the pan and cook until the shrimp are almost completely cooked, about 5 minutes. Add the lemon juice and cilantro. Serve hot with basmati rice and naan.

SEARED RAINBOW TROUT MALABAR

SERVES 4 ⚙ On the Malabar Coast in Kerala, people would use kingfish, mackerel, or pomfret for this recipe rather than rainbow trout. We like rainbow trout at Rasika because it's such a popular fish in the States. This sauce strikes a balance of sweet, salty, pungent, and sour that goes well with most fish and seafood.

It is best to use a nonstick pan for this preparation. You can use a well-seasoned skillet, but you run the risk of having the trout's skin stick and having to pry it off the bottom of the pan with a spatula. It won't affect the flavor, but the presentation will suffer.

You can make the sauce (Steps 3 and 4) the day before or earlier in the day and reheat it, but you might need to add a little water to it. You want the sauce to be the texture of crème anglaise—it should coat the back of a spoon thinly.

FISH
4 whole boned rainbow trout (10 ounces each), fins trimmed, head and tail intact
½ teaspoon ground turmeric
2 teaspoons salt
2 teaspoons Ginger-Garlic Paste (page 27)
2 tablespoons fresh lemon juice

SAUCE
1 tablespoon fennel seeds
10 whole cloves
1-inch cinnamon stick, broken into pieces
2 tablespoons coconut oil
1 teaspoon black or brown mustard seeds
1 cup finely chopped yellow onion

2 teaspoons Ginger-Garlic Paste (page 27)
½ teaspoon ground turmeric
1 teaspoon finely chopped fresh Thai green chili
10 (1½-inch) fresh curry leaves (more if smaller), cut into very thin strips
One 13½-ounce can unsweetened coconut milk
2 teaspoons malt vinegar
2 tablespoons Tamarind Pulp (page 24)
2 teaspoons salt
¼ cup water

6 tablespoons canola oil
Chopped cilantro or sprigs, for garnish
Lemon Cashew Rice (page 224), for serving

1 PREP THE FISH: To allow the marinade to seep in, cut three evenly spaced diagonal slits (½ inch deep) into the skin sides of all the trout. Transfer them to a large bowl and coat them with the turmeric, salt, ginger-garlic paste, and lemon juice. Cover and refrigerate while you make the sauce.

2 Preheat the oven to 425°F.

3 MAKE THE SAUCE: In a spice grinder, grind the fennel seeds, cloves, and cinnamon stick into a fine powder.

4 In a heavy-bottomed pot or Dutch oven, heat the coconut oil over medium heat until it shimmers. Add the mustard seeds and let them crackle. Add the onion and cook, stirring occasionally, until it just starts to brown, about 7 minutes. Add the the ginger-garlic paste and cook for 30 seconds. Add the turmeric, green chili, and curry leaves. Cook for 30 seconds. Add the coconut milk and bring to a boil. Add the malt vinegar, tamarind pulp, ground fennel/clove/cinnamon powder, salt, and water and bring to a boil. Remove from the heat.

5 Have ready a large baking sheet greased with cooking spray. In a large ovenproof nonstick skillet, heat 3 tablespoons of the canola oil over medium-high heat until it smokes. Place two trout in the pan (each closed, not splayed open) and sear on each side for 3 minutes. Transfer the fish to the baking sheet. Wipe out the skillet with a wad of paper towels and repeat the process for the remaining trout, using the 3 remaining tablespoons of oil. Once seared, transfer the fish to the baking sheet with the first two.

6 Bake the fish for 5 minutes to finish cooking them through. While they are in the oven, reheat the sauce.

7 To serve, transfer the trout to a serving platter or dinner plates and spoon some sauce over them. Garnish with cilantro and serve hot with lemon cashew rice, offering the remaining sauce on the side.

HONEY-CHILI TUNA WITH MANGO SALSA

SERVES 4 ❋ This seared tuna dish is a breeze to make and is very light—a great summertime offering, especially with the colorful and tart but sweet mango salsa with a bit of a bite.

Make sure to get the oil in the sauté pan smoking hot so that the tuna sears quickly, taking on a nice brown color on the first side. It doesn't need to brown on the other side and it won't, because there will be too much liquid in the pan. That's okay—that's the side you will serve down. The idea here is to just have a thin white line of doneness on each side and for most of the tuna's center to be a lovely medium-rare.

SALSA

¾ cup canned Alphonso mango pulp, such as Ratnā or Deep brand
¼ cup finely chopped red onion
1 tablespoon finely chopped red bell pepper
1 tablespoon finely chopped cilantro
½ teaspoon finely chopped fresh Thai green chili
2 teaspoons fresh lemon juice
½ teaspoon salt

TUNA

1½ pounds tuna
¼ cup honey
2 teaspoons red chili flakes
1 teaspoon Ginger-Garlic Paste (page 27)
2 tablespoons fresh lemon juice
1 teaspoon salt
¼ cup canola oil

Chopped cilantro, for garnish

1 MAKE THE SALSA: In a small bowl, combine the mango pulp, red onion, bell pepper, cilantro, green chili, lemon juice, and salt. Cover and refrigerate.

2 PREPARE THE TUNA: Cut the piece of tuna into 12 fairly uniform pieces that are ½ inch thick and weigh roughly 2 ounces each. (This may take a little finesse since the piece of tuna you purchase may be larger at one end than the other, for instance.)

3 In a large bowl, coat the tuna slices well with the honey, chili flakes, ginger-garlic paste, lemon juice, and salt. Cover and refrigerate for 30 minutes.

4 In a large skillet, heat the oil over medium-high heat until it smokes. Place the tuna slices in the pan, then turn them over in the same order you put them in, and remove them in that same order.

5 To serve, overlap three pieces of tuna down the center of a dinner plate and spoon ¼ cup salsa over them. Garnish with chopped cilantro.

BLACK COD WITH HONEY AND DILL

SERVES 4 ✿ I made this dish at Bombay Brasserie in London before coming to the States to work at Rasika, where it really made its name. It is so popular that I couldn't take it off the menu even if I wanted to.

What really makes it distinctive, I think, is the vinegar bath the cod gets before it's marinated. That imbues the fish with a flavor foundation deep into its flesh. This dish is perfect for entertaining because you can, and should, marinate the fish the day before. (See Marinating, page 139.) You can have the fish ready to go on a baking sheet and then just pop it in the oven once the guests have arrived.

COD

Four 5-ounce square chunks of black cod, skin on, at least 1 inch thick
1 cup red wine vinegar
8 whole star anise
2 teaspoons fennel seeds
2 teaspoons Ginger-Garlic Paste (page 27)
1 tablespoon salt

MARINADE

¾ cup (1½ ounces) finely shredded mild white cheddar cheese
¼ cup whole-milk yogurt
½ cup heavy cream
1 teaspoon Ginger-Garlic Paste (page 27)
2 tablespoons honey
½ teaspoon deggi mirch
1½ tablespoons chopped fresh dill fronds
½ teaspoon salt

Peanut Quinoa (page 222) or Rice Vermicelli with Dill and Green Chilies (page 219), for serving

1 SEASON THE COD: In a large bowl, combine the cod, vinegar, star anise, fennel seeds, ginger-garlic paste, and salt. Refrigerate for 30 minutes.

2 MAKE THE MARINADE: In a large bowl, whisk the cheddar, yogurt, cream, ginger-garlic paste, honey, deggi mirch, dill, and salt until thick and fluffy.

3 Transfer the cod, along with the star anise and whatever fennel seeds are attached, to the marinade and coat the pieces well. Cover and marinate in the refrigerator for at least 4 hours, but preferably overnight. (Discard the vinegar.)

4 Preheat the oven to 450°F. Line a small baking sheet with foil and place the cod fillets on it, skin side down. Top each one with a star anise. It's fine that there is a lot of marinade on the fish. Bake until the fish is browned on the edges and feels set but soft, like custard, when you poke it with your finger, 15 to 17 minutes.

5 Serve with peanut quinoa or rice vermicelli.

GOAN HALIBUT CURRY

SERVES 4 ✿ In Goa, this dish is a staple—people have a coconut-based fish curry like this one frequently, using whatever the fresh catch is, such as mackerel, shrimp, and *surmai,* also known as kingfish. They also may add kokum to it, a fruit indigenous to India that is dried and added to dishes for its sweet and sour notes and as a cooling agent.

The sauce should be a nice bright orange from the Kashmiri chili paste. You can make this curry up to 2 days ahead (Steps 1 and 3), then, when you're ready to serve it, marinate the fish (Step 2) for 15 minutes, bring the sauce to a boil, and proceed with Step 4.

CURRY BASE

1½ cups grated coconut, fresh or frozen
3 tablespoons Ginger-Garlic Paste
   (page 27)
¾ teaspoon ground turmeric
3 tablespoons coriander seeds
2¼ teaspoons cumin seeds
1 teaspoon black peppercorns
9 tablespoons Kashmiri Chili Paste
   (page 28)
3 cups water

FISH

1½ pounds halibut fillet, about 2 inches
   thick, cut into 12 (1 x 2-inch) pieces
½ teaspoon ground turmeric
3 teaspoons salt
2 tablespoons fresh lemon juice
2 tablespoons canola oil
½ medium yellow onion, halved and
   thinly sliced
2 fresh Thai green chilies, halved
   lengthwise
½ cup Tamarind Pulp (page 24)

Plain Basmati Rice (page 217),
   for serving

1 MAKE THE CURRY BASE: In a blender, combine the coconut, ginger-garlic paste, turmeric, coriander seeds, cumin seeds, peppercorns, Kashmiri chili paste, and 1½ cups of the water and puree on high for 5 minutes. Pass through a sieve into a bowl, scraping and pressing on the solids with a rubber spatula until mostly what is left is coconut pulp. Return the solids to the blender with the remaining 1½ cups water. Blend on high for another 5 minutes. Strain as before into the bowl. Discard the solids. You will have about 3 cups of liquid. If you have a little more or less, that's fine.

Among the curries, kormas, and other specialties in this chapter, we include a smoked rack of pork that is an interpretation of a vindaloo dish we sometimes have on the Rasika menu.

Many people think of vindaloo as just a spicy sauce, but don't know that it originates with Columbus, who, when he returned to Spain from the Americas, introduced the European continent to chili peppers, which are native to South America. Once Portuguese explorer Vasco da Gama discovered the ocean route to India at the end of the fifteenth century, Spanish and Portuguese traders began to introduce chili peppers to Asia, where they proliferated.

The Portuguese conquered Goa, on India's west coast, in the sixteenth century, and turned it into the base of operations for its spice trade. They had a tremendous influence on Indian food as we know it today. In addition to chili peppers, the Portuguese introduced such items as sweet potatoes, tomatoes, potatoes, cashews, pineapples, and carrots.

The word *vindaloo* derives from the Portuguese *carne de vinha d'alhos*, which means, literally, "meat made with garlic wine." They used a red-chili-and-vinegar-based paste not only as flavoring, but also as a natural preservative—they pickled food with it. That is the foundation for what we know as the Goan specialty vindaloo today.

8

POULTRY, GAME, AND
MEAT ENTRÉES

Lamb Shank Raan-E-Rasika (page 205)

2 MARINATE THE FISH: In a medium bowl, coat the fish with the turmeric, 1 teaspoon of the salt, and the lemon juice. Cover and refrigerate while you finish the curry.

3 In a large saucepan, heat the oil over medium-high heat until it shimmers. Add the onion and green chilies and cook, stirring occasionally, until the onion is translucent and just beginning to brown, about 4 minutes. Stir in the tamarind pulp and curry base and bring to a boil. Cook, stirring occasionally, for 5 minutes.

4 Stir in the fish and remaining 2 teaspoons salt. Reduce the heat to medium, cover, and cook until the fish is cooked through, about 10 minutes. Serve hot with rice.

CHICKEN TIKKA MASALA

SERVES 4 ⊛ *Tikka* are pieces of meat cooked on skewers and *masala* is the spiced tomato and cream sauce in which they are served.

There are a lot of theories about the derivation of this dish. Some people think that it was created in New Delhi. In England, Brits claim it. The British Foreign Secretary in 2001 called it the British national dish.

Many new chefs don't want it on the menu because they think it is too pedestrian, but we don't agree. The sauce, made with tomatoes, cream, butter, and fenugreek, is rich and appealing. Full of calories, yes, but so very good. —ASHOK

For best results and optimal flavor, marinate the chicken the day before. (See Marinating, page 139.) You can make the masala (Step 3) the day before, then bring it to a simmer and finish the dish (Step 4) when ready to serve. —VIKRAM

CHICKEN

1 cup whole-milk yogurt
¼ cup Kashmiri Chili Paste (page 28)
1 tablespoon Ginger-Garlic Paste (page 27)
1 teaspoon garam masala
¼ teaspoon ground turmeric
2 tablespoons fresh lemon juice
2 tablespoons mustard oil
2 teaspoons salt
2 pounds boneless, skinless chicken breast and/or thigh, cut into 2-inch pieces

MASALA

1¼ pounds tomatoes, coarsely chopped
1 tablespoon canola oil
6 tablespoons unsalted butter
½ teaspoon cumin seeds
2 cups finely chopped yellow onions

2 teaspoons Ginger-Garlic Paste (page 27)
1 teaspoon deggi mirch
1 tablespoon finely chopped fresh ginger
1 teaspoon finely chopped fresh Thai green chili
¼ cup tomato paste

FOR FINISHING

2 cups heavy cream
2 teaspoons fenugreek leaf powder*
1 teaspoon salt
½ green bell pepper, diced
½ red bell pepper, diced

Chopped cilantro, for garnish
Jeera or Saffron Pulao (page 220), for serving
Naan (page 247) or Mint Paratha (page 242), for serving

*To make fenugreek leaf powder, grind dried fenugreek leaves in a spice grinder, using enough so that the blades can pulverize them into a fine powder.

1 MARINATE THE CHICKEN: In a large bowl, whisk together the yogurt, Kashmiri chili paste, ginger-garlic paste, garam masala, turmeric, lemon juice, mustard oil, and salt. Add the chicken and coat the pieces well. Cover and refrigerate for at least 4 hours, but preferably overnight.

2 Preheat the oven to 425°F. Spread the chicken on a baking sheet in an even layer and bake until cooked through, 18 to 20 minutes. When the chicken is cool enough to handle, halve all the pieces.

3 MAKE THE MASALA: Puree the tomatoes in a food processor. In a large pot or Dutch oven, heat the canola oil and butter over medium-high heat until they shimmer. Add the cumin seeds and let them crackle. Add the onions and cook, stirring constantly, until dark brown, about 12 minutes. (The butter will smell nutty.) Stir in the ginger-garlic paste and cook for 30 seconds. Add the pureed tomatoes and deggi mirch and cook for 15 minutes, until most of the tomatoes' liquid has evaporated. Reduce the heat to medium and add the ginger, green chili, and tomato paste. Cook for 2 minutes.

4 FINISH THE DISH: Stir the cream, fenugreek leaf powder, salt, cooked chicken, and bell peppers into the masala. Cover and simmer for 5 minutes so the flavors meld. Garnish with chopped cilantro. Serve hot with *pulao* and naan or paratha.

MOHAMED ISSAK QURESHI

In India's restaurant and hotel kitchens, the tandoor and curry chefs are greatly valued and even revered because they bring with them treasured recipes handed down from generation to generation. Mohamed Issak Qureshi is a master curry chef who started cooking when he was a child in Lucknow, the epicenter of Mughlai cuisine. He worked in hotels and restaurants all over the world, including Mumbai, London, Berlin, Johannesburg, and Dubai and came to Rasika Penn Quarter in 2008 with a repertoire of curries, Kashmiri kormas, and other specialties. He helps Vikram create recipes by sharing his knowledge of Indian curries and cooking and then executes Vikram's vision perfectly.

—Ashok

CHICKEN GREEN MASALA

SERVES 4 ⚙ This is a riff on a Goan dish called chicken *cafreal,* which was brought to Western India by the Portuguese from their African colonies. (*Cafreal* is a Portuguese word meaning "in the African way.") In the traditional recipe, chicken, whole or cut into bone-in pieces, is marinated in spicy green masala paste and then roasted. We decided to use the same ingredients and flavors, but to cut the chicken into bite-size, boneless pieces. This makes a much cleaner presentation and provides plenty of sauce for rice and bread. Despite its spiciness, or maybe because of it, Chicken Green Masala is one of the most popular dishes at Rasika.

Cooking the chicken uncovered rather than covered after the cilantro puree is added helps maintain its brightness.

For optimal flavor, make this dish many hours in advance, preferably the day before, and reheat it, although the sauce's color will become darker.

CILANTRO PUREE
4 cups coarsely chopped cilantro, including stems
1 cup packed mint leaves
10 medium fresh Thai green chilies, coarsely chopped
10 garlic cloves, coarsely chopped
½ teaspoon ground turmeric
½ cup fresh lemon juice
1 cup water

CHICKEN
1 tablespoon green cardamom pods
1 teaspoon whole cloves
2-inch cinnamon stick, crushed
2 tablespoons canola oil
1 cup finely chopped yellow onion
2 pounds boneless, skinless chicken (breast and/or thigh), cut into 1-inch cubes
½ teaspoon ground turmeric
1½ teaspoons salt
1 cup unsweetened coconut milk

Cucumber Raita (page 269), for serving
Plain Basmati Rice (page 217) and Naan (page 247), for serving

1 MAKE THE CILANTRO PUREE: In a blender, combine the cilantro, mint, green chilies, garlic, turmeric, lemon juice, and water and blend on high speed to make a smooth puree. Run the blender for several minutes; the finer and smoother the puree, the better.

2 MAKE THE CHICKEN: In a spice grinder, grind the cardamom pods, cloves, and cinnamon stick into a powder.

3 In a heavy-bottomed pot or Dutch oven, heat the oil over medium-high heat until it shimmers. Sauté the onion, stirring frequently, until soft but not browned, about 3 minutes. Stir in the chicken, turmeric, and salt. Cover the pot and parcook the chicken for 5 minutes, stirring occasionally. Stir in the cilantro puree, coconut milk, and cardamom/clove/cinnamon powder and bring to a boil. Cook uncovered for 5 minutes, stirring occasionally, until the chicken is cooked through.

4 Serve with cucumber raita, rice, and naan.

CHICKEN PISTA KORMA

SERVES 4 ❃ The rich yogurt-and-nut-based kormas on our menus are always in demand for those who prefer milder dishes. This version is made with pistachio nuts, which lend a pleasant green hue.

For optimal flavor, make this dish many hours in advance, preferably the day before, and reheat it.

2 cups diced yellow onions
2 cups water
1 cup whole-milk yogurt
1 cup raw pistachios, preferably skinned (see Note)
½ small green bell pepper, coarsely chopped (about ½ cup)
2 fresh Thai green chilies, coarsely chopped
½ cup coarsely chopped cilantro
2 tablespoons canola oil
1 tablespoon Ginger-Garlic Paste (page 27)

⅛ teaspoon ground turmeric
2 tablespoons unsalted butter
½ cup heavy cream
2 pounds boneless, skinless chicken (breast and thigh), cut into 2-inch pieces
2½ teaspoons salt
1 teaspoon ground cardamom, preferably freshly ground*
Chopped pistachios, for garnish
Chopped cilantro, for garnish (optional)

*Make ground cardamom by grinding whole green cardamom pods into powder in a spice grinder.

1 In a medium saucepan, combine the onions and 1 cup of the water. Cover the pan and bring to a boil over medium-high heat. Cook until the onions are soft, about 10 minutes. Transfer the onions to a blender with the cooking liquid and puree until smooth. Pour the puree into a bowl and whisk in the yogurt.

2 In the blender, combine the pistachios, bell pepper, green chilies, cilantro, and remaining 1 cup water and blend until smooth.

3 In a large saucepan, heat the oil over medium-high heat until it shimmers. Stir in the ginger-garlic paste and cook for 30 seconds. Stir in the onion/yogurt mixture and cook, stirring constantly so the sauce doesn't break. Once it comes to a boil, after about 5 minutes, stir in the turmeric and pistachio puree. Cook for 5 minutes, stirring constantly, then reduce the heat to medium. Stir in the butter and cream.

4 Add the chicken, salt, and cardamom and cook, stirring occasionally, until the chicken is cooked through, about 15 minutes. Garnish with chopped pistachios and chopped cilantro, if desired.

NOTE: *To skin pistachios, pour boiling water over them and let them sit for 2 minutes. Drain and rub them vigorously in a kitchen towel until all the skins have come off.*

RASIKA

HOME-STYLE CHICKEN CURRY (TARIWALA MURGH)

SERVES 6 ✿ This simple dish showcases an elemental component of many basic curries: a tomato masala flavored with whole-spice garam masala, ground spices, ginger, and deeply browned onions and garlic. Every household in India serves it, but no two make it the same way. Everyone has their own particular way of preparing it, usually passed down through the family. And everyone says theirs is the best.

You can make this curry with lamb, bumping up the cooking time in Step 4 to 35 to 40 minutes, until the lamb is tender.

Not only can this curry be made a day or two ahead of time, but it should be. At the very least, it is best to make it in the morning and then reheat when you are ready to serve. The extra time gives all of the flavors a chance to soak into the chicken and deepens the sauce.

This curry also freezes well.

RASIKA

MASALA
1 pound tomatoes, quartered
2 cups water
6 tablespoons canola oil
½ teaspoon cumin seeds
4 green cardamom pods
4 whole cloves
1-inch cinnamon stick
2 large dried Indian bay leaves
1 large yellow onion, halved and thinly
     sliced
1 tablespoon finely chopped garlic
2 tablespoons Ginger-Garlic Paste
     (page 27)
1 teaspoon ground turmeric
1 teaspoon deggi mirch
1 tablespoon ground coriander

CHICKEN
2 pounds boneless, skinless chicken
     (breast and/or thigh), cut into 2-inch
     cubes
2 tablespoons finely chopped fresh
     ginger
1 tablespoon salt
1 cup hot water
2 tablespoons fresh lemon juice
2 teaspoons garam masala

Plain Basmati Rice (page 217) and
     Naan (page 247), for serving

1 MAKE THE MASALA: In a blender, liquefy the tomatoes and water.

2 In a large heavy-bottomed pot or Dutch oven, heat the oil over medium-high heat until it shimmers. Stir in the cumin seeds, cardamom pods, cloves, cinnamon stick, and bay leaves and let the cumin crackle. Add the onion and cook, stirring occasionally, for 10 minutes. Add the chopped garlic and continue to cook and stir until the onions and garlic are well browned, about 5 minutes. Add the ginger-garlic paste and cook for 30 seconds.

3 Stir in the pureed tomatoes and bring to a boil. Add the turmeric, deggi mirch, and coriander and cook for 15 minutes, stirring occasionally. The masala will be quite thick.

4 COOK THE CHICKEN: Add the chicken, ginger, and salt. Cover the pot and cook for 5 minutes, stirring occasionally. Add the hot water, lemon juice, and garam masala. Reduce the heat to medium, cover, and cook, stirring occasionally, for 10 minutes. Serve hot with rice and naan.

CHICKEN MAKHANI (BUTTER CHICKEN)

SERVES 6 ❁ *Makhan* in Hindi means "butter," hence its butter chicken appellation. The major difference between this dish and chicken tikka masala is that the latter is made with a lot of onions and the texture is chunkier and thicker.

For best results and optimal flavor, marinate the chicken the day before. (See Marinating, page 139.) You can make the makhani sauce a day or two ahead and bring it to a boil before adding the chicken.

1 cup whole-milk yogurt
¼ cup Kashmiri Chili Paste (page 28)
1 tablespoon Ginger-Garlic Paste
   (page 27)
1 teaspoon garam masala
¼ teaspoon ground turmeric
2 tablespoons fresh lemon juice
2 tablespoons mustard oil

2 teaspoons salt
2 pounds boneless, skinless chicken
   (breast and/or thigh), cut into 2-inch
   pieces
Makhani Sauce (page 34; see Note)
Jeera or Saffron Pulao (page 220) and
   Naan (page 247), for serving

1 In a large bowl, whisk together the yogurt, Kashmiri chili paste, ginger-garlic paste, garam masala, turmeric, lemon juice, mustard oil, and salt. Add the chicken and coat the pieces well. Cover and marinate in the refrigerator for at least 4 hours, but preferably overnight.

2 Preheat the oven to 425°F. Spread the chicken on a baking sheet in a single layer and bake until cooked through, 18 to 20 minutes. When it is cool enough to handle, halve all the pieces.

3 In a large saucepan, bring the makhani sauce to a boil over medium heat (see Note). Stir in the chicken and return the sauce to a boil. Add salt if necessary. Serve hot with *pulao* and naan.

NOTE: *If you are using makhani sauce that you have made ahead and frozen (which you would have done without adding the heavy cream), when you bring it to a boil as directed, add the ¾ cup heavy cream at the same time that you add the chicken.*

RASIKA

STUFFED SAFFRON AND ALMOND CHICKEN (MURGH MUSSALLAM)

SERVES 4 TO 6 ⚙ This royal festive dish, credited as having its origins in Lucknow, is a perfect special-occasion offering. For the impressive presentation, a whole chicken (*murgh musallam* means "whole chicken") spends the night in a yogurt, almond, and saffron marinade; gets stuffed with saffron *pulao* and a hard-boiled egg; and is roasted, swathed with a rich yogurt sauce, and decorated with quartered eggs and edible silver leaf.

There is no denying that this dish is a lot of work, so here's a strategy for making it easy to tackle:

- ⚬ SEVERAL DAYS OR EVEN WEEKS BEFORE: Make the Caramelized Onion Paste (page 26).
- ⚬ ONE OR TWO DAYS BEFORE: Make the marinade, the Saffron Pulao (page 220), and the Musallam spice mix. Make the sauce, Steps 8 and 9 only. Hard-boil (see Note) and peel the 3 eggs.
- ⚬ THE DAY BEFORE: Marinate the chicken.
- ⚬ DAY OF: Bake the chicken. Reheat the sauce and add the saffron and kewra water. Reheat the saffron pulao and finish the dish (Steps 11 and 12).

ALMOND PASTE
½ cup plus 2 tablespoons blanched
    sliced almonds
½ cup whole-milk yogurt

MARINADE
1¾ cups whole-milk yogurt
1 tablespoon Ginger-Garlic Paste
    (page 27)
½ teaspoon deggi mirch
½ teaspoon ground turmeric
½ teaspoon garam masala
2 tablespoons fresh lemon juice
¼ teaspoon saffron threads
2 teaspoons salt
2 tablespoons canola oil

CHICKEN
1 whole chicken (3½ pounds), skinned,
    wing tips and second wing joints
    removed
Saffron Pulao (page 220)
1 hard-boiled egg

MUSALLAM SPICE MIX
1-inch cinnamon stick, crushed
4 whole cloves
½ teaspoon black peppercorns
6 green cardamom pods
½ teaspoon white poppy seeds
1 teaspoon cumin seeds
3 tablespoons shredded unsweetened
    coconut
1 tablespoon charoli seeds

SAUCE
1¾ cups whole-milk yogurt
¼ cup Caramelized Onion Paste
   (page 26)
½ teaspoon deggi mirch
¼ teaspoon ground turmeric
1 teaspoon ground coriander
½ cup water
2 tablespoons canola oil

1 teaspoon Ginger-Garlic Paste
   (page 27)
¼ cup heavy cream
1½ teaspoons salt
¼ teaspoon saffron threads
½ teaspoon kewra water, such as Dabur
   brand

2 hard-boiled eggs, for serving
Naan (page 247), for serving

1 MAKE THE ALMOND PASTE: In a medium skillet, toast the almonds over medium heat, shaking the pan and tossing the nuts frequently, until golden brown, about 5 minutes. Transfer them to a bowl to cool.

2 Measure out 2 tablespoons of the toasted almonds and set aside for a garnish. In a NutriBullet or small blender, blend the remaining ½ cup almonds with the yogurt, shaking the canister or scraping down the sides a couple of times, until smooth. Refrigerate the toasted almond paste until ready to use.

3 MAKE THE MARINADE: In a large bowl, whisk together 3 tablespoons of the almond paste, the yogurt, ginger-garlic paste, deggi mirch, turmeric, garam masala, lemon juice, saffron, salt, and oil.

4 PREPARE THE CHICKEN: Splay the legs of the chicken open. Pop, but don't separate, the joint between the thigh and backbone on both sides. Cut three diagonal slits to the bone on the insides and outsides of the legs and thighs. Cut three evenly spaced diagonal slits into each breast half in a chevron pattern. The slits will allow the marinade to penetrate the flesh. (See photo, opposite.)

5 Place the chicken in the marinade and turn it to coat well on all sides. Cover and marinate in the refrigerator for at least 4 hours (breast side down is best), but preferably overnight.

6 Preheat the oven to 375°F. Line a rimmed baking sheet with foil. Remove the chicken from the marinade and place on the foil breast side up. (The legs will be splayed open and lying flat on the baking sheet.) Stuff ½ cup saffron pulao into the cavity, then 1 hard-boiled egg, then another ½ cup pulao. (Set aside the remaining rice to reheat and serve with the chicken.) Pour the chicken marinade all over the chicken. Roast for 1 hour.

7 MEANWHILE, MAKE THE MUSSALLAM SPICE MIX: In a medium skillet, toast the cinnamon stick, cloves, peppercorns, cardamom pods, poppy seeds, cumin seeds, coconut, and charoli seeds over medium heat, shaking the pan and tossing the spices frequently, until the coconut is golden brown, about 5 minutes. Grind the mixture in a spice grinder. (It will clump and be the texture of wet sand because of the oil in the coconut.)

8 MAKE THE SAUCE: In a medium bowl, whisk together the yogurt, caramelized onion paste, ¼ cup of the toasted almond paste, the deggi mirch, turmeric, coriander, and water.

9 In a medium saucepan, heat the oil over medium heat until it shimmers. Stir in the ginger-garlic paste (it may spatter) and cook for 30 seconds. Add the yogurt mixture and cook, stirring constantly, until it comes to a boil, about 7 minutes. Reduce the heat to medium-low and whisk in the musallam spice mix. Cook for another 10 minutes, stirring occasionally, to thicken the sauce. Add the cream and salt and bring to a simmer, about 3 minutes. Cook, stirring, for another 2 minutes.

10 Strain the sauce into another saucepan. Stir in the saffron and kewra water. Keep the sauce warm over very low heat. (Or set aside and reheat before serving.)

11 When the chicken is done, transfer it to a serving platter. Ladle some of the sauce over it to coat it. Quarter the two hard-boiled eggs lengthwise and place the wedges around the chicken. Garnish with the reserved toasted almonds.

12 Present the chicken whole and carve at the table, offering the remaining sauce on the side, along with the remaining saffron pulao (reheated in the microwave or oven) and naan.

NOTE: *To hard-boil the eggs, bring a small saucepan of water to a boil with 1 teaspoon vinegar. Add 3 eggs and boil for 8 minutes. Drain the eggs and rinse in cool water until cool enough to peel.*

ORANGE DUCK (NARANGI DUCK)

SERVES 4 ⚙ *Narangi* is "orange" in Hindi. I had the classic dish duck à l'orange in mind when I came up with this dish, pairing it with velvety korma sauce. At Rasika, we use mandarin orange puree from Boiron, a French company that specializes in high-quality fruit and vegetable purees. It only comes in 1-kilo containers, so in this recipe we suggest using fresh orange juice in its place. (You can buy Boiron purees at www.amazon.com.)

For precision, use a remote thermometer to guard against overcooking the duck.

You can make the Korma Sauce (page 32) called for in this recipe up to 3 days ahead.

SAUCE
2 tablespoons unsalted butter
1 teaspoon Ginger-Garlic Paste
(page 27)
¼ teaspoon deggi mirch
¼ teaspoon ground turmeric
1 cup Korma Sauce (page 32)
1 cup orange juice or mandarin orange
puree, such as Boiron brand
1 tablespoon tomato paste
½ cup heavy cream
½ teaspoon Mace-Cardamom Powder
(page 23)
1 teaspoon salt

DUCK
4 boneless, skinless duck breasts
(6 ounces each)
1 teaspoon salt
2 teaspoons Ginger-Garlic Paste
(page 27)
1 orange
2 tablespoons canola oil

Orange Pulao (page 221) and
Naan (page 247), for serving

1 MAKE THE SAUCE: In a small saucepan over medium heat, heat the butter until it melts. Add the ginger-garlic paste and cook for 30 seconds. Stir in the deggi mirch, ground turmeric, korma sauce, orange juice, tomato paste, and cream. Bring to a boil. Add the mace-cardamom powder and salt and cook for 5 minutes to thicken. Keep the sauce warm over very low heat.

2 Preheat the oven to 400°F.

3 MEANWHILE, PREP THE DUCK: Place the duck breasts in a medium bowl and coat with the salt and ginger-garlic paste.

4 Use a zester to pull off long, thin strands of zest from the orange and set aside for garnish. Use a serrated knife to slice off the ends of the orange and stand it on

a cutting board. Slice off its peel and pith, leaving as much of the fruit intact as possible. Cut between the membranes to separate the segments. Place them in a bowl and reserve.

5 In a medium ovenproof skillet, heat the oil over medium-high heat until it shimmers. Place the duck breasts in the pan and brown for 1 minute. Turn them over and brown for another minute.

6 Transfer the pan to the oven and roast the duck to 145°F for medium, about 5 minutes. Remove the pan from the oven and let the duck rest for 5 minutes.

7 To finish the dish, cut the breasts into ½-inch-thick crosswise slices and fan them on each of four dinner plates. Spoon some sauce over the meat, just enough for a light coating, and garnish with the reserved orange segments and orange zest strips.

8 Serve with *pulao* and naan and offer the remaining sauce on the side.

SMOKED RACK OF PORK VINDALOO

SERVES 6 TO 8 ⊙ This rack of pork—smoky, adobe red, caramelized from the grill, and majestic—makes a sensational presentation at a dinner party.

The base of the vindaloo sauce and the pork marinade is Peri-Peri Paste, named after fiery hot bird's eye chili peppers known as peri-peris. (I use dried Kashmiri chilies.) This gives the sauce heat and tang. Pearl onions add sweetness to help balance the heat. (Frozen onions work well and save a lot of time and effort, but feel free to use blanched fresh pearl onions.)

Optimally, you should make the vindaloo sauce (Step 4), which is also great for lamb and chicken dishes, at least a day in advance to mellow and deepen its flavors. You will need 2 cups (a double batch) of peri-peri paste: 5 tablespoons for the wet rub and the rest for the sauce. You can make the peri-peri paste well in advance.

Have the butcher trim the ends of the rack's bones of all fat and meat to expose them. (This is called "frenching.")

PORK

1 tablespoon Ginger-Garlic Paste (page 27)
5 tablespoons Peri-Peri Paste (page 29)
2 tablespoons canola oil
1 teaspoon salt
One 6-bone rack of pork (3½ to 4 pounds), trimmed to ¼ inch of fat on top and frenched
2 cups warm water
2 cups hickory chips

SAUCE

3 tablespoons canola oil
2 cups finely chopped yellow onions
¼ cup finely chopped garlic
1 cup plus 11 tablespoons Peri-Peri Paste (page 29)
2½ cups water
6 tablespoons Tamarind Pulp (page 24)
2 tablespoons malt vinegar
2½ teaspoons salt
2 teaspoons sugar
½ cup frozen pearl onions

Plain Basmati Rice (page 217) and Ladi Pao (page 252), for serving

1 PREP THE PORK: In a small bowl, mix together the ginger-garlic paste, peri-peri paste, oil, and salt. In a large bowl, coat the rack of pork on all sides with the mixture. Cover the bowl and refrigerate the loin for at least 12 hours, but preferably 24.

2 Prepare a charcoal grill for indirect grilling. Fill a chimney starter with charcoal and light it. Let it burn until the flames subside and a light layer of ash covers it, 20 to 25 minutes. Dump the coals in two mounds (or into two half-moon-shaped briquette baskets) on opposite sides of the grill. Place a drip pan filled with the warm water between the coals. Place 1 cup of the wood chips on top of each pile of coals. Put the grate on the grill.

3 Place the pork loin on the center of the grill, over the drip pan (not over the coals). Use a rubber spatula to scrape out any marinade left in the bowl and slather it over the pork. Close the grill lid and roast/smoke the pork until it reaches an internal temperature of 145°F, 70 to 80 minutes.

4 MEANWHILE, MAKE THE SAUCE: In a heavy-bottomed pot or Dutch oven, heat the oil over medium-high heat until it shimmers. Stir in the onions and garlic and cook, stirring occasionally, until lightly browned, about 10 minutes. Reduce the heat to medium and stir in the peri-peri paste, water, tamarind pulp, vinegar, salt, and sugar. Cook for 10 minutes, stirring occasionally. Remove from the heat.

5 Transfer the pork to a plate and loosely cover with foil. Let it rest for 15 minutes. While the pork is resting, finish the sauce. Bring it to a simmer over medium heat. Add the pearl onions and cook for 5 minutes.

6 Carve the roast into thick rib chops or remove the loin from the rack so you can carve it into smaller portions (to feed more guests) and serve the ribs along with it—they're the best part.

7 Serve the pork with the warm vindaloo sauce, rice, and *ladi pao*.

KERALA BISON

SERVES 4 ✣ A good indicator of trends comes in the form of requests that we get from our guests. I noticed that more and more of them were asking if we had any dishes with bison, which is leaner than beef. This dish is our interpretation of Kerala beef fry, in which pieces of beef are cooked separately in a pressure cooker and then stir-fried into a spicy masala. It is called a dry stir-fry, meaning the sauce with which the meat is cooked is more paste-like than liquid. We put the dish on the winter menu regularly because its heartiness is more suited to that time of year.

You can make the masala (Steps 1 through 4) a day ahead.

MASALA
2 pounds tomatoes, coarsely chopped
2 teaspoons fennel seeds
2 teaspoons black peppercorns
6 tablespoons canola oil
2 large yellow onions, halved and thinly sliced
2 tablespoons Ginger-Garlic Paste (page 27)
1 teaspoon ground turmeric
2 teaspoons deggi mirch
2 teaspoons ground coriander
4 medium fresh Thai green chilies, thinly sliced at an angle
10 (1½-inch) fresh curry leaves (more if smaller)
1 teaspoon garam masala
2 teaspoons salt
2 tablespoons fresh lemon juice

BISON
4 bison (or beef tenderloin) filets (6 ounces each), 2 inches thick
1 tablespoon Ginger-Garlic Paste (page 27)
¼ teaspoon ground turmeric
1 teaspoon deggi mirch
1 teaspoon salt
1 tablespoon fresh lemon juice
2 tablespoons canola oil

1 MAKE THE MASALA: Puree the tomatoes in a food processor. Set aside.

2 In a spice grinder, grind the fennel seeds and black peppercorns into a fine powder.

3 In a heavy-bottomed pot or Dutch oven, heat the oil over medium-high heat until it shimmers. Add the onions and cook, stirring occasionally, until dark brown, about 20 minutes.

4 Stir in the ginger-garlic paste and cook for 30 seconds. Add the reserved tomato puree, the turmeric, deggi mirch, and coriander. Cook, stirring occasionally, until most of the tomatoes' liquid has evaporated, about 20 minutes. Add the green chilies, curry leaves, fennel/pepper powder, garam masala, salt, and lemon juice. You will have a thick paste. Remove from the heat.

5 MEANWHILE, SEASON AND MARINATE THE BISON: In a medium bowl, coat the bison fillets with the ginger-garlic paste, turmeric, deggi mirch, salt, and lemon juice and let them sit for 15 minutes.

6 In a medium skillet, heat the oil over medium-high heat until it shimmers. Add the bison steaks to the pan and brown them for 3 minutes on each side for medium-rare. Remove from the heat and let the steaks rest in the pan for 10 minutes.

7 To serve, reheat the masala over medium heat while the steaks are resting. Cut the steaks into ½-inch-thick slices and transfer them to the sauce, stirring to coat all of them. Serve immediately.

LAMB WITH APRICOTS AND MATCHSTICK POTATOES (SALLI BOTI)

SERVES 4 ⚙ *Salli* means "sticks" and *boti* are cubes of meat. This dish could also be called *jardaloo salli boti,* which adds the Hindi word for apricots. The Parsi (*Parsi* is the Gujarati word for "Persian") community makes this dish on festive occasions, like weddings, or for their New Year celebrations. Zoroastrian Parsis celebrate the New Year (Nowruz) in July or August, according to the Shahenshahi calendar.

The boldness of the whole-spice and preground garam masalas in this recipe complements the gaminess of the lamb, which in turn is balanced by bursts of sweetness from the apricots. Apricots that have been treated with sulphur dioxide in the drying process retain their bright orange color and soft texture. That's what we use at Rasika. Apricots that haven't been treated are brown and chewier than treated apricots. You are welcome to use them, but the dish will not be as pretty.

At Rasika, I love to pile the matchstick potatoes high because it makes a dramatic effect, but feel free to use fewer of them if you want. (Parsis wouldn't even consider eating the dish without them.) It's a good idea to make the lamb curry the day before to make serving this dish a lot easier. Don't stir in the preground garam masala until after you've reheated it, just before serving.

LAMB
3 medium tomatoes, quartered
¼ cup canola oil
1 teaspoon cumin seeds
4 green cardamom pods
4 whole cloves
1-inch cinnamon stick
2 large dried Indian bay leaves
2 medium yellow onions, halved and
   thinly sliced
2 tablespoons Ginger-Garlic Paste
   (page 27)
½ teaspoon ground turmeric
1 teaspoon deggi mirch
1 tablespoon ground coriander
1 cup whole-milk yogurt
10 (1½-inch) fresh curry leaves
   (more if smaller)

2 pounds boneless leg of lamb, fat
   removed, cut into 1½-inch pieces
1½ cups water
4 teaspoons salt
½ cup (3 ounces) sulphurated dried whole
   apricots (see headnote)
2 tablespoons tomato paste
2 tablespoons malt vinegar
1 tablespoon sugar

POTATOES
3 medium russet (baking) potatoes
2 cups canola oil, for deep-frying
Salt

2 teaspoons garam masala
Jeera or Saffron Pulao (page 220),
   for serving

1 MAKE THE LAMB: Puree the tomatoes in a food processor. Set aside.

2 In a heavy-bottomed pot or Dutch oven, heat the oil over medium-high heat until it shimmers. Add the cumin seeds, cardamom pods, cloves, cinnamon stick, and bay leaves and let the cumin crackle. Add the onions and cook, stirring occasionally, until dark golden brown, 15 to 18 minutes.

3 Stir in the ginger-garlic paste and cook for 30 seconds. Add the reserved pureed tomatoes, the turmeric, deggi mirch, and coriander. Cook for 5 minutes, stirring occasionally, until most of the liquid from the tomatoes has evaporated. Stir in the yogurt and curry leaves and cook for 1 minute.

4 Stir in the lamb, water, and salt. Bring to a boil, cover, reduce the heat to medium, and cook for 20 minutes, stirring occasionally. Add the apricots, tomato paste, vinegar, and sugar. Cover the pot and cook until the lamb is tender, another 30 minutes.

5 MEANWHILE, FRY THE POTATOES: Have ready a large bowl of cool water and line a baking sheet with paper towels. Peel and rinse the potatoes and cut them into long, thin matchsticks. Using a Japanese slicer or mandoline on the julienne setting makes fast work of this. Hold the potato at a 45-degree angle to get long, thin sticks. (Or by hand, slice the potato at an angle into very thin slices. Stack several and cut the stack into very thin, long matchsticks.) As you work, submerge the matchsticks in the water. Once you have finished, use your hands to separate any sticks that are still stuck together. Drain the potatoes well.

6 Pour the oil into a wok or *kadai* and heat over medium-high heat to 375°F. Working in six batches, fry the potatoes until golden brown and crispy. This will take anywhere from 2 to 6 minutes, depending on the starchiness of the potatoes and the varying heat of the oil. With each batch, use a spider strainer or skimmer to stir the potatoes and keep them from sticking. Then continue to stir frequently so they brown evenly. Once they are golden brown, transfer them to the baking sheet with the strainer or skimmer. When all of the potatoes are fried, lightly salt them.

7 When ready to serve, stir the garam masala into the lamb. Divide among four soup or dinner plates and top each with a heaping mound of potato sticks. Serve with *pulao*.

LAMB SHANK ROGAN JOSH

SERVES 4 ✤ This recipe is our version of the classic Kashmiri dish brought to India by the Persians. *Rogan* means "oil" or "fat" in Persian and *josh* means "hot" or "passionate." Its hallmarks are caramelized onion paste, warm spices, and Kashmiri chili paste.

Use a pot just large enough to fit the shanks so they will be submerged in the sauce during cooking. For optimal flavor, make the dish a day or two ahead.

1¼ pounds tomatoes, quartered
3½ cups water
½ cup Crispy Fried Onions (page 25)
1 cup whole-milk yogurt
¼ cup canola oil
5 green cardamom pods
5 whole cloves
½ teaspoon cumin seeds
2 large dried Indian bay leaves
1-inch cinnamon stick
2 tablespoons Ginger-Garlic Paste (page 27)

¼ cup Kashmiri Chili Paste (page 28)
¼ teaspoon ground turmeric
1 tablespoon ground coriander
1 tablespoon salt
4 lamb hind shanks (1 pound each)
½ teaspoon Mace-Cardamom Powder (page 23)
2 teaspoons garam masala
½ teaspoon saffron threads
Jeera or Saffron Pulao (page 220) and Naan (page 247), for serving

1 In a medium saucepan, combine the tomatoes and 2 cups of the water and bring to a boil over medium-high heat. Cook until soft, about 10 minutes. Puree in a blender and strain into a bowl, using a spatula to press down on the solids and extract as much juice and pulp from them as you can. Discard the solids. You will have about 3 cups of liquid.

2 In a NutriBullet or small blender, puree the fried onions and yogurt until smooth.

3 In a heavy-bottomed pot or Dutch oven, heat the oil over medium heat until it shimmers. Stir in the cardamom pods, cloves, cumin seeds, bay leaves, and cinnamon stick. Stir in the ginger-garlic paste and Kashmiri chili paste and cook for 1 minute, stirring constantly. Add ½ cup of the water and cook for another 2 minutes, stirring occasionally, to cook the ginger-garlic and chili pastes. Add

the turmeric, coriander, and reserved tomato puree. Cook for 5 minutes. Add the reserved yogurt and onion puree. Stir in the remaining 1 cup water and the salt. Bring to a boil.

4 Lay the lamb shanks in the pot, submerging them in the sauce. Return to a boil and cover the pot. Reduce the heat to medium-low and simmer until fork tender, about 1 hour 10 minutes.

5 To finish the dish, stir in the mace-cardamom powder, garam masala, and saffron. Serve with *pulao* and naan.

LAMB AND PINEAPPLE KORMA (ANANAS GOSHT)

SERVES 4 ❖ This recipe is a variation of a classic korma dish in which meat or vegetables are braised slowly in a yogurt-and-nut-based sauce and seasoned with warming spices. We developed this dish for a summer menu when pineapples were in season. (*Gosht* is the Persian word for "meat" or "flesh." *Ananas* is Hindi for "pineapple.") The fruit acts as a tenderizer and lends sweetness that complements the lamb's bold flavor.

For optimal flavor, make this dish a day ahead and reheat it when ready to serve.

2½ cups fresh pineapple chunks
    (1 pineapple)
1½ cups water
3 cups Korma Sauce (page 32)
¼ teaspoon ground turmeric
¼ teaspoon deggi mirch
½ cup Caramelized Onion Paste
    (page 26)
2 pounds boneless leg of lamb, cut into
    1-inch pieces

½ cup heavy cream
2½ teaspoons salt
1 teaspoon Mace-Cardamom Powder
    (page 23)
1 teaspoon garam masala
Chopped cilantro, for garnish
Plain Basmati Rice (page 217) and
    Naan (page 247), for serving

1 In a blender, puree 2 cups of the pineapple and ½ cup of the water until smooth. Dice the remaining ½ cup pineapple and set aside.

2 In a heavy-bottomed pot or Dutch oven, heat the korma sauce and remaining 1 cup water over medium heat until it begins to bubble, stirring constantly. Add the turmeric, deggi mirch, and caramelized onion paste and cook for 2 minutes.

3 Stir in the lamb. Cover the pot and cook at a rolling simmer for 20 minutes, stirring occasionally. If it is boiling too vigorously, reduce the heat a little.

4 Stir in the pineapple puree, cream, salt, mace-cardamom powder, and garam masala. Cover the pot and cook for 30 minutes, stirring occasionally, until tender.

5 Garnish with chopped cilantro and the reserved diced pineapple. Serve hot with rice and naan.

LAMB SHANK RAAN-E-RASIKA

SERVES 4 ❀ *Raan* means "leg of lamb," but this dish is a trompe l'oeil version of that. We cut the meat off lamb shanks, mince it, and mold it back over the bottom of the bone. It's a dramatic presentation because the denuded bone looks so impressive when it comes to the table. The maharajas of the kingly states of India commonly used gold and silver leaf (*vark*) as food decoration because silver was thought to be antimicrobial and gold an aphrodisiac. Silver leaf foil is also a very popular garnish for sweets.

You can blanch the bones, make the ground lamb mixture, assemble the shanks for cooking, and make the sauce the day before, adding the saffron to the sauce before serving.

LAMB
4 lamb hind shanks (1 pound each)
3 tablespoons Ginger-Garlic Paste (page 27)
1 cup shredded mild white cheddar cheese
½ teaspoon ground turmeric
1 teaspoon deggi mirch
1 teaspoon garam masala
2 teaspoons Rose Petal Spice Mix (recipe follows)
1 teaspoon salt

SAUCE
½ cup Crispy Fried Onions (page 25)
½ cup whole-milk yogurt

2 tablespoons canola oil
2 tablespoons Ginger-Garlic Paste (page 27)
2 tablespoons Kashmiri Chili Paste (page 28)
2 cups water or meat broth
3 tablespoons tomato paste
2 tablespoons malt vinegar
¼ cup heavy cream
1½ teaspoons Rose Petal Spice Mix (recipe follows)
1½ teaspoons salt
¼ teaspoon saffron threads
Edible gold or silver leaf, for garnish (optional)

1 PREPARE THE LAMB: With a chef's knife, cut the meat off the lamb shanks. Use the blade of the knife to scrape off all the membrane from the bones above the joints to totally denude them. Don't worry if you don't manage to scrape off all of it; it will come off easily once the bones are blanched in Step 3. Use a paring knife to get off as much meat as possible from around the joint but, again, don't worry if you don't get all of it.

2 Cut away and discard tendons, sinew, silverskin, and fat from the meat and cut it into rough 2-inch chunks. You should have about 2 pounds of meat. If you have more, reserve it for another use. Cover and refrigerate the lamb.

3 Bring a small stockpot of water to a boil. Submerge the bones in it and blanch them for 15 minutes. Drain and pat dry with paper towels. Scrape off any membranes left on the shank bones.

4 Preheat the oven to 450°F.

5 Put the lamb pieces through a meat grinder fitted with a medium-coarse grinding plate. In a large bowl, combine the ground lamb, ginger-garlic paste, cheddar, turmeric, deggi mirch, garam masala, rose petal spice mix, and salt.

6 Divide the mixture into four even portions and form each around the thicker end of a shank bone, encasing the shank and leaving the bone exposed at the top. (If the butcher cut the bones short, try to leave at least 1 inch of bone exposed.) The meat should be packed tight and pear-shaped, mimicking the shape of the lamb shank before it was denuded.

7 Cut off four 12-inch squares of foil. Center a shank on each one and bring the foil up to encase the meat like a sock, but leaving the bone exposed. Place the

shanks in a deep, straight-sided, ovenproof skillet or sauté pan. Pour 1 inch of water into the pan and bring it to a boil over high heat. Transfer the pan to the oven and bake the shanks for 30 minutes.

8 MEANWHILE, MAKE THE SAUCE: In a NutriBullet, small blender, or mini food processor, puree the fried onions and yogurt.

9 In a medium saucepan, heat the oil over medium heat until it shimmers. Add the ginger-garlic paste and Kashmiri chili paste and cook, stirring occasionally, until the oil separates from the mixture, about 5 minutes. Stir in the water.

10 Increase the heat to medium-high and bring the liquid to a boil. Whisk in the reserved yogurt/onion puree, the tomato paste, and vinegar. Whisk constantly until the mixture comes to a boil. Reduce the heat to medium and cook for 5 minutes, stirring occasionally. Stir in the cream, rose petal spice mix, and salt. Cook for another 3 minutes. Keep warm over very low heat.

11 Remove the lamb from the oven and let it rest for 10 minutes.

12 To finish the dish, strain the sauce through a course sieve into a decorative Dutch oven or deep-welled serving plate. Stir in the saffron. Remove the foil from the shanks and place them on top of the sauce. If desired, garnish with edible gold or silver leaf, wrapping some around part of the exposed bone. (See photos, opposite.) Serve immediately.

ROSE PETAL SPICE MIX MAKES ABOUT 3 TABLESPOONS

2½ tablespoons (½ ounce) dried culinary rose buds
1 tablespoon black peppercorns

1 teaspoon mace (javitri)
1 teaspoon green cardamom pods

Remove and discard the stems from the rose buds. In a spice grinder, grind the petals, peppercorns, mace, and cardamom pods into a fine powder. Store in an airtight container for up to 1 month.

SMOKED VENISON CHOPS LAAL MAAS

SERVES 4 ⚬ *Laal maas* means "red meat," which refers to the fiery color of the sauce. The curry originates from Rajasthan, where it is traditionally made with mutton, whose strong flavor (it comes from an older animal) is a good match for the sauce's heat. They likely use local mathania chilies when making the dish there, whereas we use Kashmiri chilies.

At Rasika, we often serve venison chops prepared in this manner, especially in the fall and winter. An important element of the dish is smoke. (See Smoking, page 229.)

Have the butcher trim the ends of the bones of venison rib chops to expose them (this is called "frenching") or cut chops from a 2¾- to 3-pound eight-bone rack of venison and trim them. Of course, you can substitute whatever kind of chop you wish.

You can make the sauce the day before and reheat it before searing and smoking the chops.

RASIKA

SAUCE
6 tablespoons canola oil
½ teaspoon cumin seeds
2 black cardamom pods
4 green cardamom pods
4 whole cloves
2 large yellow onions, halved and thinly sliced
3 tablespoons finely chopped garlic
1 tablespoon Ginger-Garlic Paste (page 27)
5 tablespoons Kashmiri Chili Paste (page 28)
2 cups water
2 cups whole-milk yogurt
¼ teaspoon ground turmeric
2 tablespoons ground coriander
¼ teaspoon ground cloves
1 teaspoon garam masala
1½ tablespoons salt

VENISON
8 venison chops (5 ounces each), ½ inch thick and frenched
1 tablespoon Ginger-Garlic Paste (page 27)
1 tablespoon Kashmiri Chili Paste (page 28)
1 tablespoon fresh lemon juice
1 teaspoon salt
¼ cup canola oil

SMOKING
2 charcoal briquettes
One 4-inch double-thick square of heavy-duty foil
6 whole cloves
1 teaspoon ghee or unsalted butter, melted

Saffron Pulao (page 220) and Naan (page 247), for serving
Cucumber Raita (page 269), for serving

1 MAKE THE SAUCE: In a heavy-bottomed pot or Dutch oven, heat the oil over medium-high heat until it shimmers. Add the cumin seeds, black and green cardamom pods, and whole cloves and let the cumin crackle. Add the onions and garlic and cook, stirring occasionally, until dark golden brown, 20 to 25 minutes.

2 In a small bowl, whisk together the ginger-garlic paste, Kashmiri chili paste, and 1 cup of the water and stir it into the pot. Cook for 5 minutes.

3 Stir in the yogurt, turmeric, and coriander and cook for 5 minutes, stirring constantly. Add the ground cloves, garam masala, salt, and remaining 1 cup water and cook for 1 minute. Keep warm over very low heat.

4 SEASON THE VENISON: Place the venison chops in a large bowl and coat them well with the ginger-garlic paste, Kashmiri chili paste, lemon juice, and salt. Let them sit for 30 minutes.

5 In a large skillet, heat the oil over medium-high heat until it shimmers. Lay the chops flat in the pan and brown them for 3 minutes on each side.

6 Transfer the chops to the sauce. Cover the pot and remove it from the heat.

7 SMOKE THE CHOPS: Place 2 charcoal briquettes over a high open flame on the stove for 10 minutes, using tongs to turn them over halfway through, until they are gray all round. You can also light a briquette on the coil of an electric stove, which will likely take less time.

8 Place the square of foil directly on top of the chops in the pot and make sure it lies flat. Place the cloves in the center of the foil and place the briquettes on top of them. Pour the melted ghee or butter over the briquettes and cover the pot quickly. Wait for the smoke to dissipate, about 10 minutes.

9 Discard the foil, charcoal, and cloves and serve the chops warm with *pulao*, naan, and raita.

GOAT OR LAMB BIRYANI

SERVES 8 ⚙ We have always had biryani, the layered rice dish beloved by the Moghuls, on the menu at Rasika, whether with chicken, lamb, goat, or vegetables. We serve it in individual copper pots sealed with a naan dough crust. For the home cook, we have left the crust off. (See On Biryanis, page 135.) If well made, you should be able to smell the rich spices of a biryani from far away.

In India, goat is more popular and prevalent than lamb. It's funny to me that many people associate lamb with Indian cuisine. This probably comes from the proliferation of Indian cooking in Great Britain, where lamb is consumed more widely.

You can usually find goat meat at a halal market, where butchers cut legs from young goats into bone-in pieces. (The bones enhance the flavor.) The cooking of the meat may vary, depending on the goat. Baby goat meat is more tender than meat from an older animal.

There is no getting around the fact that making biryani involves a lot of steps and patience. You can make the lamb or goat a day or two ahead (Steps 1 through 4) as well as the Crispy Fried Onions (page 25) and the Tomato and Red Onion Raita (page 269). Have your mise en place in order before you start making the rice.

GOAT (OR LAMB)
1 quart whole-milk yogurt
½ teaspoon ground turmeric
1 teaspoon deggi mirch
1 tablespoon ground coriander
¼ cup canola oil
4 green cardamom pods
4 whole cloves
1-inch cinnamon stick
½ teaspoon cumin seeds
2 large dried Indian bay leaves
1 large yellow onion, quartered and thinly sliced
4 teaspoons Ginger-Garlic Paste (page 27)
2 pounds bone-in baby goat leg, cut into rough 1-inch pieces (or 2 pounds boneless leg of lamb, trimmed of fat and sinew, cut into 1-inch cubes)

3 teaspoons salt
4 medium fresh Thai green chilies, thinly sliced at an angle
One 2 x 1-inch piece fresh ginger, thinly sliced and cut into very thin julienne strips
1 teaspoon Mace-Cardamom Powder (page 23)
1 teaspoon garam masala

RICE
3 cups basmati rice
½ cup whole milk
½ teaspoon saffron threads
¼ teaspoon ground turmeric
1 tablespoon kewra water, such as Dabur brand
3 quarts water
¼ cup canola oil

2 teaspoons fresh lemon juice
4 green cardamom pods
4 whole cloves
1-inch cinnamon stick
½ teaspoon black cumin seeds
2 large dried Indian bay leaves
3 tablespoons salt

¼ cup ghee

Crispy Fried Onions (page 25),
for garnish
Cucumber Raita (page 269) or Tomato
and Red Onion Raita (page 269),
for serving

1 PREPARE THE GOAT: In a medium bowl, whisk together the yogurt, turmeric, deggi mirch, and coriander.

2 In a heavy-bottomed ovenproof pot or Dutch oven, heat the oil over medium-high heat until it shimmers. Add the cardamom pods, cloves, cinnamon stick, cumin seeds, and bay leaves. Let the cumin seeds crackle. Add the onion and sauté, stirring occasionally, until dark golden brown, about 20 minutes. Reduce the heat to medium. Stir in the ginger-garlic paste and cook for 30 seconds.

3 Add the yogurt mixture and cook for 10 minutes. The yogurt may look grainy, as if it has broken. Don't worry about it.

4 Stir in the goat and 2 teaspoons of the salt. Cover the pot and let simmer, still over medium heat, until the goat is tender, 45 to 55 minutes (45 minutes for lamb). Give the meat a stir from time to time while it's cooking. When the meat is tender, stir in the green chilies, ginger, mace-cardamom powder, garam masala, and remaining 1 teaspoon salt. Remove from the heat.

5 MEANWHILE, START THE RICE: In a very large bowl, cover the rice with cool water. Tip the bowl to drain as much water out as you can without letting any grains fall into the sink. Repeat three or four times, or until the water is clear. Once it is, cover the rice with water and let it soak for at least 30 minutes.

6 Preheat the oven to 375°F.

7 In a small glass bowl, microwave the milk, saffron, and turmeric for 1 minute to warm the milk. Stir in the kewra water. Let the saffron steep while the rice is cooking.

8 In a small stockpot, combine the water, oil, lemon juice, cardamom pods, cloves, cinnamon stick, black cumin seeds, bay leaves, and salt and bring to a boil over high heat. Drain the rice and stir it into the water. Return to a boil and cook, stirring once or twice, for 1 to 5 minutes. You want the rice to be partially cooked and al dente. When you taste a piece you should definitely sense a bit of hardness in the center of the grain. The cooking time varies depending on the age of the rice you have (and who knows how old it is) and how long it has been soaked. To be on the safe side, start checking it after 1 minute and keep checking until it is just right.

9 Drain the rice and cover the meat with half of it. Drizzle the steeped saffron milk all over, then top with the remaining rice.

10 In a small saucepan, heat the ghee over medium heat until it is hot. Drizzle it all over the rice. Cover the pot with foil and a tight lid. Transfer to the oven and bake for 25 minutes. Remove from the oven and let rest for 5 minutes.

11 Fluff the rice with a serving spoon to jumble the meat and rice. Serve hot directly from the pot or pile onto a serving platter. Garnish with crispy fried onions and serve with raita on the side.

Rice Vermicelli with Dill and Green Chilies (page 219)

9

RICE, GRAINS, AND LEGUMES

There is nothing more satisfying than ladling a delectable curry over the fragrant, delicate long-grain basmati rice India is known for, especially the dishes known as *pulaos*. *Pulao* derives from *pilav,* the Turkish word for this rice dish, but similar words exist in Persian (*polou*), Spanish (*paella*), French (*pilau*), and English (pilaf). Pulaos differ from biryanis in that the latter are layered dishes in which the rice is parboiled before being cooked together with its other components, often a highly spiced meat stew.

Pulaos are basically one-pot dishes. You use rice and whatever aromatics, vegetables, or cooked meat you wish to add and cook them all together in just enough liquid necessary to cook the rice completely. The liquid can be water (Jeera or Saffron Pulao, page 220), but can also be something more full-flavored, perhaps a stock, broth, or even fruit juice, such as the orange juice used in Orange Pulao (page 221).

PLAIN BASMATI RICE

BOILED BASMATI RICE
VEGAN

SERVES 6 TO 8 ⚙ This rice accompanies most curries, so you don't want too much salt in it—just a hint will do. The oil keeps the grains separate. To halve the recipe, use a smaller pot and halve all the ingredients.

Cooking time varies with the age of the rice—you basically have no idea how old the rice is when you buy it in a store—so you just have to keep your eye on it while it's cooking and taste it often until the texture is just right. This, of course, is second nature to those of us who eat and cook rice every day of our lives. There comes a day when you can tell the precise moment when the grain has crossed over from al dente to cooked all the way through and you're destined to lead a life accompanied by perfect rice from there on out.

You can make this rice a day ahead and reheat it in a covered dish in the microwave.

2 cups basmati rice
1 tablespoon salt

2 tablespoons canola oil

1 Clean and soak the rice (see Note). Drain well.

2 In a heavy-bottomed 5-quart pot or Dutch oven, combine 3 quarts water, the salt, and oil. Cover and bring to a boil over high heat. Add the drained rice and stir it into the water. Return to a boil and cook the rice until just tender and no longer al dente at all. This will take 3 to 5 minutes, so start tasting it often after the 2-minute mark to make sure you get the texture right. Drain well and serve hot.

NOTE: *In a very large bowl, combine the rice with cool water to cover. Tip the bowl to drain as much water out as you can without letting any grains fall into the sink. Repeat three or four times, or until the water is clear. Once it is, cover the rice with water and let it soak for 30 minutes.*

MICROWAVE BASMATI RICE
VEGAN (SUBSTITUTE CANOLA OIL FOR THE BUTTER)

SERVES 8 TO 10 ✷ My wife, Anjali, always makes rice this way at home. She learned it from my uncle Balaram, known as Uncle B, who developed the recipe through trial and error. The water used to prepare it this way is always double the volume of the rice, plus ½ cup. So 1 cup of rice takes 2½ cups water and 3 cups of rice calls for 6½ cups water. I'm not really sure why it works this way, but it does. Feel free to add any flavorings you wish, such as saffron threads or turmeric, cardamom pods, cinnamon stick, cumin seeds, and/or cloves.

You need a large microwave-safe casserole or bowl with a lid to make this rice. (A 2½-quart glass casserole with a glass lid, such as Corningware, is perfect.)

You can make the rice a day ahead and reheat it in the microwave in the same dish.

2 cups basmati rice
2 tablespoons unsalted butter, cut
  into small pieces

1 teaspoon salt

1 Clean and soak the rice (see Note, page 217). Drain well.

2 Put the drained rice in a large glass bowl with 4½ cups water, the butter, and salt and give it a stir. Cover the bowl and microwave for 10 minutes. Stir the rice. Re-cover and cook another 12 minutes. Let the rice rest, still covered, for 5 minutes. Fluff with a large spoon and serve hot.

RICE VERMICELLI WITH DILL AND GREEN CHILIES

SERVES 8 ✺ When we were working on the original Rasika menu, we wanted to come up with an accompaniment for Black Cod with Honey and Dill (page 169), something more unexpected than rice but not heavy. The thin rice vermicelli used in Asian cooking seemed like a perfect solution. Turmeric and fresh dill add bright yellow and green vibrancy and Thai chili gives the dish a bit of heat.

You can make the vermicelli the day before and reheat it in a covered dish in the microwave.

½ pound rice vermicelli
4 tablespoons unsalted butter
½ teaspoon finely chopped fresh Thai green chili

1 teaspoon finely chopped fresh ginger
½ teaspoon ground turmeric
1 teaspoon salt
¼ cup chopped fresh dill

1 Bring a large saucepan of water to a boil over high heat. Remove from the heat and submerge the vermicelli to soften them, 3 to 4 minutes. Drain the noodles, return them to the pot, and keep covered.

2 In a skillet, heat the butter over medium heat until it sizzles. Reduce the heat to medium-low and add the green chili, ginger, turmeric, and salt. Cook for 30 seconds and fold into the noodles. Fold in the dill and serve.

RICE, GRAINS, AND LEGUMES

JEERA OR SAFFRON PULAO
VEGAN (SUBSTITUTE CANOLA OIL FOR THE BUTTER)

SERVES 8 ❧ *Jeera* is "cumin" in Hindi, a derivation of the Persian word for the spice. This recipe calls for black cumin seeds, so it could more accurately be called *shahi jeera pulao*. By adding saffron and turmeric to the cooking liquid, it becomes saffron pulao, which is a lovely vibrant yellow. These rices, obviously, have more flavor than plain boiled rice, which is why people often prefer them.

You can make this rice a day ahead and reheat it in a covered dish in the microwave.

RASIKA

2 cups basmati rice
2 tablespoons canola oil
1 teaspoon black cumin seeds
4 green cardamom pods
4 whole cloves
2-inch cinnamon stick
2 large dried Indian bay leaves

3 cups water
1 tablespoon unsalted butter
1½ teaspoons salt
½ teaspoon saffron threads
    (for Saffron Pulao)
½ teaspoon ground turmeric
    (for Saffron Pulao)

1 Preheat the oven to 375°F.

2 Clean and soak the rice (see Note, page 217). Drain well.

3 In a heavy-bottomed ovenproof pot or Dutch oven, heat the oil over medium-high heat until it shimmers. Add the black cumin seeds, cardamom pods, cloves, cinnamon stick, and bay leaves and let the cumin seeds crackle. Add the water, butter, and salt (plus the saffron and turmeric if making saffron pulao) and bring to a boil.

4 Stir the drained rice into the pot and return the liquid to a boil. Stir the rice again, cover the pot, and cook, stirring occasionally, until the water is mostly absorbed and the rice looks thick and soupy, 2 to 3 minutes.

5 Transfer to the oven and bake, covered, until the liquid has been absorbed, about 10 minutes. Remove the pot from the oven and let the rice rest for 5 minutes. Fluff with a large spoon and serve hot.

ORANGE PULAO (NARANGI PULAO)
VEGAN (SUBSTITUTE CANOLA OIL FOR THE BUTTER)

SERVES 8 ⚙ I created this dish to accompany Orange Duck (page 192), my take on duck à l'orange, but the customers liked it so much we decided to put it on the menu as a side dish.

You can make this rice a day ahead and reheat it in a covered dish in the microwave.

2 cups basmati rice
1 tablespoon canola oil
1 tablespoon unsalted butter
½ medium yellow onion, halved and thinly sliced
One 1 x ½-inch piece fresh ginger, finely julienned

1 medium fresh Thai green chili, thinly sliced at an angle (1 teaspoon)
2 strips of orange zest (see Note), slivered
3 cups fresh orange juice
¼ teaspoon ground turmeric
1 teaspoon salt

1 Clean and soak the rice (see Note, page 217).

2 Preheat the oven to 350°F.

3 In a heavy-bottomed ovenproof pot or Dutch oven, heat the oil and butter over medium-high heat until they sizzle. Stir in the onion and cook, stirring occasionally, until translucent but not browned, about 2 minutes. Add the ginger and green chili and cook, stirring, for 1 minute. Add the orange zest slivers, orange juice, turmeric, and salt. Bring to a boil.

4 Drain the rice, stir it into the pot, and return the liquid to a boil. Stir the rice again, cover the pot, and cook, stirring occasionally, until the water is mostly absorbed and the rice looks thick and soupy, 2 to 3 minutes.

5 Transfer to the oven and bake, covered, until the liquid has been absorbed, about 10 minutes. Remove the pot from the oven and let the rice rest for 5 minutes. Fluff with a large spoon and serve hot.

NOTE: *Using a vegetable peeler, cut off two large strips of zest from the orange and slice them lengthwise into very thin slivers. You can then juice the orange to use as part of the 3 cups orange juice called for in the recipe. Or, better yet, just eat the orange.*

PEANUT QUINOA

SERVES 6 ❖ When people fast in India for religious holidays, such as Navratri and Shivratri, they often don't eat grains and cereals. There are plenty of allowable foods to enjoy instead. One of them is pearl tapioca (*sabudana*). A classic Maharashtrian (Western India) dish made with tapioca, along with peanuts and potatoes, is called *sabudana khichdi*. For my interpretation of the dish, I use quinoa, which would not be eaten during fasting periods in India. Quinoa, though, has become so popular in the United States that I wanted to come up with some way to feature it.

You can make the quinoa a day in advance and reheat in a microwave.

1½ cups white quinoa
3 cups water
⅓ cup chopped unsalted roasted peanuts
¾ teaspoon salt
1½ tablespoons ghee
½ teaspoon cumin seeds

12 (1½-inch) fresh curry leaves (more if smaller), chopped (1 tablespoon, packed)
2 teaspoons finely chopped fresh Thai green chili

1 In a large saucepan, stir together the quinoa and water. Cover and bring to a boil over medium-high heat. Cook the quinoa for 10 minutes, stirring occasionally, until the water is mostly absorbed. Remove from the heat and stir in the peanuts and salt. Cover the pan and let stand for 5 minutes.

2 In a small skillet, melt the ghee over medium-high heat until it begins to smoke. Add the cumin seeds and let them crackle, then remove from the heat and add the curry leaves and green chili. Stir the cumin mixture into the quinoa. Cover the pan and let stand for 5 minutes. Fluff with a fork and serve warm.

RASIKA

LEMON CASHEW RICE
VEGAN

SERVES 4 ❂ In Southern India, you often find dishes in which flavorings are folded into boiled rice. Mustard seeds, curry leaves, urad dal, and chana dal are common additions. The dal imparts an extra dimension of nuttiness and a bit of crunch.

This rice would be served with South Indian dishes such as Mixed Vegetable Curry with Mango (page 131), Seared Rainbow Trout Malabar (page 164), and Lobster Moilee (page 161). If you have nut allergies, you can leave the cashews out.

You can make this rice a day ahead and reheat it in a covered dish in the microwave. You can also reheat plain leftover rice and fold the flavorings into it or fold the flavorings into cold, plain leftover rice and then microwave it.

RASIKA

3½ cups freshly cooked Plain Basmati
    Rice (page 217)
¼ cup canola oil
1 teaspoon black or brown mustard seeds
1 teaspoon urad dal
1 teaspoon chana dal
¼ chopped unsalted raw cashews
½ teaspoon ground turmeric

¼ teaspoon asafetida
15 (1½-inch) fresh curry leaves
    (more if smaller)
¼ teaspoon finely chopped fresh Thai
    green chili
½ teaspoon finely chopped fresh ginger
¼ cup fresh lemon juice
½ teaspoon salt

1 Prepare the basmati rice and keep it covered so it stays hot.

2 In a small skillet, heat the oil over medium heat until it shimmers. Add the mustard seeds, urad dal, chana dal, and cashews and cook, stirring constantly, until the dals and nuts are golden brown, about 1 minute. Stir in the turmeric, asafetida, curry leaves, green chili, and ginger.

3 Fold the mixture into the rice with the lemon juice and salt. Serve hot.

KIDNEY BEANS IN TOMATO MASALA (RAJMA MASALA)

VEGAN

SERVES 6 ❖ *Rajma* is Hindi for "kidney beans."

There is no oil or butter in this dish, a Northern Indian favorite, so it is an excellent source of protein without guilt. That is why my wife, Anjali, makes it at home often. Rajma masala goes especially well with Saffron Pulao (page 220).

The beans freeze well. Thaw in the refrigerator and reheat over medium heat, stirring occasionally.

½ pound dried red kidney beans
½ cup finely chopped yellow onion
1 tablespoon finely chopped garlic
½ teaspoon finely chopped fresh Thai green chili
1½ tablespoons finely chopped fresh ginger
4 whole cloves
4 green cardamom pods

½ teaspoon cumin seeds
1 dried Indian bay leaf
1-inch cinnamon stick
½ teaspoon deggi mirch
¼ teaspoon asafetida
2 teaspoons salt
3 tablespoons tomato paste
1 teaspoon garam masala

1 Pick over the kidney beans, discarding any stones or dirt. Rinse them and place in a large bowl. Pour in enough water to submerge them by 4 inches and leave them on the counter uncovered to soak overnight. (Or use the quick-soak method. See Note, page 78.)

2 Drain and rinse the beans and put them a medium saucepan with 1 quart water, the onion, garlic, green chili, ginger, cloves, cardamom pods, cumin seeds, bay leaf, cinnamon stick, deggi mirch, asafetida, and salt.

3 Bring to a boil over medium-high heat. Skim off any foam that rises to the surface. Cover the pot, reduce the heat to medium, and simmer until the beans are falling apart, about 45 minutes. Stir in the tomato paste and garam masala and cook for another 15 minutes, covered, still over medium heat. There should be plenty of gravy in the pot. Serve hot.

CHANA DAL WITH ZUCCHINI AND COCONUT

SERVES 6 ❁ This lovely zucchini dal is a variation of *cholar dal* from West Bengal. It's a great way to use up some of the summertime surplus of zucchini, and ladled over plain rice, it makes a hearty but simple meal.

The seeds that imbue the dish with flavor are cooked in mustard oil. Before frying spices in mustard oil, you must first heat it to the smoking point and let it cool slightly. This removes its caustic property and brings its pungency forward.

1 cup chana dal
6 cups water
1 teaspoon ground turmeric
1½ pounds zucchini, trimmed
One 2 x 1-inch piece of skin-on fresh coconut (see Note)
½ teaspoon nigella seeds
½ teaspoon black or brown mustard seeds

½ teaspoon cumin seeds
½ teaspoon fennel seeds
¼ teaspoon fenugreek seeds
2 tablespoons mustard oil
2 medium fresh Thai green chilies, halved lengthwise
2 teaspoons salt
¼ cup golden raisins

OPENING COCONUTS

To open a coconut, hold it over a bowl. In your other hand, hold a heavy chef's knife upside down. With the back of the knife, whack the shell all around its circumference until the shell and fruit break in half. (By the way, drink the water—it's good for you.)

To remove the flesh, work an oyster knife in between the flesh and the shell and pry it back and forth until the flesh releases. Or hold the coconut half in your hand flesh side down and whack the shell all over with the back of the knife until you can pull the flesh out easily from the shell.

1 Pick over the chana dal, discarding any stones or dirt, and rinse it. In a medium saucepan, combine the chana dal and 4 cups of the water and bring to a boil over medium-high heat. Skim off any scum that rises to the surface. Stir in ½ teaspoon of the turmeric. (If you add it before skimming, you will lose all of it.) Cover the pan, reduce the heat to medium, and cook until soft, about 40 minutes. Remove from the heat and set aside.

2 Halve the zucchini crosswise. Stand a half up and cut four ½-inch-thick slices of flesh from around the seeds in the center. Cut the flesh into ½-inch cubes. (Discard the seeds.)

3 Cut the coconut piece lengthwise into ½-inch-wide strips, then thinly slice the strips crosswise. (You need ¼ cup.)

4 In a small bowl, mix together the seeds: nigella, mustard, cumin, fennel, and fenugreek.

5 In a heavy-bottomed pot or Dutch oven, heat the mustard oil over medium-high heat until it smokes. Remove the pan from the heat and let it cool for 1 minute. Add the seeds and let them crackle.

6 Return the pot to medium heat. Stir in the green chilies and coconut and cook for 30 seconds. Stir in the zucchini, the remaining ½ teaspoon turmeric, and the salt and cook for 1 minute.

7 Add the cooked dal, remaining 2 cups water, and the raisins. Cover and simmer, stirring occasionally, until the zucchini is soft and the dal has thickened from a broth into a soup, about 15 minutes. Serve hot.

NOTE: *The recipe calls for a small piece of fresh coconut. I think it's worth the trouble to break down a fresh coconut (see Opening Coconuts, opposite), because you can freeze the rest of the pieces and have them on hand to use for this and other dishes, such as Coconut Chutney (page 259). Or for snacking. To use a frozen piece, microwave it for 15 seconds and blot it on a paper towel.*

SMOKED DAL (DAL DHUNGAREE)

SERVES 6 TO 8   ❧ *Dal* is technically split dried legumes, but this recipe includes whole gram and whole kidney beans. (See Legumes, Pulses, Gram, Besan, and Dal, page 15.)

Dhungar means "to smoke." This dish is basically *dal makhani,* the notable Northern Indian dish of pulses and kidney beans, but with the addition of perfumed smoke created by lit charcoal. (See Smoking, opposite.)

Feel free to leave out the smoke if you wish, but it's so spectacular that a better idea is to wait to do the smoking just before serving and remove the lid at the table. (Have a plate ready so you can put the foil and briquette on it.)

The dish is pretty rich, considering it is has cream and butter in it, which of course makes it irresistible. The recipe can be doubled and made a day or two ahead of time. It freezes nicely through step 4. You may want to add some water to it as you reheat it because the legumes may have absorbed some of their liquid.

LEGUMES
½ cup black gram
¼ cup chana dal
¼ cup dried red kidney beans

TOMATO MASALA
2 tablespoons canola oil
½ teaspoon cumin seeds
1 tablespoon finely chopped garlic
¼ teaspoon asafetida
1 tablespoon finely chopped fresh ginger
1 teaspoon finely chopped fresh Thai
   green chili
1 teaspoon deggi mirch

1 cup finely chopped tomato
⅓ cup tomato paste
5 tablespoons unsalted butter

SMOKING AND FINISHING
1 charcoal briquette
2 teaspoons fenugreek leaf powder*
¼ cup heavy cream
1 tablespoon salt
One 4-inch double-thick square of
   heavy-duty foil
6 whole cloves
1 teaspoon ghee or unsalted butter,
   melted

*To make fenugreek leaf powder, grind dried fenugreek leaves in a spice grinder, using
 enough so that the blades can pulverize them into a fine powder.

1 PREPARE THE LEGUMES: Pick over the black gram, chana dal, and kidney beans, discarding any stones or dirt. Rinse them and place in a large bowl. Pour in enough water to submerge them by at least 4 inches and leave them on the counter uncovered to soak overnight. (Or use the quick-soak method. See Note, page 78.)

2 Drain and rinse the legumes several times. Put them in a 3-quart heavy-bottomed saucepan with 6 cups water. Bring to a boil over high heat. Skim any foam that rises to the surface. Reduce the heat to medium, adjusting it to maintain a vigorous simmer. Cover the saucepan and cook until the kidney beans are completely soft and their skins are split, about 1 hour 15 minutes.

3 MEANWHILE, MAKE THE TOMATO MASALA: In a medium nonstick skillet, heat the oil over medium heat until it shimmers. Add the cumin seeds and let them crackle. Add the garlic and stir until well browned, about 1 minute. Stir in the asafetida, ginger, green chili, and deggi mirch and cook for 30 seconds. Add the tomato, increase the heat to medium-high, and cook, stirring constantly, until the tomatoes are an adobe-colored cohesive mush, not dry and pasty, about 8 minutes.

SMOKING

We Indians have an age-old technique for smoking dishes that is really quite simple and delicious. The way we do it is to take a piece of heavy-duty foil, fold it into a square, and rest it on top of whatever food we're going to smoke in a pan or pot that has a tight lid.

Then we heat a piece of charcoal. You can do this in your house over an open gas flame or directly on an electric burner, lighting the briquette until it is ash gray all around, but ember-hot on the inside. If you use wood charcoal, small embers may fly up. This isn't a problem if you have a strong hood over your stove.

Once the briquette is hot, whole cloves are placed on the foil square and the briquette goes on top of them. Then we pour melted ghee or butter over the briquette, which immediately begins to smoke. We quickly put the lid on the pot and wait for the smoke to dissipate, about 10 minutes usually. The foil, briquette, and cloves get tossed, the pot gets a stir, and the dish is imbued with a lovely touch of subtle smoke.

This method is used for Smoked Dal (opposite) and Smoked Venison Chops Laal Maas (page 208) and suggested as an option for Butternut Squash Bharta (page 104).

4 Stir the tomato masala into the cooked legumes. Add the tomato paste and butter, stirring until the butter has melted. Simmer uncovered, still on medium-high heat, for 15 minutes, stirring occasionally.

5 MEANWHILE, PREPARE TO SMOKE: Place the charcoal briquette over a high open flame on the stove for 10 minutes, using tongs to turn it over halfway through, until gray all around. You can also light a briquette on the coil of an electric stove, which will likely take less time.

6 FINISH AND SMOKE THE DAL: Stir the fenugreek leaf powder, cream, and salt into the dal and remove the pot from the heat. Float the foil square directly on top of the dal. Place the cloves in the center of the foil and the briquette on top of the cloves. Pour the melted ghee over the briquette and cover the pot quickly. Wait for the smoke to dissipate, about 10 minutes. Discard the foil, charcoal, and cloves. Stir the dal and serve with steamed rice and naan.

MOONG DAL WITH SPINACH (MOONG DAL PALAK)

SERVES 4 ⊚ Ghee, rather than oil, adds some richness and buttery flavor to this dal, which makes up for the masala being so simple.

Don't make this dish more than several hours before serving because the texture really suffers when you refrigerate it. If you must, make the dish a few hours ahead of time and reheat, adding a little bit of water if it is too thick. (Cooked dal continues absorbing water as it sits.)

DAL
1 cup moong dal
3 cups water
½ teaspoon ground turmeric

MASALA
¼ cup ghee
1 teaspoon cumin seeds
1 cup finely chopped yellow onion

1 tablespoon finely chopped garlic
1 cup finely chopped tomato
½ teaspoon ground turmeric
1 tablespoon finely chopped fresh ginger
2 teaspoons finely chopped fresh Thai
    green chili
½ pound baby spinach leaves
1½ teaspoons salt

1 PREPARE THE DAL: Pick over the moong dal, discarding any stones or dirt. Rinse it and put in a large heavy-bottomed saucepan with 2 cups of the water. Bring to a boil over high heat. Skim off any foam that rises to the surface. Stir in the turmeric.

2 Reduce the heat to medium-low. Cover the pot and simmer, stirring occasionally, until the dal is completely soft, about 20 minutes. Most of the water will have evaporated and the dal will be a mush. Remove the pan from the heat and leave it covered while you prepare the masala.

3 MAKE THE MASALA: In a heavy-bottomed pot or Dutch oven, heat the ghee over medium-high heat until it shimmers. Add the cumin seeds and let them crackle. Stir in the onion and garlic and cook, stirring occasionally, until the onion is golden brown, about 5 minutes. Stir in the tomato, turmeric, ginger, and green chili. Cook the masala, stirring occasionally, until the tomatoes are completely soft and all their liquid has evaporated, about 2 minutes.

4 Stir the spinach into the masala and cook until wilted, about 1 minute. Stir in the cooked moong dal, the remaining 1 cup water, and the salt. Serve warm.

SPICY KADAI CHICKPEAS
VEGAN

SERVES 6 ✻ *Kadai* refers to the vessel in which these chickpeas are traditionally cooked. A kadai resembles a wok, but is much heavier because it's made from thick cast iron. A heavy-bottomed Dutch oven more closely approximates the vessel than the woks usually found in American kitchens, which are much thinner.

Toasted and ground coriander seeds, dried fenugreek leaves, and Kashmiri chilies are characteristics of kadai cooking. The masala used here can be used for lamb, chicken, or paneer.

To learn more about pulses used in Indian cooking, see Legumes, Pulses, Gram, Besan, and Dal, page 15.

You can make the chickpeas up to 2 days ahead. They also freeze well. Thaw in the refrigerator and reheat over medium heat, stirring occasionally.

½ pound dried kabuli chickpeas
    (garbanzo beans)
2½ teaspoons salt
1 pound tomatoes, coarsely chopped
2 tablespoons coriander seeds
1 tablespoon coarsely chopped dried
    Kashmiri chilies (with seeds)
2 tablespoons canola oil
½ teaspoon cumin seeds

1 tablespoon Kashmiri Chili Paste
    (page 28)
1 tablespoon Ginger-Garlic Paste
    (page 27)
1 tablespoon finely chopped fresh ginger
1 teaspoon finely chopped fresh Thai
    green chili
1½ teaspoons fenugreek leaf powder*
¼ cup tomato paste

To make fenugreek leaf powder, grind dried fenugreek leaves in a spice grinder, using enough so that the blades can pulverize them into a fine powder.

1 Pick over the chickpeas, discarding any stones or dirt. Rinse and place them in a large bowl. Pour in enough water to submerge the chickpeas by 4 inches and leave them on the counter uncovered to soak overnight. (Or use the quick-soak method. See Note, page 78.)

2 Drain and rinse the chickpeas and place them in a medium saucepan with 6 cups water and 1½ teaspoons of the salt. Bring to a boil over medium-high heat. Skim off any foam that rises to the surface. Cover the pot and cook until the chickpeas

are very soft, about 30 minutes. Transfer the chickpeas and liquid to a large bowl and return the pan to the stove.

3 In a food processor, finely chop the tomatoes and set aside.

4 In a small dry skillet, toast the coriander seeds and Kashmiri chilies over medium heat, shaking the pan frequently, until the seeds are lightly browned and fragrant, about 5 minutes. Transfer them to a bowl to cool for 5 minutes. In a spice grinder, grind them into a powder. Measure out 1½ tablespoons of the chili-coriander powder and set aside. (Save the remainder for another use.)

5 Turn the heat under the saucepan to medium and heat the oil until it shimmers. Add the cumin seeds and let them crackle. Stir in the Kashmiri chili paste, ginger-garlic paste, and ½ cup water. Cook, stirring occasionally, for about 3 minutes to thicken the mixture.

6 Stir in the reserved chopped tomatoes and increase the heat to medium-high. Cook, stirring occasionally, until the liquid has evaporated, 15 to 20 minutes. The tomatoes will be a thick mush and you will see oil separating from them in the bottom of the pan. (The cooking time here will depend on how juicy your tomatoes are.) Remove the pan from the heat.

7 Reserving the cooking liquid, drain the chickpeas. Add them to the tomatoes along with ½ cup of the cooking liquid. Stir the ginger, green chili, fenugreek leaf powder, tomato paste, remaining 1 teaspoon salt, and the reserved 1½ tablespoons chili-coriander powder into the chickpeas.

8 Return the pan to medium-high heat and cook, stirring occasionally, until thick, 10 to 15 minutes. Serve hot.

From top: Naan (page 247) sprinkled with red chili flakes, Red Onion and Sage Naan (page 249), Mint Paratha (page 242)

10

BREADS

All of the breads at Rasika are made to order in the tandoor or on the *tawa* (griddle) and served immediately so they are piping hot. The naans, whether plain or with garlic or dried chilies, are the most popular, followed by the combination we offer of mint paratha and red onion and sage naan. On a busy night, we can sell two hundred to three hundred orders of the various breads, so you can imagine the flurry of constant activity taking place in the kitchen to produce them.

CHAPATI
VEGAN (WITHOUT THE BUTTER)

MAKES SIX 8-INCH CHAPATIS ⚙ Before making chapati, read On Making Indian Breads (page 246) thoroughly.

Chapati is an unleavened, whole wheat flatbread perfectly suited to scooping up curry sauces and gravies. That's why it's a staple on Indian tables, especially in Northern India, where wheat is grown. At Rasika, we make chapatis in the tandoori oven and so call them roti. When made on a *tawa,* a wide, shallow griddle, they're called chapati. Both use the same dough. A cast iron skillet is an excellent stand-in for a tawa. Do NOT use a nonstick skillet; it will impede the bread's browning.

Indians use *atta* flour for breads, which is whole meal (whole wheat to Americans) flour. It's much lighter in color than the whole wheat flour we are used to in America. You can find atta flour at stores or online sites that sell Indian products, but using a good-quality American whole wheat flour, such as King Arthur, is fine.

The word *chapati* comes from the Hindi word for "to slap." When we make these breads, we slap them back and forth a few times between our open palms before we put them on the tawa. Feel free to use this technique to take out your aggressions, but also to rid the chapatis of excess flour that may be left on them from the rolling process.

Chapatis should be soft, not crispy or dry. That's why you need to keep them wrapped up as you make them.

After the dough has rested, it can be refrigerated for a day. Bring it to room temperature before rolling. You can make chapatis ahead of time, even the day before, and reheat them by sprinkling a bit of water on them, stacking them, wrapping them in foil, and putting them in a 300°F oven for 5 to 10 minutes. Or wrap the stack in damp paper towels and microwave for 20 to 30 seconds.

½ pound (225 grams) whole wheat flour (about 1¾ cups)
½ teaspoon salt
1 tablespoon canola oil

½ cup plus 2 tablespoons water
All-purpose flour, for dusting
2 tablespoons melted ghee or butter, for brushing (optional)

1 In a medium bowl, use your hand to combine the flour, salt, oil, and water. The dough should come together in a ball with no traces of flour in the bottom or on the sides of the bowl. It should be quite firm, but not dry. Knead it aggressively several times, using your knuckles. The dough should be very slightly tacky, not sticky. Cover with plastic wrap and let it rest for 30 minutes.

2 Once the dough has rested, weigh it and divide the weight by 6. Then weigh out 6 portions of equal weight (about 2 ounces each). Roll them into balls using the palms of your hands, returning each to the bowl and covering it as you go along.

3 To roll and stack the chapatis, have ready a small bowl of all-purpose flour to use for dusting and six squares of wax paper or parchment. Dust a ball of dough completely. With the palm of your hand, flatten it on the counter (or *chakla*) into roughly a 3-inch-diameter round. Use a rolling pin (or *belan*) to enlarge the round a little. Turn it over, enlarge the round a little more, and repeat the process of rolling, turning over, and rolling until you have an 8-inch round. This rolling method keeps the dough from sticking to the counter. Use more flour to dust if you must, but use it as sparingly as possible. Transfer the chapati to one of the sheets of wax paper or parchment placed on the counter or a plate.

4 Roll out the remaining chapatis, stacking them with paper between each one.

5 To griddle the chapatis, have ready a cutting board, the melted ghee (if using), a pastry brush, and a tortilla warmer or serving bowl or plate lined with napkins or kitchen towels (for keeping the chapatis warm).

6 Get a 10-inch cast iron skillet quite hot over medium heat. (A few drops of water sprinkled on it should spatter.) Place a chapati in the pan and cook for 1 minute, pressing down on it lightly with a wide spatula to keep air bubbles from forming. Turn it over (you should see some nice brown spots on it) and brown on the other side for 1 minute, pressing down on it again.

7 Transfer the chapati to the cutting board and brush it on each side with melted ghee. This step is optional, but recommended. Place the chapati in the tortilla warmer or napkin-lined bowl and cover to keep it warm.

8 Repeat the griddling process with the remaining chapatis. Adjust the heat under the skillet if necessary so it doesn't get too hot. Serve the chapatis warm.

CAULIFLOWER DILL PARATHA

VEGAN

MAKES TEN 6-INCH ROUNDS ❋ Before making this paratha, read On Making Indian Breads (page 246) thoroughly.

These parathas are so good they could be a meal with plain yogurt or Cucumber Raita (page 269). They make an impressive addition to bread baskets because your guests discover the fresh dill and cauliflower stuffing hidden within the paratha when they take the first bite.

You can make these through Step 9 in advance, even a day before. After they are browned in a dry pan, let them cool and then wrap them in foil. Refrigerate them if using the next day. When you are ready to eat them, brush with canola oil on each side and crisp them up per the recipe's instructions. Cold leftover parathas, brushed with oil, can be crisped up and reheated in a skillet.

A tortilla warmer is a good vessel to use to keep the parathas warm as you make them. Or you could line a bowl with a cotton napkin and fold the napkin over the finished parathas while you cook the rest of them.

The recipe halves easily.

DOUGH
1 pound (450 grams) whole wheat flour
   (about 3½ cups)
1 teaspoon salt
2 tablespoons canola oil
1¼ cups water

FILLING
½ pound cauliflower florets
1¼ teaspoons salt

¼ cup chopped fresh dill
4 teaspoons finely chopped fresh ginger
1 tablespoon chopped fresh Thai green
   chili
1 teaspoon Toasted Cumin Powder
   (page 23)

All-purpose flour, for dusting
½ cup canola oil

1 MAKE THE DOUGH: In a medium bowl, use your hand to combine the flour, salt, oil, and water. The dough should come together in a ball with no traces of flour in the bottom or on the sides of the bowl. It should be quite firm, but not dry. Knead it aggressively several times, using your knuckles. The dough should be very slightly tacky, not sticky. Cover with plastic wrap and let it rest for 30 minutes.

2 MEANWHILE, MAKE THE FILLING: Using the coarse side of a box grater, grate the cauliflower and transfer it to a bowl. Finely chop whatever bits of cauliflower you can't get through the grater and add them to the bowl. Stir in 1 teaspoon of the salt and let the cauliflower sit for 10 minutes. Place the cauliflower in a cotton kitchen towel and squeeze as much water out as you can. It should be the consistency of wet sand.

3 Transfer the cauliflower to a bowl and stir in the dill, ginger, green chili, toasted cumin powder, and remaining ¼ teaspoon salt.

4 Once the dough has rested, weigh it and divide the weight by 10. Then weigh out 10 portions of equal weight (about 2.4 ounces each). Roll them into balls using the palms of your hands, returning each to the bowl and covering it as you go along.

5 Take a ball of dough and crimp the circumference of it with your fingers to create a rough 4-inch round, making sure the dough in the center remains thick. (It should look like a flying saucer or a filled raviolo.)

6 Lay the dough round in the palm of your hand. Put 2 tablespoons of the cauliflower filling in the center. With the tips of your fingers, press the filling into the center of the dough. As you press, cup the dough more and more so the outside edges of the round begin to meet each other. Pinch those edges together to enclose the filling securely in a neat ball. (See photos, opposite.) Transfer to a plate and cover loosely with plastic wrap. Stuff the remaining balls of dough, covering them as you go along.

7 Dust a ball lightly with all-purpose flour. Put the ball on the counter and, using the palm of your hand, flatten it into a (roughly) 3-inch-diameter round. Use a rolling pin to enlarge the round a little. Turn it over, enlarge the round a little more and repeat that process until you have a 6-inch round. This rolling method keeps the dough from sticking to the counter. Roll the remaining balls of dough, stacking the rounds on a plate with parchment paper between each one as you go along.

8 To griddle the parathas, have ready the oil, a pastry brush, and a tortilla warmer or a bread basket lined with napkins or kitchen towels (for keeping the parathas warm).

9 Get a 10-inch cast iron skillet quite hot, over medium heat. (A few drops of water sprinkled on it will spatter.) Place the dough round in the dry pan. Cook for

1 minute, until large spots of brown form on the bottom. With a wide spatula, flip it over and cook for another minute to lightly brown on the other side. Transfer to a plate and repeat with all the rounds, stacking them loosely as you go along.

10 Now griddle the parathas a second time. Brush the entire surface of one of them with oil on both sides and place it in the hot skillet. Cook for 1 minute, using the spatula to press down on it to create more contact with the pan, which ensures crispiness. Flip it over. Cook for 1 minute, pressing down on it as before. Transfer the paratha to the tortilla warmer or bread basket lined with napkins.

11 Repeat with the remaining dough rounds, adjusting the heat under the skillet if necessary so it doesn't get too hot.

12 Serve the parathas in the lined bread basket, folding the napkins' edges over the breads to keep them warm.

MINT PARATHA
VEGAN (WITHOUT THE BUTTER)

MAKES EIGHT 7-INCH PARATHAS ✣ Before making this paratha, read On Making Indian Breads (page 246) thoroughly.

This paratha is a round of irresistible flakiness that involves pleating the dough and then rolling it up in a pinwheel before rolling it out and griddling it. After it's cooked, pushing the outside edges toward the center with your fingers makes the layers pop up and separate.

The smaller you make the pleats, the flakier, and therefore better, the parathas will be because you are creating more layers. You will get a rhythm with practice and will be able to roll out one paratha while one is in the pan. If you have a griddle that covers two burners on your stove, you can even make two parathas at a time once you get the hang of it.

The recipe halves easily.

DOUGH
1 pound (450 grams) whole wheat flour
   (about 3½ cups)
1 teaspoon salt
2 tablespoons canola oil
1¼ cups water
All-purpose flour, for dusting

FILLING
2 cups packed mint leaves
½ cup canola oil
¼ teaspoon ground turmeric
½ teaspoon salt

¾ cup all-purpose flour, for rolling
6 tablespoons canola oil
Melted butter or ghee, for brushing
   (optional)

1 MAKE THE DOUGH: In a medium bowl, use your hand to combine the flour, salt, oil, and water. The dough should come together in a ball with no traces of flour in the bottom or on the sides of the bowl. It should be quite firm, but not dry. Knead it aggressively several times, using your knuckles. The dough should be very slightly tacky, not sticky. Cover with plastic wrap and let it rest for 30 minutes.

2 MAKE THE FILLLING: In a NutriBullet or small blender, combine the mint, oil, turmeric, and salt and puree until smooth. You may have to shake the canister several times or scrape it down in the process. Use a rubber spatula to transfer the puree to a small bowl.

3 Once the dough has rested, weigh it and divide the weight by 8. Then weigh out 8 portions of equal weight (about 3 ounces each). Roll them into balls using the palms of your hands, returning each to the bowl and covering it as you go along.

4 Put the all-purpose flour in a small bowl. Dust a ball of dough lightly in it. With the palm of your hand, flatten the ball on the counter into a (roughly) 3-inch-diameter round. Use a rolling pin to enlarge the round a little. Turn it over, enlarge the round, and repeat the process of rolling, turning over, and rolling until you have a 10-inch round. This rolling method keeps the dough from sticking to the counter.

5 Spread 1 tablespoon of mint puree over the entire dough round. Dust the puree-covered round with 2 teaspoons all-purpose flour.

6 Lift the edge of the dough closest to you off the counter and make a 1½-inch fold away from you, toward the other side of the round. Now pick the edge up that you started with and fold it back toward you to be flush with the edge of the fold you just made. You just made a ¾-inch pleat. Pick that entire pleat up and make another ¾-inch pleat the same way. Continue until you can't make any more pleats. You should have a vertical stack six pleats high. Rotate the stack toward you ninety degrees and stand it on the counter. (The herb-covered folds should be facing up.)

7 Stretch the dough so it is roughly 12 inches long. With one hand, hold an end of the dough stationary but lifted off the counter about ¾ inch. With your other hand, roll the dough around the center to create a tight pinwheel that looks like a rose, with the center "bud" higher than the outside "petals." Place the pinwheel on a large plate and cover loosely with plastic wrap.

8 Repeat Steps 4 through 7 with the remaining seven balls of dough. (You can make the parathas through this step several hours in advance and keep them covered and refrigerated. You don't want to make the dough the day before—the parathas will not be as flaky.)

9 To griddle the parathas, have ready a cutting board, a bowl with 6 tablespoons oil in it, a pastry brush, and a wide spatula for flipping. Also have a tortilla warmer or a bread basket lined with napkins or kitchen towels to keep the parathas warm.

10 Heat a 10-inch cast iron skillet over medium heat until quite hot. (A few drops of water sprinkled on it should spatter.)

11 Lightly dust the counter with flour and roll a pinwheel, mint side up, into a 7-inch-diameter round. Peel the paratha off the counter and place it in the pan mint side down. Cook for 1 minute, until large spots of brown form on the bottom. Flip the paratha over with the spatula and cook for another minute. Press down on the bread with the spatula throughout the process from here on out to keep the edges from puffing up. This will also help to achieve maximum browning by creating more contact with the pan.

12 Brush the entire surface with oil, flip it over, and cook for 1 minute. Brush the surface with oil, flip it over again, and cook for 1 minute. (Total cooking time is 4 minutes.)

13 Transfer the paratha to a cutting board. (The mint side should be facing up. You can tell because the mint-side layers will appear more separated than the other sides.) With the tips of your fingers, push the edges of the round aggressively toward the middle—the layers you created by pleating the dough should separate. Brush with melted butter or ghee, if you wish, and put the paratha in a tortilla warmer or bread basket lined with napkins.

14 Wipe out the pan with a wad of paper towels. Repeat with the remaining pinwheels of dough. Adjust the heat under the skillet if necessary so it doesn't get too hot. Serve the parathas in the lined bread basket, folding the napkins' edges over the breads to keep them warm.

VARIATION: *To make plain parathas, brush the rolled out dough with plain canola oil instead of the mint puree in Step 5 and proceed with the rest of the recipe.*

Bread is as much a staple on the Indian table as on the French table, especially in the North where wheat is grown. Some kind of bread, be it naan, roti, chapati, *phulka* (chapati puffed up over an open flame), *kulcha*, or paratha, shows up at the table with every meal. What those breads are will vary from region to region. For instance, in Gujarat and Maharashtra, chapati and phulka are more prevalent, whereas in Punjab and points north, roti, kulchas, and naan are favorites.

In the South, rice is the number one staple, so bread with meals is not a mainstay and the bread people do make is often made with rice. Those include *appam*, dosa, and *iddyappam*. Malabari parathas, made with wheat flour, are also popular.

Making bread is second nature to Indian cooks, but even we Indians started somewhere. At Rasika, we have cooks whose only job is to make bread, so don't worry if it takes you a little while to get the knack of it. With practice, you will know when the dough feels just right or needs a little more water. You will realize when the pan is hot enough to begin griddling and when to adjust the heat because it's getting too hot or not hot enough. You will know when it's time to turn a paratha over without eyeing a clock.

In restaurants, we have the wherewithal to make several breads at the same time, but the recipes in this book are made one at a time. If you have a griddle that accommodates making more than one at a time, by all means do it if you can keep up with them.

Three things are crucial to success in bread making: having the necessary equipment, setting up your workstation properly, and getting a good rhythm going. You'll be surprised by how quickly you'll become adept at it.

Setting Up the Workstation:

- A 10-inch cast iron skillet (for Chapati, page 237; Mint Paratha, page 242; and Goat Cheese Kulcha, page 250)
- A pizza stone (for Naan, opposite; Garlic Naan with Cilantro, page 249; and Red Onion and Sage Naan, page 249)
- A digital kitchen scale—this takes the guesswork out of portioning and is more reliable than using cup measures.
- A cooking thermometer
- A 12-inch ruler
- A timer with a "counting up" function. That way you don't have to start and stop a timer—you can keep your eye on the stopwatch and take note of where a minute starts and stops. (Or use the timer, set to 1 minute, and keep restarting it.) Of course, you can just watch the clock on your stove, but without the seconds displayed, it is difficult to time a minute.
- A rolling pin and cutting board, or, preferably, an Indian *belan* and *chakla* marked with 6-inch, 7-inch, 8-inch, 9-inch, and 10-inch circles.
- A small bowl of all-purpose flour, for dusting
- A wide spatula, for flipping
- Kitchen tongs
- A small bowl of melted butter or ghee with a pastry brush, if the recipe calls for it
- A small jar of canola oil with a 1-teaspoon measuring spoon in it
- A tortilla warmer, to keep breads warm as you make them. Or a bread basket, plate, or serving bowl lined with cotton napkins or kitchen towels to fold over finished breads as you prepare them.
- Paper towels and kitchen towels

NAAN

 ○ Before making naan, read On Making Indian Breads (opposite) thoroughly.

Flour varies, so weighing is more precise than measuring. At Rasika, we use King Arthur Sir Galahad flour, which is for professional use. It is 11.7 percent protein, and so is their all-purpose flour, which is available in grocery stores and is a fine substitute.

Naan is made in a tandoori oven, so cooks in less than a minute. For home use, we use a pizza stone. The end result is not exactly the same as you would get at Rasika, in the same way that you won't get the same kind of pizza at home that you would from a wood-burning, 800-degree oven. But that doesn't mean that your home pizza isn't wonderful—and so is this homemade naan.

If you have a convection oven, use it—the faster the bread bakes, the softer it will be. Adjust cooking time accordingly and keep your eye on it so it doesn't bake beyond lightly browned.

Preferably, naan should be eaten hot out of the oven. The dough, though, is very forgiving. You can make it through Step 3 and store it covered in the refrigerator for a day or two. You can also form the balls through Step 5 the day before. Bring the dough to room temperature before continuing with the recipe.

1 pound (450g) unbleached all-purpose flour (about 3½ cups), preferably King Arthur, plus more for dusting
2½ teaspoons baking powder
1 teaspoon salt
1 large egg, beaten

1 cup plus 2 tablespoons warm whole milk (110°F)
2 teaspoons canola oil, plus more for brushing
1 tablespoon unsalted butter, melted

1 In a bowl, stir together the flour, baking powder, and salt.

2 In the bowl of a stand mixer, stir the egg into the milk. Fit the mixer with the dough hook. Add the flour mixture to the milk and mix on medium speed until the dough comes together around the hook and leaves the sides of the bowl.

3 Pull the dough off the hook and out of the bowl and form a large ball. Coat the entire ball with 2 teaspoons of the oil to keep it from sticking. Return the dough to the bowl, cover, and let it rest for 4 hours. (Or refrigerate it overnight.)

4 Place a pizza stone on the bottom rack of the oven and preheat the oven to 500°F.

5 Weigh the dough and divide the weight by 9. Then weigh out 9 portions of equal weight (about 3 ounces each). Roll them into balls using the palms of your hands and place them on a baking sheet dusted with flour. Brush the balls with oil and cover the pan with plastic wrap. Let the dough rest for 30 minutes.

6 Brush a little bit of oil on the counter where you plan to roll the naan. (This will keep it from sticking, but also help it to anchor to the bottom of the stone. That yields a browner bottom crust than dusting with flour does.)

7 With the palm of your hand, flatten a ball of dough on the counter into a (roughly) 3-inch-diameter round. Use a rolling pin to enlarge the round a little. Turn it over, enlarge the round a little more, and repeat the process of rolling, turning over, and rolling until you have a 7-inch round. This rolling method keeps the dough from sticking to the counter.

8 Open the oven door. Lift the dough off the counter and place it carefully on the stone. Bake until puffed and lightly browned, 3 to 4 minutes. (Keep a close eye after the 3-minute mark; this is where variances in oven temperature make a big difference.)

9 Transfer the baked naan to a cutting board and brush with melted butter. Put the naan in a tortilla warmer or a bread basket lined with napkins.

10 While one naan is baking, roll out the next. Bake, brush, and keep warm as before. With practice, you will get the rhythm of the process. With more practice, you can bake two at a time.

11 If you feel your naans aren't warm enough once they are all baked, spread them directly on an upper oven rack and let them warm them through for a minute or two. Serve in the lined bread basket, folding the napkins' edges over the breads to keep them warm.

GARLIC NAAN WITH CILANTRO

MAKES NINE 7-INCH NAANS

4 tablespoons unsalted butter
1 cup garlic cloves, very finely
  chopped, preferably in a mini food
  processor

½ cup finely chopped cilantro

1 In a skillet, melt the butter with the garlic over medium heat, stirring occasionally. Cook for 2 minutes, stirring constantly, to take some of the rawness out of the garlic without browning it at all. You should have about 9 tablespoons.

2 Prepare the naan through Step 7.

3 Spread 1 tablespoon of garlic over the entire surface of the dough. Sprinkle chopped cilantro all over it. Continue with Steps 8 through 11. (Make sure to lay the naan on the stone garlic side up.)

RED ONION AND SAGE NAAN

MAKES NINE 7-INCH NAANS

2 cups finely chopped red onion

¾ cup packed fresh sage leaves,
  thinly sliced crosswise

1 In a bowl, mix the onion and sage together.

2 Prepare the naan through Step 7.

3 Spread ¼ cup of the of the onion/sage mixture over the entire surface of each dough round. Using your fingertips, firmly press the topping into the dough so the onion sticks. Continue with Steps 8 through 11. (You will lose some of the onions on the trip from the counter to the oven.) This naan will take a little longer to bake than plain naan because of the onion.

GOAT CHEESE KULCHA

MAKES NINE 6-INCH KULCHAS ✽ *Kulcha* comes from the northern part of India, especially Punjab (Amritsar, Delhi). It is a stuffed leavened bread, made from naan dough.

Before making this kulcha, read On Making Indian Breads (page 246) thoroughly. With a little practice, you can fill and roll one ball of dough while another is cooking in the skillet.

RASIKA

FILLING
14 ounces goat cheese
4 ounces paneer, shredded
1½ teaspoons deggi mirch
1 teaspoon chaat masala
2 tablespoons chopped fresh cilantro
¾ teaspoon salt

KULCHAS
Naan (page 247), through Step 5
All-purpose flour, for dusting
6 tablespoons (18 teaspoons) canola oil

1 MAKE THE FILLING: In a medium bowl, combine the goat cheese, paneer, deggi mirch, chaat masala, cilantro, and salt well. (Your hands are the best tools for this.) Using the palms of your hands, roll the cheese mixture into nine 2-ounce balls.

2 FORM THE KULCHAS: Crimp the circumference of a ball of dough with your fingers to create a rough 4-inch round, making sure the dough in the center remains thick. (It should look like a flying saucer or a filled raviolo.) Lay the dough round in the palm of one hand. With your other hand, press a ball of cheese into the center of the dough, cupping your palm to enclose the dough around the filling. Pinch the dough together, making sure you've encased the filling completely, forming a ball.

3 Dust the area where you will roll the dough lightly with flour. With the palm of your hand, flatten the ball on the counter into a (roughly) 3-inch-diameter round. Use a rolling pin to enlarge the round a little. Turn it over, enlarge the round a little more, and repeat the process of rolling, turning over, and rolling until you have a 6-inch round. This rolling method keeps the dough from sticking to the counter. Use more flour to dust if you need to, but use it as sparingly as possible.

4 To make the kulchas, have ready a baking sheet lined with paper towels.

5 Heat a 10-inch cast iron skillet over medium heat until it is quite hot. (A drop of water will sizzle.)

6 Place a dough round in the pan. Cook for 1 minute, until large spots of brown form on the bottom. With a wide spatula, flip the round over and cook for another minute to lightly brown on the other side.

7 Spread 1 teaspoon of oil over the entire surface of the round and flip it over. Cook for 30 seconds, using the spatula to press down on the kulcha. (The baking powder in the dough tends to make the kulcha puff up.)

8 Spread 1 teaspoon of oil over the surface and flip it over again. Cook for 30 seconds, pressing down on it as before. If some filling oozes out, don't worry about it; there is still plenty inside. (Total cooking time is 3 minutes.)

9 Blot the kulcha on both sides on the paper towels and place it in a tortilla warmer. (Or on a plate and loosely covered with foil.) Wipe out excess oil or filling from the pan with a wad of paper towels.

10 Repeat with the remaining dough balls and filling, adjusting the heat under the skillet if necessary so it doesn't get too hot. Serve the kulchas in a bread basket lined with napkins, folding their edges over the breads to keep them warm.

LADI PAO

MAKES 20 ROLLS ❁ These fluffy, yeasty rolls, so easy to make, will become a favorite of yours. They'd be perfect for the Thanksgiving table.

A *ladi* is a slab—the rolls are baked touching, as Parker House rolls are, and are sold in slabs in Mumbai, with rows torn off as consumers order them. *Maska pao* and chai is a very common combination found in Iranian cafes in Mumbai. You split the warm *pao* open and slather them with butter (*maska* means "butter") while enjoying your warm, spiced chai.

These rolls freeze beautifully, wrapped in foil and then placed in a freezer-proof zip-top bag or well wrapped in plastic wrap for up to 1 month. Break the rows up and freeze in batches so you will have them on hand for Pao Bhaji (page 47), sandwiches, or meal accompaniments. To reheat, thaw in the refrigerator overnight. Remove the plastic wrap or bag, undo the foil, and sprinkle the pao with a little bit of water. Rewrap with the foil, but loosely, and reheat for 10 minutes in a 325°F oven. To reheat directly from the freezer, do the same as with the thawed pao but bake for 20 minutes or longer until warmed through.

To warm the water to 110°F takes about 10 seconds in most microwaves.

RASIKA

252

4½ teaspoons (2 packets) active dry yeast
3 tablespoons sugar
1¼ cups warm (110°F) water
20 ounces (562 grams) all-purpose flour (about 4⅓ cups), plus more for dusting
⅓ cup instant milk powder, such as Carnation brand

2 teaspoons salt
2 large eggs
2 tablespoons unsalted butter, at room temperature, plus 1 tablespoon melted unsalted butter
Cooking spray
1 teaspoon whole milk

1 In a medium bowl, combine the yeast, 1 tablespoon of the sugar, and ½ cup of the warm water. Give it a stir and let it activate for 10 minutes, until it foams vigorously.

2 In a stand mixer fitted with the dough hook, blend together the flour, milk powder, salt, and remaining 2 tablespoons sugar.

3 Add the activated yeast mixture, one of the eggs, the softened butter, and remaining ¾ cup water to the dry ingredients. Beat on medium-low until the dough comes together around the hook. Remove the dough hook. Cover the bowl with plastic wrap and let the dough rise for 40 to 50 minutes, until doubled in size.

4 Coat a 9 x 13-inch baking pan with cooking spray.

5 Dust the counter with flour, then dust your hands generously with flour to turn the dough out onto the counter. (It will be a little bit sticky.) With floured hands, knead it a few times until it is only a bit tacky.

6 Weigh the dough and divide the weight by 20. Then weigh out 20 portions of equal weight (about 1.8 ounces). Roll them into balls using the palms of your hands.

7 Fit the dough balls into the baking pan in 4 rows crosswise and 5 rows lengthwise. They will be touching each other. Cover loosely with plastic wrap and let the rolls double in size, about 30 minutes.

8 Meanwhile, preheat the oven to 350°F.

9 In a small bowl, beat the remaining egg with the milk. With a pastry brush, brush the tops of the rolls with the egg wash. Bake until golden, rotating the pan front to back halfway through so they brown evenly, about 25 minutes.

10 Remove the rolls from the oven and brush with the remaining 1 tablespoon melted butter and let them rest for 10 minutes before serving. Serve in a bread basket lined with napkins, folding their edges over the rolls to keep them warm.

11

CHUTNEYS AND CONDIMENTS

To me, an Indian meal is not complete without chutneys and pickles to add extra zest to the sundry curries, kormas, vegetables, breads, and rice.

What we Indians call pickles have nothing to do with brined pickles like the ones in the States. Indian pickles are generally a combination of spices, oils, fruits, or vegetables used as a condiment; they are not something you'd eat on their own like you would American dill pickles. Some Indian pickles contain vinegar, as the Lemon Pickle on page 267 does, but what you find more often are ingredients such as fenugreek seeds, fennel seeds, mustard seeds, mustard oil, and red chili powder mixed with fruits such as mango, lemon, and lime or vegetables such as cauliflower, carrots, and eggplant. These mixtures are often left to mature unrefrigerated in the sun for a week or two.

Chutneys tend to be less spicy and sweeter (jaggery is often an ingredient in them) than pickles and have a much smoother texture; they are never chewy.

MINT-CILANTRO CHUTNEY
VEGAN

MAKES ABOUT 1 CUP ◦ Mint-cilantro chutney is served with many Indian snacks, such as Potato Patties with Spiced Yellow Peas (page 76), Lamb Patties (page 96), samosas, and pakoras (fritters). We even like mint-cilantro chutney sandwiches—we butter bread, spread the chutney on it, top with another piece of bread, and that's it.

Made with yogurt (see following variation), this chutney accompanies grilled dishes and kebabs, such as Paneer Shashlik (page 143), Tandoori-Style Mango Shrimp (page 140), Kashmiri Cinnamon Salmon (page 148), Creamy Tandoori-Style Chicken Kebabs (page 145), and Grilled Cashew Cardamom Lamb Chops (page 154). The yogurt softens the spices a bit and makes the chutney a bit milder.

If you want to use a full-size blender, double the recipe; otherwise there isn't enough in one batch for the blades to work effectively.

1¼ cups coarsely chopped cilantro, including stems
½ cup packed mint leaves
¼ cup water
3 tablespoons fresh lemon juice
1 tablespoon Ginger-Garlic Paste (page 27)

2 teaspoons coarsely chopped fresh Thai green chili
½ teaspoon cumin seeds
½ teaspoon salt
½ teaspoon sugar

In a NutriBullet, small blender, or mini food processor, puree all the ingredients until smooth. Store in an airtight container (or containers) in the refrigerator for up to 3 days or in the freezer for up to 3 months.

VARIATION
MINT, CILANTRO, AND YOGURT CHUTNEY

Fold 3 tablespoons of whole-milk yogurt into the Mint-Cilantro Chutney and adjust the salt if necessary. Store in an airtight container (or containers) in the refrigerator for up to 3 days. Do not freeze. However, you can freeze the Mint-Cilantro Chutney, then thaw it and fold in the yogurt.

TAMARIND-DATE CHUTNEY

VEGAN

MAKES ABOUT 2 CUPS ⚙ This chutney is a main ingredient in chaats because of its sweet, sour, and spicy notes. It's also a nice complement for appetizers, such as Potato Patties with Spiced Yellow Peas (page 76); Crispy Fried Spinach with Tomato, Onion, Tamarind, and Yogurt (page 53); and Avocado Chaat with Banana (page 59).

Tamarind (see page 14), including its seeds, is dehydrated and comes in a dense, tar-like block. As it cooks, it falls apart and its pulp becomes soft. Good tamarind chutney has a nice glaze to it and a rich, dark color that comes from a long cooking time and using block tamarind instead of a concentrate.

4 ounces dried tamarind block, such as Laxmi brand
½ cup (3 ounces) pitted Deglet Noor dates
2 tablespoons coarsely chopped unpeeled fresh ginger
2 tablespoons coarsely chopped garlic
3 ounces jaggery
1 cup sugar
2 dried Kashmiri chilies, stemmed

1 large dried Indian bay leaf, crushed
2 teaspoons fennel seeds
6 cups water
2 teaspoons ground ginger
1 teaspoon Toasted Cumin Powder (page 23)
½ teaspoon deggi mirch
1 teaspoon black salt
½ teaspoon salt

1 In a heavy-bottomed pot or Dutch oven, combine the tamarind, dates, fresh ginger, garlic, jaggery, sugar, Kashmiri chilies, bay leaf, fennel seeds, and water and bring to a boil over high heat. Reduce the heat to medium-high and boil uncovered until the dates and tamarind are soft, about 40 minutes. Cool to room temperature.

2 Puree the tamarind mixture in a blender for 20 seconds. (You will hear the tamarind seeds hitting the blades.) Strain the mixture into a bowl through a coarse sieve or a colander, pressing the solids with the back of a spoon to extract as much liquid and pulp as possible. The texture will be like that of apple butter. Discard the solids.

3 Whisk the ground ginger, toasted cumin powder, deggi mirch, black salt, and salt into the chutney. Store in an airtight container (or containers) in the refrigerator for up to 3 weeks or in the freezer for up to 3 months.

COCONUT CHUTNEY

VEGAN

MAKES ABOUT 2 CUPS ✦ This is an ideal accompaniment for many South Indian appetizers, such as Rice and Dal Pancakes with Asparagus (page 65), idli (steamed rice and dal cakes), and *medu vada* (dal doughnuts).

Roasted chana dal is chana dal that is dry-roasted. But you really can't make it yourself from chana dal. In the commercial process manufacturers start with whole Bengal gram, roast them with the skin, and then husk them. Even though you will find recipes for making homemade roasted chana dal, they do not yield the same product as what you can buy commercially.

1 cup grated coconut, fresh or frozen
1 cup coarsely chopped cilantro, including stems
¼ cup Tamarind Pulp (page 24)
1 tablespoon roasted chana dal
1 teaspoon finely chopped fresh Thai green chili
1 tablespoon finely chopped fresh ginger
1 cup water
¼ teaspoon ground turmeric
2 tablespoons canola oil

½ teaspoon black or brown mustard seeds
½ teaspoon chana dal
½ teaspoon urad dal
2 dried Kashmiri chilies, stemmed, broken into rough 1-inch pieces
10 (1½-inch) fresh curry leaves (more if smaller)
¼ teaspoon asafetida
½ teaspoon salt

1 In a blender, puree the coconut, cilantro, tamarind pulp, roasted chana dal, green chili, ginger, water, and turmeric on high speed to form a thin paste. (It will not be smooth.) Transfer the chutney base to a bowl.

2 In a small skillet, heat the oil over medium heat until it shimmers. Add the mustard seeds, chana dal, urad dal, and dried chilies and cook, stirring, until the dals are browned, about 1 minute. Add the curry leaves, asafetida, and salt. Use a silicone spatula to add the pan's contents to the chutney base. Store in an airtight container (or containers) in the refrigerator for up to 4 days or in the freezer for up to 3 months.

CRANBERRY CHUTNEY

VEGAN

MAKES ABOUT 3/4 CUP ⚙ Cranberries are not something you'd find in India. I associate them with Thanksgiving, so I created this chutney to go with fall dishes, such as Sweet Potato Samosa Purses (page 70). By the way, try this chutney as a stand-in for cranberry sauce on your Thanksgiving table.

1 cup cranberries, fresh or frozen
1½ cups white grape juice
4 ounces jaggery
1 medium fresh Thai green chili, stemmed, halved lengthwise
1 dried Indian bay leaf, torn into pieces

5 green cardamom pods
3-inch cinnamon stick, broken into pieces
5 whole cloves
Strips of zest* from ½ orange
¼ teaspoon salt

*Use a vegetable peeler to pull off strips of zest, just the thin orange layer of the peel.

In a small saucepan, combine the cranberries, grape juice, and jaggery. On a 6-inch square of cheesecloth, place the green chili halves, bay leaf, cardamom pods, cinnamon stick, cloves, and orange zest. Fold the cheesecloth's corners up to form a sachet and tie it closed with kitchen twine. Add the sachet to the pan. Bring to a boil over medium-high heat. Reduce the heat to medium and cook, stirring occasionally, until thick, about 40 minutes. Discard the sachet. Stir in the salt. Cool completely. Store in an airtight container (or containers) in the refrigerator for up to 1 week or in the freezer for up to 3 months.

MANGO CHUTNEY

VEGAN

MAKES 2 CUPS ⚙ This chutney is by far the most popular one at Rasika. The recipe is a take on a *murabba,* fruit preserves common in India and Central Asia. Its beautiful color, bright orange-yellow speckled with red saffron, is striking.

The yield of a mango varies depending on its variety and the size of its seed. You don't want the mango to be too soft. The flesh should yield to pressure when you press a finger into it, but still be a bit firm. You want there to be little pieces of the fruit in the chutney so it has texture. If the mango is too ripe, the fruit will turn to mush when you pulse it in the food processor.

2½ pounds just-ripe mangoes
1 cup water
1 cup sugar
¼ teaspoon deggi mirch
¼ teaspoon ground turmeric

½ teaspoon saffron threads
½ teaspoon ground cardamom,
    preferably freshly ground*
1¼ teaspoons salt
3 tablespoons fresh lemon juice

Make ground cardamom by grinding whole green cardamom pods into powder in a spice grinder.

1 Peel the mangoes. Cut the flesh from around the hard center seeds and coarsely chop it. You should have 3 cups chopped mango. Discard the seeds. Transfer the fruit to a food processor and pulse it until it is finely chopped.

2 In a medium saucepan, combine the water and sugar. Bring to a boil over medium heat, stirring to dissolve the sugar. Add the deggi mirch, turmeric, and chopped mango. Continue boiling, stirring occasionally, for 15 minutes.

3 Stir in the saffron, cardamom, salt, and lemon juice and cook for another 2 minutes. The chutney will be the consistency of applesauce. Cool completely. Store in an airtight container (or containers) in the refrigerator for up to 3 weeks or in the freezer for up to 3 months.

TOMATO CHUTNEY

VEGAN

✱ As this chutney cools, the flavors really mellow. Try it with anything you'd put ketchup on—French fries, hamburgers, even scrambled eggs. It's also great as a dip with pappadums. And, of course, as a condiment to go with any Indian meal.

Before frying spices in mustard oil, you must first heat it to the smoking point and let it cool slightly before proceeding. This removes its caustic property and brings its pungency forward.

1 pound tomatoes
½ teaspoon black or brown mustard seeds
½ teaspoon fennel seeds
½ teaspoon cumin seeds
½ teaspoon nigella seeds
¼ teaspoon fenugreek seeds
2 tablespoons mustard oil
½ teaspoon deggi mirch

¼ teaspoon ground turmeric
½ cup water
2 tablespoons tomato paste
1 ounce jaggery, coarsely chopped or grated
¼ cup golden raisins, chopped
1 teaspoon salt

1 Have ready a large bowl of ice water. Bring a large pot of water to a boil over high heat.

2 Use a sharp paring knife to cut out the cores of the tomatoes and cut a shallow "X" through the skin on the bottom of each tomato. Boil the tomatoes for 2 minutes, until the skins begin to peel back where the Xs are cut. Transfer the tomatoes to the ice bath just long enough to cool them down. Remove and pull off their skins.

3 Cut the tomatoes into rough 1-inch chunks and puree them in a food processor. Transfer the puree to a bowl.

4 In a small bowl, combine the mustard seeds, fennel seeds, cumin seeds, nigella seeds, and fenugreek seeds.

5 In a medium saucepan, heat the mustard oil over medium heat until it smokes. Remove the pan from the heat and let it cool for 1 minute. Return it to the heat, add the seeds, and let them crackle. Stir in the pureed tomatoes, deggi mirch, turmeric, water, tomato paste, and jaggery. Bring to a boil and simmer, stirring occasionally, until the jaggery is dissolved and the chutney has thickened, about 10 minutes.

6 Add the raisins and salt and cook for another 5 minutes, stirring occasionally. Cool completely. Store in an airtight container (or containers) in the refrigerator for up to 3 weeks or in the freezer for up to 3 months.

EGGPLANT AND GINGER CHUTNEY

VEGAN

MAKES 1 CUP ❋ This chutney is great as a condiment with breads, pita chips, or pappadums. It's a variation of South Indian ginger chutney, with the eggplant giving it a hint of smoky flavor.

1-pound Italian eggplant
3 tablespoons canola oil
⅓ cup (about ⅓ ounce) coarsely chopped dried Kashmiri chilies (with seeds)
½ cup Tamarind Pulp (page 24)
½ teaspoon cumin seeds
½ teaspoon urad dal

½ teaspoon chana dal
1 tablespoon finely chopped fresh ginger
10 (1½-inch) fresh curry leaves (more if smaller)
2 ounces jaggery, coarsely chopped or grated
¾ teaspoon salt

1 Place the eggplant directly over a medium flame, be it directly on one of your gas stove's burners or on a charcoal or gas grill. (This can also be done under a broiler. See Note.) Cook it for about 20 minutes, turning it often to char the skin on all sides. Move it around over the flame so it cooks evenly. When the flesh has deflated and the eggplant is completely soft, transfer it to a bowl and cover with plastic wrap. Let it steam for 10 minutes.

2 Remove and discard the eggplant's skin and stem and transfer the flesh and whatever juices have accumulated in the bowl to a food processor. Puree until smooth and transfer to a bowl.

3 In a small skillet, preferably cast iron, heat 1 tablespoon of the oil over medium heat. Add the Kashmiri chilies and sauté for 30 seconds, stirring constantly, to toast the peppers and plump them. (Don't let the oil get too hot. You want to toast the peppers, not burn them.) Transfer them to a small blender or NutriBullet. Add the tamarind pulp and puree for a full minute until smooth.

4 In a medium saucepan, heat the remaining 2 tablespoons oil over medium heat until it shimmers. Add the cumin seeds, urad dal, and chana dal and cook, stirring constantly, until the dals are golden brown, about 1 minute. Add the ginger and cook for 30 seconds. Add the curry leaves and the Kashmiri puree. Cook for 2 minutes, stirring. Add the jaggery, eggplant puree, and salt. Cook, stirring frequently, until the jaggery is dissolved and the puree has reduced to 1 cup and is a deep adobe color. This can take anywhere from 5 to 15 minutes, depending on how much water is in your eggplant.

5 Cool completely. Store in an airtight container (or containers) in the refrigerator for up to 1 week or in the freezer for up to 3 months.

NOTE: *To roast eggplant under the broiler, halve it lengthwise and place the halves cut sides down on a baking sheet. Broil until the skin is charred and the flesh is completely soft, 20 to 25 minutes.*

RHUBARB CHUTNEY

VEGAN

MAKES ABOUT 1¼ CUPS ❁ Rhubarb is an ingredient I associate with American cooking, but it perfectly suits Indian chutneys because of its sour quality. The pink hue is appealing, especially when contrasted with magenta Beet and Goat Cheese Tikki (page 67). As a dipping sauce, it has qualities similar to those of Thai sweet chili sauce: sweet, sour, hot, and acidic.

½ cup sugar
½ cup water
4 stalks (7 ounces) fresh rhubarb, cut into 1-inch cubes (about 2 cups)
¼ teaspoon deggi mirch

⅛ teaspoon ground turmeric
2 tablespoons fresh lemon juice
¼ teaspoon green cardamom powder*
¼ teaspoon freshly ground black pepper
¼ teaspoon salt

*Make cardamom powder by grinding whole green cardamom pods into powder in a spice grinder.

1 Set up a bowl of ice water. In a small saucepan over medium-high heat, bring the sugar and water to a boil, stirring until the sugar is completely dissolved. Boil until a drop of syrup put into the ice water forms a soft ball (220°F), about 4 minutes. Add the rhubarb, deggi mirch, and turmeric. Reduce the heat to medium and cook at a simmer until the rhubarb is just soft, about 5 minutes.

2 In a blender, puree the rhubarb mixture until smooth. Stir in the lemon juice, cardamom, black pepper, and salt. Cool completely. Store in an airtight container (or containers) in the refrigerator for up to 1 week or in the freezer for up to 3 months.

LEMON PICKLE

VEGAN

MAKES 2 1/2 CUPS ⊕ In India, it's common to serve pickles with meals so people can add more spice to a dish as they prefer. Pickles serve the same purpose as putting mustard on foods in America—to provide pungency.

In India, homemade pickles are usually made in April or May, when it's very hot but before the monsoon season. That's because you cure them in the sun, making big batches in earthenware jars covered in muslin.

This pickle is acidic and spicy and a good accompaniment for simple dishes, such as boiled rice and yogurt and *khichdi,* a South Indian rice and dal porridge, similar to congee.

As the pickle cools, the cooking liquid, red from deggi mirch, thickens. You must use thick-skinned, pithy lemons for this recipe; if they are thin-skinned and have too much juice, the pickle will be too thin.

1 pound whole lemons, stem ends
   removed (see headnote)
1½ cups distilled white vinegar
4 teaspoons deggi mirch

½ teaspoon garlic powder
2 tablespoons salt
½ teaspoon toasted fenugreek powder*

Toast ½ teaspoon fenugreek seeds in a dry pan over medium heat for 2 to 3 minutes until fragrant. Grind in a spice grinder.

1 In a medium saucepan, combine the lemons with water to cover and bring to a boil over high heat. Drain and transfer the lemons to a cutting board to cool for a few minutes. Finely dice them and don't worry about the seeds. You should have about 2 cups.

2 Return the lemons to the saucepan and stir in the vinegar, deggi mirch, garlic powder, and salt. Bring to a boil over medium heat. Stir in the toasted fenugreek powder and remove from the heat.

3 Cool completely. Store in airtight jars (such as three 8-ounce mason jars) in the refrigerator for up to 1 year.

KACHUMBER

VEGAN

MAKES ABOUT 1 1/2 CUPS (SERVES 4) ✲ Indians who come to Rasika ask for something called chili plate, which consists of sliced red onion rings, whole green chilies, and lemon wedges. They squeeze the lemons over the onions and eat pieces of it, and the chilies, during the meal. Others love kachumber, which is a chopped salad made from diced raw vegetables, like Mexican salsa fresca or pico de gallo, but with cucumber. We serve it as a little side dish with the Lamb Kathi Roll (page 93), much in the same way Americans would offer coleslaw. *Kacha,* by the way, is a Hindi word meaning "raw" or "uncooked."

Serve kachumber cold, but don't prep the salad ingredients too far ahead of time because the onions become acrid after a few hours. Don't dress the salad until the last minute; if you do so earlier, the salt will extract water from the vegetables and the lemon will lose its brightness.

½ cup finely chopped tomato
½ cup (4 ounces) finely chopped
    unpeeled English cucumber
½ cup finely chopped red onion

½ teaspoon finely chopped fresh Thai
    green chili
1 tablespoon finely chopped cilantro
½ teaspoon salt
1 tablespoon fresh lemon juice

In a medium bowl, combine the tomato, cucumber, red onion, green chili, and cilantro. Cover and refrigerate for up to 3 hours and serve chilled. Just before serving, mix in the salt and lemon juice.

CUCUMBER RAITA

MAKES ABOUT 2 CUPS ✿ You can use this raita as a condiment with bread or with a meal, especially to cool down and balance spicy foods, such as Chicken Green Masala (page 179), Smoked Venison Chops Laal Maas (page 208), Jalapeño in Gravy (page 124), and with any biryani, such as Vegetable Biryani (page 133) and Goat or Lamb Biryani (page 210).

1 cup whole-milk yogurt
½ pound unpeeled English cucumber,
  coarsely shredded (about 1 cup)
½ teaspoon Toasted Cumin Powder
  (page 23)

½ teaspoon salt
½ teaspoon sugar

In a large bowl, combine all the ingredients well. Store in the refrigerator for up to 1 day.

TOMATO AND RED ONION RAITA

MAKES 1½ CUPS ✿ This raita goes especially well with biryanis, such as Vegetable Biryani (page 133) and Goat or Lamb Biryani (page 210). In Southern India people make something similar, called *pachadi,* but top it with mustard seeds, curry leaves, hot chilies, and hing (asafetida) tempered in hot oil.

1 cup whole-milk yogurt
½ cup finely chopped tomato
½ cup finely chopped red onion
1 tablespoon chopped cilantro

½ teaspoon Toasted Cumin Powder
  (page 23)
½ teaspoon salt
½ teaspoon sugar

In a large bowl, mix all the ingredients well. Store covered in the refrigerator for up to 1 day, but it is best to consume the same day because the onions will begin to take on an acrid flavor.

Chcolate Samosas (page 284)

12

DESSERTS

Desserts are where we really like to mix the traditional with the modern. We imbue the French classic crème caramel with the warm spices of our chai, such as cardamom, black peppercorn, anise, ginger, cloves, and fennel seed, and give a nod to France's famous upside-down apple tarte Tatin by using mangoes for it instead. Dreamy ganache fills triangular samosas made with Greek phyllo. Still, you can't go wrong with silken carrot halwa, basmati rice pudding enriched with white chocolate, or a jaw-dropping sixteen-layer cake perfumed with coconut oil.

MANGO KULFI WITH SAFFRON SAUCE AND PISTACHIOS

SERVES 6 TO 8 ❀ *Kulfi* is a frozen treat, similar to ice cream, that was introduced to the subcontinent by the Moghuls in the sixteenth century, by way of the Persians. (*Kulfi* is derived from a Persian word meaning "covered cup.") Rather than being made with eggs, the kulfi base is made with *rabdi,* milk and sugar that has been cooked and reduced until thick.

In India, kulfi cups, made of aluminum, are conical. By all means use them if you have them. This recipe calls for freezer pop molds, which are more easily found and make a fun presentation, and makes enough to fill eight 3-ounce molds or six 4-ounce molds.

DESSERTS

RABDI AND SAFFRON RABDI SAUCE
1 quart whole milk
1 cup heavy cream
¾ cup sugar
1 teaspoon pure vanilla extract
¼ teaspoon chopped saffron

KULFI
1 cup canned Alphonso mango pulp, such as Ratnā or Deep brand
1 teaspoon grated lemon or lime zest
1 tablespoon dark rum
1 tablespoon honey
1 teaspoon pure vanilla extract
½ cup heavy cream
¼ cup chopped pistachios, preferably Sicilian

1 MAKE THE RABDI: In a heavy-bottomed pot or Dutch oven, combine the milk, cream, sugar, and vanilla and bring to a boil over high heat, stirring to dissolve the sugar. Reduce the heat to medium and cook uncovered until the liquid has reduced to just over 2 cups and is slightly thick and custard colored, 50 minutes to 1 hour. Strain into a bowl.

2 Measure out 1 cup of the rabdi, transfer it to a large bowl, and refrigerate it to cool completely.

3 Stir the saffron into the remaining 1 cup warm rabdi. Let cool, then cover and refrigerate the saffron rabdi sauce.

4 MAKE THE KULFI: In a large bowl, combine the cooled rabdi, the mango pulp, lemon zest, rum, honey, and vanilla.

5 In a bowl, beat the cream with an electric mixer into soft peaks. (Do not overbeat.) Fold the whipped cream into the mango mixture until completely combined. Fill freezer pop molds with the kulfi mixture. (See headnote.) Or line six 6-ounce ramekins with plastic wrap and fill them each with ½ cup of the mixture. Freeze for at least 8 hours, but preferably overnight.

6 To serve, unmold each kulfi by dipping the mold or ramekin in a bowl of hot water long enough for the kulfi to release. (If using lined ramekins, peel off and discard the plastic wrap.) Serve on a dessert plate with part of the kulfi overlapping a small pool (2 tablespoons) of saffron rabdi sauce. (If your sauce is too thick, thin it out with a little bit of heavy cream.) Sprinkle with chopped pistachios and serve immediately.

RASIKA

CARROT HALWA (GAJAR KA HALWAR)

SERVES 6 TO 8 ✣ *Halwa* derives from an Arabic word that means "sweetmeat" and can refer to various sweetened candies or dessert confections throughout the Middle East, Central Asia, and India. Halwa come in many forms and variations—some are flour-based, some nut-based, and others are fruit- or vegetable-based.

Through the influence of the Moghuls, halwa took off in Northern India. Carrot halwa became popular when the Dutch developed orange carrots. Before then, carrots were purple, with yellow or white mutants, and not sweet like the new orange carrots. Cooks in Northern India turned them into a confection by cooking them slowly with sugar and milk until thick, rich, and concentrated. Then additions would be made, such as nuts and dried fruit, spices or other flavorings (such as rose water), and often *khoya,* cooked milk solids pressed into dry curds.

This version of halwa, with no khoya added, lets the carrots' sweetness shine through. For a more professional look, you can pack each serving of halwa into a ½-cup measuring cup and unmold it onto a dessert plate. Cardamom-laced whipped cream or a simple drizzle of heavy cream over and around the halwa are nice alternatives to ice cream as accompaniments.

You can make the halwa a day or two in advance and reheat it in the microwave or in a pot over low heat until warmed through.

3 cups whole milk
2 pounds carrots, coarsely shredded
  (about 7 cups)
¾ cup sugar
¼ cup golden raisins
2 teaspoons ground cardamom,
  preferably freshly ground*

¼ cup ghee
¼ cup unsalted raw cashew pieces
Cardamom Ice Cream (page 294) or
  vanilla ice cream, for serving
Chopped pistachios, for garnish

Make ground cardamom by grinding whole green cardamom pods into powder in a spice grinder.

1 Put the milk in a small saucepan and set it over low heat.

2 Meanwhile, in a heavy-bottomed pot or Dutch oven, sweat the carrots over medium-high heat, stirring frequently, until they are soft and resemble hash

browns, about 10 minutes. Stir in the warm milk and cook, stirring frequently, until the liquid has evaporated, about 15 minutes. Stir in the sugar, raisins, and cardamom. Continue cooking, stirring frequently, until the mixture is quite thick, about 8 minutes.

3 In a small skillet, melt the ghee over medium heat. Add the cashews and cook, stirring frequently, until golden, about 1 minute. Stir the ghee and nuts into the carrots and cook for another couple of minutes to glaze the carrots nicely.

4 Divide the halwa among four dessert plates and serve warm with scoops of ice cream. Sprinkle with chopped pistachios.

CHAI MASALA CRÈME CARAMEL

SERVES 6 ✿ This recipe is basically a dessert version of chai masala, the hot Indian beverage made with sweetened milk, brewed black tea, and a spice blend that often includes those spices/ingredients listed in our Chai Masala recipe (page 279): cardamom, cinnamon, fennel seeds, ginger, star anise, cloves, and black peppercorns.

Caramel custards should be made a day or two ahead of time so they are well set and cold; this factor makes custard a convenient and stress-free dessert to serve for company. At Rasika, we also make a chai masala crème brûlée.

You don't have to use the pistachio brittle garnish. You could garnish with chopped pistachios or not use a garnish at all. The custard is still delicious without it, but it does add a nice touch of color and an element of crunch.

CARAMEL AND BRITTLE
¾ cup sugar
¼ cup water
¼ cup salted roasted pistachios

CUSTARD
2 cups whole milk
½ cup heavy cream

3 tablespoons loose black tea, such as
    Assam or Darjeeling
1 vanilla bean or 1 teaspoon pure vanilla
    extract
1 tablespoon Chai Masala (recipe follows)
3 large eggs
2 large egg yolks
½ cup sugar

1 Preheat the oven to 325°F.

2 MAKE THE CARAMEL: In a small saucepan, stir together the sugar and water. Bring it to a rolling boil over medium-high heat. Leave the syrup be until you notice that it has started to turn light amber, about 6 minutes. Stir briefly. When the caramel is medium amber, about another 30 seconds, remove it from the heat—it will continue to cook and turn darker without burning.

3 Spoon 1 tablespoon of caramel into each of six 6-ounce custard cups and rotate it to coat the bottom evenly with it. Work quickly to coat the bottoms of all the cups. Set the cups in a 9 x 13-inch baking dish lined on the bottom with a double thickness of paper towels to anchor the cups during baking.

4 MAKE THE BRITTLE: Coat a small baking sheet with cooking spray and set aside. Add the pistachios to the caramel that remains in the pan and stir to coat them. If

the caramel is too hard to stir, reheat it over medium heat until it melts enough for you to coat the nuts. Turn the mixture out onto the baking sheet, using the back of the spoon to press it into as flat a layer as you can. Let the caramel cool and harden into brittle. (To clean the pot, boil water in it to melt the caramel residue.)

5 Put a kettle of water on to boil.

6 MAKE THE CUSTARD: In a small saucepan, combine the milk, cream, and tea. Split the vanilla bean lengthwise and use the tip of a paring knife to scrape the seeds out of each side into the pan. Add the scraped pod to the pan. (If you're using vanilla extract, you'll add it later.) Cook over medium heat, stirring once or twice, until the mixture is just about to boil. Remove from the heat and stir in the chai masala. While you perform the next tasks, let the mixture steep for 5 minutes, but no longer or the tea will make the mixture bitter.

7 In a large bowl, whisk together the whole eggs, egg yolks, and sugar until lemon colored. Slowly stir the hot milk mixture into the egg mixture. Strain the custard through a coarse sieve into a 1-quart measuring cup. (You want the vanilla seeds and masala to pass through the sieve, but not the vanilla pod or the tea leaves. Discard those.) If you are using vanilla extract, add it to the custard now. Ladle off and discard any foam floating on top of the cup.

8 Fill the custard cups with custard (about ½ cup in each one), stirring as you go along so that all the spices don't wind up in the last cup.

9 Transfer the baking dish to a pulled-out oven rack and pour in enough boiling water to come halfway up the sides of the cups. (It's easier to do this by removing one of the cups closest to you, pouring the water there, and then returning the cup to the dish.) Center the baking dish on the rack and push the rack back into the oven. Bake until the custards are just set, 35 to 40 minutes. When you poke the side of a ramekin, the custard should jiggle like Jell-O rather than undulate beneath the surface.

10 Transfer the custards to a wire rack and cool completely. Wrap each with plastic wrap and refrigerate for at least 4 hours, but preferably overnight. The custard should be ice cold when you serve it.

11 To serve, coarsely chop the pistachio brittle. Dip the bottom of a custard cup briefly in very hot water to melt the caramel on the bottom. Run a sharp paring knife around the inside of the custard cup to separate the custard from the cup and invert the custard onto a dessert plate. Pour any caramel left in the cup over the top. Repeat with all the custards and garnish each with chopped brittle.

CHAI MASALA MAKES ABOUT 2 TABLESPOONS

4 green cardamom pods
2-inch cinnamon stick, crushed
1 teaspoon fennel seeds
1 teaspoon ground ginger

1 star anise
2 whole cloves
½ teaspoon black peppercorns

In a spice grinder, grind all ingredients to a fine powder. Sift and store in an airtight container for up to 1 month.

DATE AND TOFFEE PUDDINGS

SERVES 12 ✿ This pudding—moist individual cakes studded with chopped dates and drenched in toffee syrup—is a signature dish at Rasika. It is a take on the English standard, sticky toffee pudding.

You can refrigerate the undipped cakes for 2 days or freeze them for up to 1 month. The toffee syrup will keep for 1 month refrigerated. To serve, warm the cakes (thawed, if frozen) briefly in the microwave before dipping them in the warmed toffee (Step 9).

PUDDINGS
Cooking spray
8 ounces pitted Deglet Noor dates
1½ teaspoons baking soda
1 cup hot water
1⅓ cups all-purpose flour
1¼ teaspoons baking powder
⅛ teaspoon salt
1 stick (4 ounces) unsalted butter,
    at room temperature

6 tablespoons light brown sugar
2 large eggs, at room temperature

TOFFEE SYRUP
1 cup heavy cream
1 stick (4 ounces) unsalted butter
¾ cup packed light brown sugar

Vanilla ice cream or Cardamom Ice
    Cream (page 294), for serving
Fresh berries, for serving (optional)

1 Preheat the oven to 350°F. Coat a 12-cup muffin pan with cooking spray.

2 MAKE THE PUDDINGS: In a food processor, finely chop the dates. This can be done by hand, but the machine does a better job.

3 In a bowl, stir together the dates, baking soda, and hot water. Let rest for 10 minutes.

4 In a small bowl, mix together the flour, baking powder, and salt.

5 In a stand mixer fitted with the paddle attachment, cream the butter and brown sugar on medium speed until fluffy, about 3 minutes. Add the eggs, one at a time, scraping down the bowl after each addition. Add the flour mixture in two additions. Scrape down the bowl.

6   Stir in the date mixture in three additions until completely incorporated.

7   Fill each muffin cup three-fourths full. Bake until a toothpick inserted into the center of one of the puddings comes out clean, 20 to 25 minutes. Transfer the pan to a wire rack and cool for 10 minutes. Carefully remove the cakes from the muffin pan and onto the rack.

8   MEANWHILE, MAKE THE TOFFEE SYRUP: In a saucepan, combine the cream, butter, and brown sugar and stir over medium heat until the butter is melted and the sugar is dissolved.

9   Remove the syrup from the heat. Poke the puddings all over with a skewer and dip each cake one at a time into the syrup, turning them over and over to soak them well before transferring them to a (microwavable) serving plate.

10   To serve, heat the cakes in the microwave for 20 seconds. Serve warm with ice cream and fresh berries (if using). Warm any remaining toffee syrup and serve on the side.

WHITE CHOCOLATE RICE PUDDING

SERVES 4 TO 6 ⚙ This is a rich, but not stodgy, version of rice pudding, made all the better by the addition of white chocolate, saffron, golden raisins, and cashews.

It is best to make fresh cardamom powder (from green cardamom pods) rather than using something that has been hanging around your spice cabinet for a long time. Many people in India grind the cardamom pods with granulated sugar. The friction of the crystals makes the cardamom finer. Make sure to use real white chocolate.

Once the pudding has chilled, you may want it thinner, depending on your preference. Simply stir in some milk and serve it hot or cold. You can make the pudding 2 days in advance.

½ cup basmati rice
6 cups whole milk
¼ cup sugar
½ teaspoon plus ¼ teaspoon ground cardamom, preferably freshly ground*
½ teaspoon saffron threads

2 tablespoons golden raisins
2 tablespoons unsalted butter or ghee
2 tablespoons unsalted raw cashew pieces
3 ounces white chocolate chips (about ½ cup)
Chopped pistachios, for garnish

*Make ground cardamom by grinding whole green cardamom pods into powder in a spice grinder.

1 Rinse the rice in cool water. In a large saucepan, combine the rice and milk and bring to a boil over medium-high heat, stirring frequently. Reduce the heat to medium and stir in the sugar, ½ teaspoon of the cardamom, and the saffron. Cook, stirring occasionally, until the rice has broken down completely and the milk is thickened, about 25 minutes. It may seem thin to you—it will thicken as it cools. Remove from the heat and stir in the raisins.

2 In a small skillet, heat the butter over medium heat until it sizzles. Add the cashews and cook, stirring frequently, until golden, 3 to 4 minutes. Stir the butter and cashews into the rice. Stir in the white chocolate and remaining ¼ teaspoon cardamom.

3 Transfer the pudding to a bowl. Press a piece of plastic wrap directly onto the pudding to keep a skin from forming. Cool completely, then refrigerate for several hours, or overnight, until chilled. Serve cold, garnished with chopped pistachios.

CHOCOLATE SAMOSAS

❖ Samosas are savory triangular-shaped pastries usually filled with vegetables or meat. This is a dessert rendition.

We like to use ganache—a smooth, luscious cream and chocolate filling—in these buttery, crunchy phyllo triangles. When you cut into one with the side of your fork, the filling oozes out and melds into the ice cream like hot fudge.

Ganache is a snap to make, but it is also tricky to work with. It thickens and hardens as it cools and there is a window of opportunity where it is stiff enough to work with but still malleable. The best strategy is to scoop out portions of the filling and form them into capsule shapes before you start dealing with the phyllo dough. That makes working with the chocolate easier and tidier when you form the triangles.

I find frozen phyllo dough to be very inconsistent—sometimes you get a great box where none of the sheets stick together and sometimes you get one where they all do. There are about twenty-eight 12 x 17-inch sheets in a one-pound box and you only need twelve for this recipe, but I would lay out the entire stack to make your chances of coming up with twelve perfect sheets better.

This recipe makes 12 samosas, but you can halve it. I suggest you assemble the full batch because they are great to have on hand in a pinch. Use what you need or refrigerate them, well wrapped, for up to 2 days. Then freeze the rest. Thaw them completely before baking; if you bake them frozen, they will brown before the inside layers of phyllo are cooked.

½ cup heavy cream
3 cups (about 15 ounces) bittersweet or
   semisweet chocolate chips
12 phyllo sheets, such as Apollo brand
1 stick (4 ounces) unsalted butter, melted

Powdered sugar, for serving (optional)
Vanilla ice cream or Cardamom Ice
   Cream (page 294), for serving
   (optional)

1 In a small saucepan, bring the cream to a boil over medium heat. Remove from the heat and stir in the chocolate until smooth. If the chocolate doesn't melt completely, whisk it briefly over very low heat until it does. Transfer the melted chocolate to a large bowl. Leave the ganache out on the counter to thicken to the consistency of thick icing, about 1 hour.

2   Line two baking sheets with parchment. Spoon twelve 2-tablespoon (1.25-ounce) dollops of ganache onto one baking sheet. (An easy, and less messy, way to do this is to put the baking sheet on a scale and spoon out exact 1.25-ounce portions, zeroing the scale after each one.) Use the spoon to shape the piles into capsule shapes about 2 x 1 inch and ¾ inch thick.

3   Preheat the oven to 375°F.

4   Stack the phyllo sheets (or the entire stack from a whole box—see headnote) on the counter.

5   Place a phyllo sheet on the counter with a short side facing you. Brush it all over with melted butter. Top it with another sheet and butter it. Repeat with two more sheets, buttering the top sheet. Cover the remaining phyllo with a damp cloth so they don't dry out while you're working on the first batch.

6   Using a pizza wheel or paring knife, trim the rectangle, if necessary, to 16 x 12 inches. Cut the rectangle lengthwise into four equal 4 x 12-inch strips. Place a ganache portion at a 45-degree angle at the bottom of each strip.

7   To fold a strip into a triangle, lift the bottom corner of phyllo opposite the chocolate and fold it diagonally over the chocolate to form a perfect 4-inch right triangle with the edges perfectly aligned. Use your fingertips to maneuver the chocolate so it fills its triangular encasement. Fold that triangle vertically and then repeat that pattern (diagonal, vertical, diagonal, vertical) until you reach the end. Repeat with the other three strips. If any of the triangles have seams, turn them over so the pretty sides are facing up. Brush them all with melted butter and transfer them to the second lined baking sheet.

8   Repeat the process to make the remaining 8 triangles, 4 at a time. (Remember to cover the stack of remaining sheets with the damp cloth while you're making the second batch.) If you're planning to bake all of the samosas, you may need another baking sheet.

9   To freeze the samosas, cover them with plastic wrap and place the baking sheet in the freezer. Once they are frozen, you can transfer them to freezer storage bags or containers.

10   Bake the samosas until golden brown, 13 to 15 minutes. Serve hot as is, sprinkled with powdered sugar, or with ice cream.

LAYERED COCONUT CREPE CAKE (BEBINCA)

SERVES 16 ❀ This traditional Goan dessert has a presentation that is about as magnificent as can be. What resembles a one-layer cake in dimension is a sixteen-layer showstopper.

You make *bebinca* one layer at a time. The first one starts on the stove so that you can brown what will become the top of the finished cake once it is inverted. From there, you ladle on a layer's worth of batter, broil it to golden brown, lace it with luscious coconut oil, and continue building the cake in that fashion. The thin, crepe-like layers are interspersed with caramelized striations.

The process is really quite simple. Bebinca requires time and attention rather than baking skills beyond the rudimentary. The trick is to keep a watchful eye as each layer is under the broiler and move it around under the flame so the top gets evenly browned. It takes a bit of babysitting, but the payoff is totally worth it. Plus, the cake is so rich that one recipe can serve sixteen guests.

You can make bebinca a day or even a week ahead of time or freeze it, well wrapped, for up to 1 month. The coconut oil keeps the cake moist. To reheat, bring to room temperature, wrap the cake loosely in foil, and bake at 200°F for 20 minutes to warm it through. Or, cut individual slices and microwave for 15 to 20 seconds.

12 large egg yolks
3⅔ cups unsweetened coconut milk
2½ cups sugar
1 teaspoon freshly grated nutmeg
½ teaspoon salt
1½ teaspoons pure vanilla extract

2 cups all-purpose flour
1 cup plus 1 tablespoon coconut oil at
    room temperature
Cardamom Ice Cream (page 294),
    for serving (optional)

1 In a large bowl, whisk together the egg yolks, coconut milk, sugar, nutmeg, salt, and vanilla to dissolve the sugar. Add the flour 1 cup at a time, whisking until smooth after each addition. Cover with plastic wrap and refrigerate overnight.

2 Remove the batter from the refrigerator and let it come to room temperature for 1 hour.

3 Position a rack in the top third of the oven (see Note). Preheat the broiler to high.

4 Spread 1 tablespoon of the coconut oil evenly in the bottom of a nonstick 9-inch cake pan. Place the pan over medium heat until the oil shimmers. Using a potholder, remove the pan from the heat with one hand; with the other, ladle in ½ cup of batter. (Use a 4-ounce ladle or a ½ cup measuring cup.) Turn the pan to evenly coat the bottom. Return it to the heat and cook for 2 minutes to caramelize the layer on the bottom. It will start to bubble up. Move and rotate the pan around the burner so the bottom browns evenly.

5 Center the pan under the broiler and broil, moving the pan around under the flame or element so it turns golden brown all over, 4 to 5 minutes.

6 Remove the pan from the oven. (If the layer puffed up during broiling, wait for it to deflate before adding a new layer.) Spread 1 tablespoon coconut oil over the entire surface of the layer (use the back of the measuring spoon to do this). Make another layer as before with another ½ cup of batter. Return the pan to the broiler and brown for 4 to 5 minutes as before.

7 Repeat with the coconut oil, batter, and broiling until all the batter is gone. (You should have 16 layers.) As the layers build up, the batter gets closer and closer to the flame, so layers may take less time to brown. (Or may not.)

8 When the last layer is done, spread the remaining 1 tablespoon coconut oil over it. Let the cake rest for 10 minutes. To serve, run a knife around the edge of the pan to loosen the cake. Invert onto a cake plate and slice. Serve plain or with ice cream.

NOTE: *Every broiler is different and this affects total cooking time and how evenly each layer browns. Gas broilers have a rod with two jets of flames running down the middle and electric ovens have elements that cover more surface area. Some broilers run hot, whereas others don't. Most have hot spots.*

With most broilers, the rack is between 3 and 4 inches from the heat source. Adjust the rack if the layers are cooking too fast or burning, or not browning quickly enough, until you find the sweet spot. And move the cake pan around to get even browning. The bottom line is this: Don't even think of walking away while you're making these layers!

MANGO TARTE TATIN

SERVES 8 TO 12 ⚙ I love mangoes, which in India are called the king of fruits. Every year during my childhood in Mumbai, my grandmother would send me a crate of Alphonso mangoes when they came into season in April or May. They were packed in hay, handpicked by a mango trader who brought her only the best of the best.

This gorgeous dessert is a riff on the well-known French dessert tarte Tatin, an upside-down caramelized apple tart. We serve them individually at Rasika; you could make them that way at home, too, but preparing one large tart and slicing it into portions is much less fuss.

To make the tart, you place half-moon mango slices in a skillet, making concentric circles from the edge of the pan to the center of it so that the slices resemble the petals of an open rose.

To do this successfully, it is important that the mangoes be about 12 ounces each—those will yield the size of slice that works best for this recipe. Consult the photo on page 291 to visualize how to construct the tart.

It is also important that the mangoes be ripe, but still firm. That is, when you press your thumb into the side of one, it should not be hard; it should yield to some pressure on the surface, but not be so soft that you can easily push your thumb in more than a quarter inch. If the mangoes are too ripe, you will not be able to cut nice, neat slices and they will disintegrate during cooking.

You can bake the tart several hours ahead of serving and enjoy it at room temperature, but I prefer to pop it into a low (200°F) oven to warm it. That way the ice cream melts and creates a bit of a sauce as guests are eating it.

DOUGH

1 large egg
1 tablespoon milk
1¾ cups all-purpose flour, plus more for dusting
1½ teaspoons sugar
1 teaspoon salt
1½ sticks (6 ounces) cold unsalted butter, cut into ½-inch cubes

TART

8 large (12-ounce) firm-ripe mangoes, preferably Alphonso
5 tablespoons unsalted butter, at room temperature
½ cup sugar

Cardamom Ice Cream (page 294), for serving

1 MAKE THE DOUGH: In a small bowl, beat together the egg and milk.

2 In a stand mixer fitted with the paddle attachment, give the flour, sugar, and salt a stir.

3 Add the cubed butter and mix on low speed, until the flour resembles cornmeal, about 4 minutes. Add the egg and milk mixture and let the dough come together around the paddle, about 30 seconds. Form the dough into a rough 5-inch-diameter disk. Wrap in plastic wrap and refrigerate it while you perform the next tasks.

4 MAKE THE TART: Peel the mangoes. Stand a mango on a cutting board lengthwise so the stem end is facing away from you. There is a wide seed running down the middle of most of the length of the mango. Using a chef's knife, begin to slice through the fruit ½ inch to the left of center. If the blade hits the seed, maneuver the knife to the left only as much as necessary to clear it and slice all the way through. Repeat on the other side. Cut all of the mangoes this way.

5 Around the seeds are two strips of flesh about 1 inch wide that run the length from the stem end down. Slice them off from around all of the seeds. Dice and reserve them.

6 To make the mango petals, hold your knife at a 45-degree angle to the cutting board and cut each mango half crosswise into ¼-inch-thick slices.

7 To build the tart, lightly grease the sides of an 11-inch-diameter (measure across the top) cast iron skillet with a little bit of the 5 tablespoons softened butter, then smear the rest of it thickly on the bottom of the pan. Cover the butter with the sugar and shake the pan to distribute the sugar evenly.

8 Line the inside of the skillet with side-by-side mango half-moons, their flat edges resting on the sugar. Create a second row of mango slices the same way, but offset it by making sure its slices are centered where the half-moons of the previous row touch each other rather than right in front of them. Continue to build circles this way concentrically, working toward the center so that the mango slices resemble open petals of a rose.

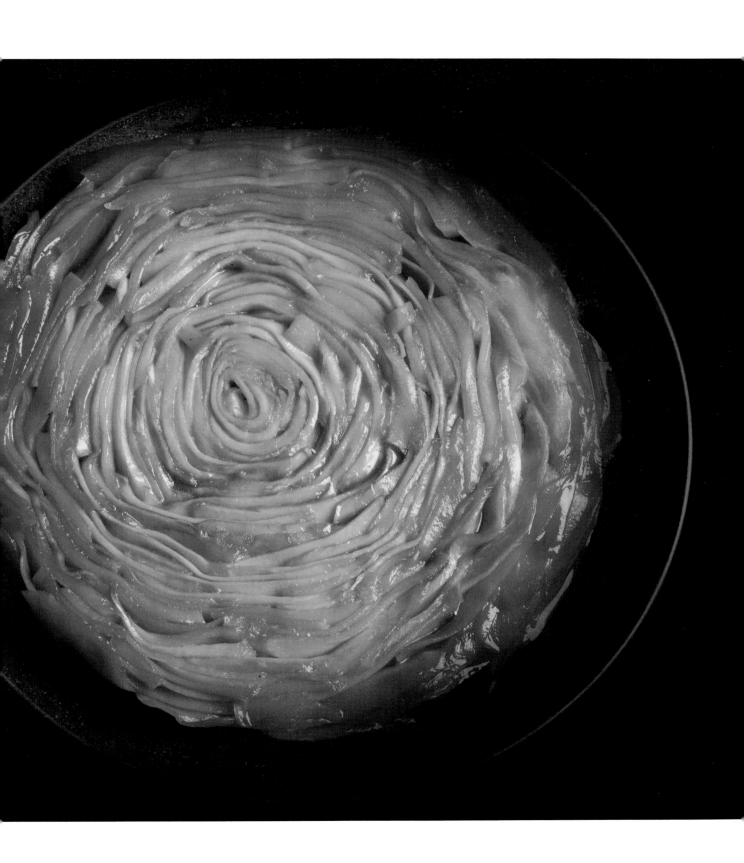

9 Once you get to the point where there is a 1-inch circle left in the center, fill the center hole abundantly with the reserved diced mango. Save any remaining diced mango for snacking or another use. Work any remaining half-moons into your flower among the other petals.

10 Preheat the oven to 375°F.

11 Place the skillet on the stove over medium-high heat. Cook the mango for 10 minutes undisturbed to allow the fruit's juices to leach from it, boil, and evaporate. While it's bubbling away, roll out the crust.

12 Dust the counter with flour and knead the refrigerated dough for a minute until pliant. Dust the counter again and roll the dough, dusting it with a little flour if you need to, into a ¼-inch thickness. Using a 12-inch-diameter bowl or plate as a template, cut out a 12-inch round. Prick it all over with the tines of a fork, transfer it to a baking sheet, and refrigerate. Discard any extra dough.

13 At the 10-minute mark, check the mangoes. Continue to let the juices boil, keeping a watchful eye, until the juices are syrupy instead of watery and begin to turn a light amber color. This could take up to 10 more minutes, depending on how much juice was in the mangoes. Remove the pan from heat.

14 Place the dough round (pricked side up) over the fruit and fit it inside the pan. It may seem a little too big, but make it work—the crust will shrink some in the oven.

15 Transfer to the oven and bake until the crust and caramel are golden brown, about 40 minutes. Cool for 30 minutes.

16 Run a paring knife around the inside of the skillet to free any mango slices stuck to the sides. Then shake the skillet vigorously on the counter a couple of times until you feel the tart moving. (This is how you know the mango is not stuck to the bottom of the pan.) Carefully invert the tart onto a serving plate. Some mango slices might be left in the pan. Pull them out with a fork and patch the tart with them.

17 Serve the tart warm or at room temperature, with ice cream.

CARDAMOM ICE CREAM

MAKES 1 QUART ⚙ Where vanilla is a fundamental component in most American desserts, Indians use cardamom in theirs.

Cardamom ice cream is excellent on its own or as an accompaniment to many desserts, such as chocolate cake, apple pie, and pumpkin pie, and in this book: Carrot Halwa (page 275), Date and Toffee Puddings (page 280), Chocolate Samosas (page 284), and Mango Tarte Tatin (page 289).

For best results, refrigerate the custard overnight before freezing it. I highly recommend using freshly ground cardamom for this recipe.

You can make the ice cream a month ahead.

2 cups whole milk
2 cups heavy cream
1 vanilla bean or 1 teaspoon pure vanilla
   extract

5 large egg yolks
¾ cup sugar
1 teaspoon ground cardamom,
   preferably freshly ground*

*Make ground cardamom by grinding whole green cardamom pods into powder in a spice grinder.

1 In a small saucepan, combine the milk and cream. Split the vanilla bean lengthwise and use the tip of a paring knife to scrape the seeds out of each side into the pan. Add the scraped pod. (If you're using vanilla extract, you'll add it later.) Bring to a boil over medium heat. Remove from the heat.

2 Meanwhile, in a medium bowl, beat together the egg yolks, sugar, and cardamom until light yellow. With a wooden spoon, slowly stir in ¼ cup of the hot milk mixture, then another ¼ cup, into the eggs. Pour the warmed egg mixture back into the saucepan and cook the custard, stirring constantly, over medium-low heat until it coats the back of the spoon, about 2 minutes. (Do not let it boil.)

3 Strain the custard through a coarse sieve into a pitcher. (You want the vanilla seeds in the custard, but not the pod. Discard that.) If using vanilla extract, add it here. Cool to room temperature. Cover and refrigerate overnight.

4 Freeze the ice cream in an ice cream maker according to the manufacturer's instructions. (It works perfectly in a Cuisinart-style ice cream maker.) Transfer the ice cream to an airtight 1-quart container. Cover and freeze for at least 1 hour to ripen, although the ice cream is lovely served soft right out of the ice cream maker.

ROSE ICE CREAM

MAKES 1 QUART ❁ Rose flavorings, commonly used in Persian cooking, made their way into Indian cuisine, as so many ingredients and preparations did, via the Moghuls. This ice cream, bright pink from rose syrup, is an easy dessert to make using a custard base. It would look and taste great with chopped Sicilian pistachios over it.

You can make the ice cream a month ahead.

2 cups whole milk
2 cups heavy cream
1 vanilla bean or 1 teaspoon pure vanilla
   extract

5 large egg yolks
¼ cup sugar
½ cup rose syrup, such as Dabur brand

1   In a small saucepan, combine the milk and cream. Split the vanilla bean lengthwise and use the tip of a paring knife to scrape the seeds out of each side into the pan. Add the scraped pod. (If you're using vanilla extract, you'll add it later.) Bring to a boil over medium heat. Remove from the heat.

2   Meanwhile, in a medium bowl, beat the egg yolks and sugar until light yellow. With a wooden spoon, slowly stir ¼ cup of the hot milk mixture, then another ¼ cup, into the eggs. Pour the warmed egg mixture back into the saucepan and cook the custard, stirring constantly, over medium-low heat until it coats the back of the spoon, about 2 minutes. (Do not let it boil.)

3   Strain the custard through a coarse sieve into a pitcher. (You want the vanilla seeds in the custard, but not the pod. Discard that.) Stir in the rose syrup. If using vanilla extract, add it here, too. Cool to room temperature. Cover and refrigerate overnight.

4   Freeze the ice cream in an ice cream maker according to the manufacturer's instructions. (It works perfectly in a Cuisinart-style ice cream maker.) Transfer the ice cream to an airtight 1-quart container. Cover and freeze for at least 1 hour to ripen, although the ice cream is perfectly lovely served soft right out of the ice cream maker.

ACKNOWLEDGMENTS

FROM ASHOK BAJAJ

To my best friend and confidante, Andrea Reid, for all the support she has given me through the years and for encouraging me to write this book as a way to promote greater appreciation for Indian cuisine.

To Executive Chef Vikram Sunderam, for taking a leap of faith and believing in Rasika's concept enough to relocate and move his family from London to Washington, D.C. His talent, loyalty, and commitment are truly unrivaled.

To Pat Minter, controller of the Knightsbridge Restaurant Group, but also a dear friend and my right hand.

To the dedicated and hardworking staff of Rasika, who nurture our success every day, including: General Manager Atul Narain, Chef Neraj Govil, Pastry Chef Aracely Ventura, Jose Ventura (Mario), Victor Lopez, Francisco Ventura, Santosh Bodke, Daya Kotian, Michael Williams, and former employees Paul Ruttiman and Zahirul Haque.

To writer David Hagedorn, for his invaluable knowledge of food, his patience and guidance in the creation of this book, and his friendship. And to his team of recipe testers: Cathy Barrow, Sally Swift, Michaele Weissman, Tom Natan, Kelly Magyarics, and Deepa Venkataraman.

To Rasika's photographers, Shimon and Tammar, for their beautiful work.

To Dan Halpern, publisher of Ecco, for believing in Rasika and championing it, and to Gabriella Doob, our book's editor.

To literary agent, Joy Tutela, for her wise counsel and insight in making Rasika become a reality.

To John Mitchell, for helping me gather my thoughts, and for his long-term friendship.

To Harry Gregory, my UK designer, for bringing my vision of Rasika to life.

To my brother, Naresh, his wife, Seema, and their sons, Neil and Sean, for being such a supportive family.

And finally to my late parents, Amrit Lal and Kamla Bajaj, for teaching me the importance of respecting others and the value of a strong work ethic and for always standing behind me.

FROM VIKRAM SUNDERAM

To my late mother, who was my earliest inspiration in cooking.

To Mr. Ashok Bajaj, who gave me free rein in the kitchen and has always backed me wholeheartedly. It is said that when a drop of water falls in the ocean, it is just another drop of water; but when the same drop of water falls on a leaf, it shines like a diamond. In Rasika, Mr. Bajaj gave me a wonderful setting to showcase my creativity. He has been a great employer and is someone I respect and admire.

To all the chefs and cooks I have met during my professional career, who have taught, guided, and inspired me.

To my wonderful chefs and back-of-the-house staff, who are the backbone of my kitchens.

And last but not the least, to my wife, Anjali, and my children, Nidhi and Viraj, for their unstinting and unwavering support.

298

ACKNOWLEDGMENTS

BIBLIOGRAPHY

FROM VIKRAM SUNDERAM

One of the things I love to do most is lose myself in cookbooks, particularly Indian ones for obvious reasons. I never cease to find inspiration from these talented, brilliant, and awe-inspiring writers:

Awchat, Deepa Suhas. *The Goa Portuguesa Cookbook.* Batra Art Press, 2009.

Bhatnagar, Sangeeta and Saxena, R. K. *Dastarkhwan-e-Awadh: The Cuisine of Awadh.* HarperCollins, 1997.

Jaffrey, Madhur. *A Taste of India: The Definitive Guide to Regional Cooking.* Pavilion Books, 1985.

Kalra, J. Inder Singh. *Prashad: Cooking with Indian Masters.* Allied Publishers, 1986.

Kalra, Jiggs and Pushpesh Pant. *Kama Bhog: Foods of Love.* Allied Publishers, 2003.

Karan, Pratibha. *A Princely Legacy: Hyderabadi Cuisine.* HarperCollins, 1998.

Oberoi, Hemant. *The Masala Art: Indian Haute Cuisine.* Roli Books, 2011.

Padmanabhan, Chandra. *Dakshin: Vegetarian Cuisine from South India.* Thorsons, 1994.

Panjabi, Camellia. *50 Great Curries of India.* Kyle Books, 1994.

Sahni, Julie. *Classic Indian Cooking.* William Morrow and Company, 1980.

Singh, Digvijaya. *Cooking Delights of the Maharajas: Exotic Dishes from the Princely House of Sailana.* Vakils, Feffer & Simmons, 1982.

INDEX

INDEX